# THE PRICE OF
# PARADISE

# THE PRICE OF
# PARADISE

## THE COSTS OF INEQUALITY AND A VISION
## FOR A MORE EQUITABLE AMERICA

### DAVID DANTE TROUTT

NEW YORK UNIVERSITY PRESS

*New York and London*

NEW YORK UNIVERSITY PRESS
New York and London
www.nyupress.org

References to Internet websites (URLs) were accurate at the time of writing.
Neither the author nor New York University Press is responsible for URLs that
may have expired or changed since the manuscript was prepared.

LIBRARY OF CONGRESS CATALOGING-IN-PUBLICATION DATA
Troutt, David Dante.
The price of paradise : the costs of inequality and a vision for a more equitable America /
David Dante Troutt.
pages cm.
Includes bibliographical references and index.
ISBN 978-0-8147-6055-0 (cl : alk. paper)
1. Equality—United States. 2. Racism—United States. 3. Social stratification—United States.
4. Social mobility—United States. 5. Income distribution—United States. I. Title.
HN90.S6T76 2013
305.50973—dc23
2013028295

New York University Press books are printed on acid-free paper,
and their binding materials are chosen for strength and durability.
We strive to use environmentally responsible suppliers and materials
to the greatest extent possible in publishing our books.

Manufactured in the United States of America
10 9 8 7 6 5 4 3 2 1

Also available as an ebook

*For my children, Naima and Jasmine*

*In memory of my mother,*
*Dr. Bobbye Vary Troutt,*
*no clearer voice was ever missed*

# CONTENTS

# INTRODUCTION

Let's begin with a brazen assault on paradise. On June 4, 2010, eighteen-year-old Justin Hudson was the chosen student graduation speaker at Hunter College High School, a prestigious New York City high school for "intellectually gifted" students. He was to deliver a celebratory speech to the assembled recipients of the American Dream at its meritorious best. A half-black, half-Latino young man from a low-income neighborhood, Justin began by acknowledging that he had no right to be standing there before his classmates and their families. Blacks represented only 3 percent of Hunter's students, Latinos 1 percent. But then, Justin went on, neither did anyone else deserve the privilege.

"We stand on the precipice of our lives, in control of our lives, based purely and simply on luck and circumstance," he explained. "If you truly believe that the demographics of Hunter represent the distribution of intelligence in this city, then you must believe that the Upper West Side, Bayside and Flushing are intrinsically more intelligent than the South Bronx, Bedford-Stuyvesant and Washington Heights, and I refuse to accept that."[1]

You can imagine distinct segments of Justin's audience that day and their peculiar reactions to a lucky soul ambivalently, but boldly, taking aim at a whole system of sorting and mobility in which they were fully and proudly invested. Some would no doubt react angrily, convinced that the celebration that day honored true merit, the American Dream of hard work and exemplary performance on standardized tests. After all, Hunter is not an elite private school where the price of admission often determines composition. Old money and new money were in attendance, as well as working-class and immigrant families. To them the kid was all wrong.

Still others in the crowd probably wondered why underrepresented minorities exhibit such a flair for the dramatic. *You* made it, didn't you? Be a role model—or not—and quit complaining.

A third faction may have had no earthly idea what Justin was talking about. It sounded vaguely like something about race or class or other distasteful subjects mixed up with the wrong place and time. After a short groan, they went back to gazing at the new leaves dancing in the late spring breeze.

Then there were people like me. We recognize that Justin was not talking only about education, intelligence, and economic and racial segregation. He was talking about the relationship between all those things as they have become instantiated with *place*. He was making critical reference to the way that opportunity in the United States has become increasingly connected with the places where one lives. I happen to know the difference between those neighborhoods Justin mentioned. I grew up in Harlem/Washington Heights and recently lived near Bedford–Stuyvesant in Brooklyn. With the exception of gentrifying pockets, these are areas of resource struggle—high numbers of poor families, low horizons for opportunity—despite the fact that most grown folks work at least one job. The fates of those who grow up in these neighborhoods are so statistically disparate from those who grow up in the other neighborhoods he named that you can bet confidently on the outcomes.

But Justin's story is a fitting start to this book for another reason that hits close to home. I remember standing before my own New York

City elite high school assembly as a speaker almost thirty years ago, a young mixed black man in the springtime of my life, expressing the same frustration with newly discovered truths to uncomfortable friends and family, my voice trembling. Justin and I repeated so many similar observations that you might fear that nothing has changed in all that time. Indeed, too little has changed, and many things related to the distribution of opportunity and the inequality gap have gotten worse. In 1983, for example, the top 20 percent of income earners held 81.3 percent of the nation's wealth.[2] By 2010, they held 89 percent. The racial segregation index for the New York metropolitan area was 81.7 in 1980,[3] one of the highest in the land. Three decades later, it was 79.1—despite more than a generation's worth of changes in the real estate landscape, school policy, and good-faith experiments in race relations. On a map, resources still follow race, by and large, so racially segregated geographies tend to reflect economically segregated opportunities.

Yet two things have dramatically changed the prospects for every American. First, Justin now has numbers behind him, even if they were not present in *that* audience. In fact, though born a "minority," Justin will not die one. The demographic reality of a nonwhite nation is no longer a prediction but a fact in the nation's largest metropolitan areas. The places where predominantly nonwhite people still struggle for the resources to become the next generation's middle class are becoming the norm. From the South Bronx to Compton, California, and thousands of cities and inner-ring suburbs in between, the problem of racially inequitable access to the middle class will soon become one of *the* issues in this nation's quest for a politically robust, economically competitive, and environmentally sustainable future.

The second big change is the loss of the grip on middle-class status among those who once securely held it. Being a middle-class household has become as tenuous as being a middle-class community. Large structural shifts in the economy and long lags in law and policy have contributed to widespread instability and doubt about the future. Growing class inequality—and specifically the concentration of wealth and privilege among a dwindling few—reflects shrinking options. It takes a lot more to become and to stay middle class in a high-tech services economy, and there is much less government or union help to do it. Even traditional options such as going to college (if you're a young person) or fiscal zoning (if you're a growing town) carry risky expenses that no longer seem a sure investment in a stable future. What people and communities could do just a decade ago looks extravagant now. Expectations about middle-class life have fundamentally changed, and there is no good reason to assume the old paradise will return.

So, after all the years between Justin's speech and mine, these two facts—demographic transformation and broad middle-class instability—bring an ironic hope to a scary state of things. The central point of this book is that our future success as a culture depends on a greater commitment to equity and interdependency in the laws and policies responsible for creating middle-class opportunities. That sounds distinctly 1960s, I know, which is a fair criticism except that today the conditions are such that we really must be all-in about these things. In those days, we had little reason to assume more than an abstract connectedness about our lives in the United States, so we tended to hope for the principle of integration more than to actually live it. Now interdependency is a local fact for most of us despite decades of segregative policies separating us by race, class, and place. Equitable integration—sharing services, sharing classrooms, sharing regional economies, sharing sidewalks near our homes, and sharing burdens—has ripened into necessity. Being middle class is no longer the stuff of dreams. It must become the primary function of our policies at the local, state, and federal level.

This book is about how we got here from where we've been and how we can do better. It is intended as a constructive examination of the problems I described, or social stratification, which the sociologist Douglas Massey nicely defines as "the unequal distribution of people across social categories that are characterized by differential access to scarce resources."[4] Resources may be material, symbolic, or emotional. However, the book is also an analysis of our grandparents' most cherished *assumptions*, the ones they bequeathed to us and that we have faithfully, and now fatefully, followed into the current crisis about spatial inequity—or, the suspect processes that produce gross inequalities between places. Because these assumptions about people's social worth, racial identity, and economic standing have configured our most common residential patterns, we can find cures for inequity in policies that focus on the social value of places. Ultimately, this book is a rejection of our divisive assumptions, an argument about the profound interdependency of our lives, and a guidepost for regional communities of mutuality—what some call *metropolitan equity*. "Community," I know, is probably a hackneyed term by now; it was becoming so in 1980. But a *beloved* community is something few of us have tried.

## Rational Dad

Let me give you an example of how the points above intersect. Most literature in economics, geography, law, and urban planning takes as a given the behavior of so-called rational actors. Like Charles Tiebout's hypothetical "consumer–voter,"[5] rational actors are presumed to make efficient choices that maximize their interests at the lowest cost. As a society, we collectively rely upon their individual reasonableness. So for a moment call me the Rational Dad. I am relocating with my middle-class (about 120 percent of median income) family to your medium-sized city, and I want you to advise me about where to buy a home. Home ownership will redeem my sense of citizenship, making me an economic stakeholder in my community, with taxpayer standing on political issues, and, very importantly, a consumer of public and private services, like street cleaning and nice places to shop. However, *where* I own a home will determine how much support my family receives in staying middle class. Following our grandparents' script, you will avoid talk of "diversity" and point me to the suburb with the best schools, the lowest taxes, and the shortest commute to work (in that order). You will enumerate the many amenities—low property taxes and steady property values, consistently solid school rankings, good libraries, nice recreational facilities, decent shopping variety, and the reputation for good local health care—while making passing reference to the lack of negatives (like declining strip malls, high rates of foreclosure, or rampant crime). I will thank you for your careful assistance, check with a dozen other people behind your back, scour the Internet by candlelight, and eventually buy the cheapest available house in the "best" and almost certainly racially and economically homogenous neighborhood the realtor happens to show me. Paradise bought.

Because I am rational, I will not allow this investment to be colored explicitly by color, so I will let your disregard for diversity go unnoticed. Since I believe "all politics are local," I will also ignore the region around my new 'burb (at my peril). Because I am my grandparents' grandson, I will act unconsciously on my assumptions. First, I will assume that the law and government have generally worked in my best interests, helping to stabilize the life chances of contributors like me. Second, I assume that my choices and what I buy with them reflect my merit as a self-sufficient, middle-class person. Third, I will assume that the absence of any poor people around me helps to preserve my status as a self-sufficient, middle-class dad. Fourth, I will assume that racial and ethnic diversity, were it relevant, would not be an issue because segregation no longer exists unless the proverbial *they* voluntarily prefer it. Fifth, I will assume that the avenues of my new life contain none of racism's litter, because racism, I am persuaded, doesn't limit opportunity anymore (see Barack Obama!). Lastly, I will assume that I need not worry about the poor who live somewhere out of my sight because, sadly, *those people* have made poor choices born of weak values. For now, these are the core assumptions. Dream secured—for the moment.

You may have guessed that the problem with my Rational Dad began when he ignored the region, and it devolved from there. The regional economy contains a range of interlocking fiscal realities that result from entrenched social arrangements, which are in turn reflected in Rational Dad's taxes, the learning environment in his children's schools, his children's safety, the quality of the workforce that services them, and many of the prospects for overall economic decline or vitality for residents of that small part of the world. Rational Dad should have asked about median-income disparities between neighboring towns in the county, for example. Too much disparity is expensive and promotes inter-local competition for the latest office park (with the loser getting only traffic congestion). He should have asked whether the public schools are strong *throughout* the region, not just in the town he chose, since state aid to the weaker districts will come out of his state income taxes. Rational Dad should have asked for trends in racial and ethnic segregation in order to determine whether he will be paying the premium for more segregation over the years or getting the discount that comes with more evenly distributed populations of all groups. He might also wonder if his children will receive the demonstrated social benefits of a diverse educational environment. And dad was downright irrational to ignore poverty—not just the rates by race, but also whether it's concentrated. There is nothing more expensive or persistent as concentrated poverty. The Rational Dad of children born in *this* century might have concerned himself with the prospects for maintaining all those stabilizing amenities in his town *and* for other people's children across the region.

Unfortunately, Rational Dad was born in the last century. I don't mean to mock him (so was I). Like Rational Mom, he is well-intentioned and serious. Yet because their assumptions about being middle class derive from a public–private system of cities and suburbs that for generations subsidized a white middle class at the expense of central cities and nonwhites (especially blacks), they struggle with a changing narrative. We all do. This was the paradise of an American Dream that reached millions. The narrative changed.

Here's how. When the Civil Rights Movement explicitly attacked the race-based privileges of whiteness, the privileges were recreated under a regime of legal and political colorblindness that could be leveraged by some nonwhites, too. The spatial result of this counter-movement was local control at the municipal level—"localism," local sovereignty, or home rule—which fixated on property taxes (and thus property values) as the means to community well-being. The governing process took different forms around the country, whether it be in Pennsylvania, outside Detroit, metropolitan New Orleans, or Los Angeles County. But in all, the fetish of property values encouraged new barriers to entry into "have" communities, which contributed to the growth of "have-not" communities. Barriers naturally create spillover effects, and these disadvantaged certain communities more than others. Over the last generation, walls of overt racial exclusion gave way in pockets of the first-ring suburbs around Pittsburgh and Chicago, for instance. Justin's and my family moved in—along with many of our less advantaged peers. The unevenness of the situation promoted larger swaths of fiscal distress across the metropolitan region as tax bases couldn't keep up with local demands on them. Even self-contained municipalities like Bronxville, New York, could no longer sustain their normal levels of public services. Where wealth concentrated, exclusion remains—performed by the market, occasional discrimination, and the residue of land use rules that keep outsiders out. But many rational middle-class actors of more modest means fled the invasion of less affluent groups, sometimes further to the periphery, producing expensive sprawl, environmental degradation, and mind-numbing commutes. In turn, the communities they abandoned rapidly filled with the people they were fleeing—new immigrants and migrants from central cities. The weaknesses were already apparent when the final straw occurred: the Great Recession. Like the safety net for individual households that was transformed in the 1990s, the government safety net for towns and cities was transformed (if not dismantled) by the deficits that followed the housing crisis during the 2000s. In the process, whole regions are now absorbing an impact they were not designed to manage. Stubbornly sovereign for so long, they know not how to work together. So, more communities become financially unstable, and opportunities to become and stay middle class there hang by threads.

These shifts and shafts amid an inequitable landscape amount to unsustainable costs—the price, we are learning, of a paradise at risk. Such uncertainty could easily fuel a lot more division. Politically, the last two or three decades have provided a study in rising polarization, cresting perhaps during the Obama presidency. Polarization is fed by economic anger and desperation about just who are the givers (a forgotten white middle class/"one percenters") and who are the takers (people who pay no taxes/people who don't pay enough). Even this book is a chronicle of divisions, seen and unseen.

Yet the key to a reckoning with what has happened to us, I believe, is to recognize what is finally on the other side of these divisions: we can no longer avoid the presence and the desires of the Other, no matter how hard we try. Under our grandparents' assumptions we either ignored each other, expelled the Other, or ran away. Our new interdependent reality shows that we are running out of space to run. Even if we run, we can't hide from the costs. For example, it costs twice as much to educate a black child in poor Asbury Park, New Jersey, as it does to educate a white one in wealthy Holmdel a few miles away. The wealthy town's school budget comes almost 90 percent from local property taxes while the poor one's comes almost 80 percent from county and state taxpayers. Yet all of Holmdel's students graduate high school while only 60 percent of Asbury Park's students do. This makes no economic sense, and it is happening all over this country. The high price we are now paying for a history of inequitable access to an unfunded American Dream will be paid by all of us. In a way, division has produced its opposite: mutuality.

Mutuality implies Martin Luther King Jr., and Martin Luther King Jr. suggests social justice. I worry that social justice is not a subject many rational actors want to take up these days. The key may be in the difference between equality, a term associated with civil rights, and equity, a hallmark of fairness and the social contract. It reminded me of something Angela Glover Blackwell, the founder of PolicyLink, told me in an interview.

"I don't think fairness scares people," she explained. Engaging and elegant, Angela speaks with a lyrical clarity uninterrupted by doubt. "I think *justice* scares people. Everybody likes fairness. Children talk about fairness at the earliest age. PolicyLink's definition of equity is just and fair inclusion. An equitable society is one in which everyone can participate and prosper. The goals of equity are to create the conditions to allow all to reach their full potential." To her, this does not imply the sameness of equality and may even have little to do with it. "Equity says, what's the outcome that we want for everybody and what is the just and fair input it takes to get everybody there? I don't think that equity is hard for people to embrace on the fairness side of it. It's the *just* side of it that makes it challenging."

Most of this boils down to known subjects like housing and education policy, local government rules about democracy and zoning, and fiscal choices about infrastructure and transportation priorities—but that is not how the book is structured. Instead, I proceed by including these things within the rubric of our operating assumptions. We will travel around the country and see them in action, usually as a combination of short-sighted individual preferences and even shorter-sighted government policy. I try to present them in their appealing complexity, then subject them one by one to the principle of equity. It's a conversation about what you know and believe, challenged by what you suspect might also be true.

## The Assumptions That Structure the Book

Chapter 1 is an overview of paradise gained and lost in American communities. I introduce Martin Luther King's notion of mutuality and amend it. I look at the evidence of middle-class crisis and enter a brief discussion of the assumptions that led us here. Six assumptions then follow in detailed discussion. Chapter 2 begins in the single-family detached suburban home with what is the threshold assumption of the American Dream—that middle-class status is premised on self-sufficiency. Instead, we'll see the extent to which it progressed through a network of subsidies for many that was denied to others. This chapter also introduces the growth of localism as a distinct "color-blind" alternative to Jim Crow segregation after about 1965. Chapter 3 crosses the country to examine the assumption that preserving middle-class status means keeping the poor at a spatial distance. This legacy of economic separation is also a hallmark of localism, especially its legal form, despite its inequitable consequences. Chapter 4 explores the assumption that the United States has overcome its segregated past, with due exceptions for individual preferences. Facts strongly indicate otherwise, but because residential organization so often happens through assumptions it may not be clear to many of us what we're doing. I focus instead on schools. Chapter 5 examines the assumption that racism no longer limits material opportunity. After a discussion about how we've come to frame discrimination the way we do, I present the contrary evidence from environmental conditions, predatory lending, and criminal justice. Chapter 6 looks at the widely held assumption that the persistently poor remain so as a result of weak values and poor decision making—a sort of culture of poverty argument. The evidence is distressing, but it focuses mainly on public health factors that show how what outsiders perceive as dysfunctions are lived by insiders as traumas. We stay mostly in California for the final assumption, that racial labels are no longer accurate or helpful. This entails a difficult discussion in chapter 7 about the troubles with colorblindness and the profound cracks in the presumed solidarity of nonwhite people.

In the last chapter of the book I try to offer some answers. Simply ignoring our core assumptions would probably produce many long-term gains. But we need another concept of rational self-interest—and at least a framework for moving forward. Analytic conversations like this one are often long on critique and short on remedy. I propose a remedial framework embraced by a growing number of scholars called metropolitan equity. I lay it out in both general and specific approaches, with examples of particular reforms in use around the country. In general, I argue that self-interest at both the individual and community levels must aspire to a demonstrable amount of objective fairness. As Blackwell stated, we have to take equity seriously. We have to relearn equity in our policy making. But what does that really mean?

More specifically, this means enacting equitable policies sized to the region, with the goal of demonstrably expanding the resources that promote economic stability. Metropolitan equity has different variants, some appropriate to the characteristics of particular regions and not others. As a coherent approach to reform, however, it entails a focus on the things that reduce fiscal stress on municipalities, because those stresses are correlated with household economic stress. It elevates inclusiveness as a direct repudiation of the assumptions that have thus far guided residential organization in the United States. And it requires more equitable sharing of both burdens and benefits—the things we have fought over most, like affordable housing, waste treatment facilities, and school district membership—so that they are more evenly distributed among the towns and cities in a relevant metropolitan area. In the most practical terms, metropolitan equity will involve significantly curbing our system of localism and decentralized decision making.

I try to demonstrate how this works with a scenario borrowed chiefly from the work of the urban–suburban scholar David Rusk on the Camden, New Jersey, region. It starts with a goal of reducing the variables that retard opportunity—for instance, the rates of concentrated family poverty and racial segregation—by some arbitrary margin, like 5 percent. It further shows how much even a marginal improvement in these measures will affect individual as well as municipal well-being. It turns out that even modest changes at the start can produce significant benefits in a decade. Next, I discuss some of the specific policy proposals—regional tax-base sharing, for instance—that could be implemented to affect those kinds of results. It's a promising framework, not a blueprint, for regions across the country.

An ambitious project invites criticism, and I can anticipate a few here. One is that localism is a fancy word for the expression of a community's values, a pure form of democracy that is the last thing we should curtail. I am not an enemy of local participation, and many local functions can remain without promoting the constant competition to exclude undesirable uses and people. Recall that another word for local control is NIMBYism (not in my backyard), which often perverts democracy by revealing only which community is too politically weak to prevent something unwanted from happening to it.

Another criticism may be that all this ignores cities (my original love) at the expense of suburban ideals that are largely in decline. My answer is that the death of suburbs is greatly exaggerated. (People still love them, especially poor people.) More important, there remain great similarities in the inequitable relationships between wealthy and poor city neighborhoods and wealthy and poor suburbs. Large cities are forced by their boundaries to take a more "regional" approach to problem solving, unhampered by mythologies of local autonomy. Still, they mirror metro areas in their adherence to inequity. Upper-middle-class parents in New York City or San Diego are just as loathe to put their children in school beside poor kids as are parents in those cities' suburbs. Kids in Chicago die by gunfire only in certain neighborhoods. Somehow parents in all these places manage to do the same social sorting. Thus the rules of reform that create regional equity in the entire metro area have some application to reforms available in the large cities that used to be—but are increasingly not—the places where disparities in opportunity are most vis ible in the United States.

A final criticism is that all this talk of structural reform operates too high above people's actual lives. Perhaps, but that has been our chief blind spot. Metropolitan equity strategies may be called first-generation strategies; they bring about a path to a more progressive mutuality in our institutional relationships. How we actually maximize our individual relationships once we share space, benefits, and burdens entails second-generation strategies. Those, too, are critical but beyond the scope of this book. These are bold steps that most communities can take only one at a time.

Ultimately, I hope to advance a discussion that has as its goal the expansion of middle-class opportunities across our changing country. We may yet achieve a broad coalescence of two dreams—the American and Dr. King's. We can act on our best principles to stabilize economic life for many more Americans and to discover along the way our common good. Paradise may not be possible, but a beloved community may be within a generation's reach.

# 1

## MUTUALITY

## THE THIEF, THE PREACHER, AND THE LATE-NIGHT LAWYER

*All I'm saying is simply this, that all life is interrelated, that*
*somehow we're caught in an inescapable network of mutuality,*
*tied in a single garment of destiny. Whatever affects one directly*
*affects all indirectly. For some strange reason, I can never be*
*what I ought to be until you are what you ought to be. You can*
*never be what you ought to be until I am what I ought to be.*
*This is the interrelated structure of reality.*
DR. MARTIN LUTHER KING JR.

When my youngest was two years old she used to point to any American flag she saw and say, "There's that Obama thing, Dada." That alone, I realized, is why some people fear the future. Yes, a president is often seen beside the flag, but for so many children to learn about *this* flag beside *this* president is just a peek at how basic meanings about American life are changing. What's new and hopeful for her generation is still fraught and contested for mine. Beneath adult differences over who represents our national symbols, however, are more broadly shared fears about how opportunity will be constructed for our children.

Americans have good reason to worry about the way to a middle-class future. The Great Recession revealed fault lines in banking and on Wall Street, diminished home ownership as a family's central asset, weakened college prospects, and altered for millions the likelihood of a stable job or even retirement. It wiped out all the wealth gained by the middle class during the 1990s, and devastated state and local budgets.[1] Over all, these changes have shaken our personal faith in mobility by destabilizing our local faith in environments that were designed to support an American—middle-class—Dream. In particular, economic collapse pulled back the curtain on the flawed ways we finance schools, public safety, and infrastructure repair, foreshadowing decades of limited services, unstable budgets, and grossly unequal communities. At risk is not merely individual access to a middle-class life. Equally frayed are the collective means by which we get there: the social contract.

Unlike conventional approaches to the topic, I hope to demonstrate how most of these problems reflect our rules about *place*, especially how place helps to determine opportunity. Place is where opportunity in principle happens in practice. Beyond your immediate family, the tangibles of your well-being run through your home, job, schools, transportation, community organizations, food shopping, and the basic infrastructure of the landscape—all place-based needs of our lives and most of them local. If we are fortunate to live in a place high in opportunity, we get an array of supportive connections that aid in the business of life; just as important, we avoid a gauntlet of stresses that might hold us back. Things work, routines make sense, costs are reasonable, hassles few. For many of our grandparents, this was the unspoken promise of American middle-class residency, a veritable paradise of markets and merit that became the envy of the world.

Of course, places can also limit opportunity, often severely. Many communities have unstable tax bases, strained public services, and aging infrastructure needs that constrain the resources of most institutions in town. A lack of institutional cohesion usually mirrors a lack of social cohesion, and folks in less stable places spend a lot of their energy struggling to hold on to reliable options. They endure bad treatment, deferred maintenance, higher taxes and user fees, slow responses, and the obstacles can mount into traps. These are areas of lower opportunity, and right now in the United States the number of low-opportunity environments is outpacing the number of high. Residents of areas with such limited capacity come disproportionately from groups my generation still calls "minorities." The other big change occurring—the population shift to majority minority—will happen by the time my child can vote. For the country as a whole, the miracle of becoming a racial plurality comes just when opportunity is in steep decline.

So, we are challenged but not doomed. In fact, these two indisputable forces in the United States—the growing instability of the middle class and the rising proportion of previously excluded groups—inspired this book. Lurking in the antagonism is an untapped alliance of interests rooted in our geography.

I found that the key is to begin every inquiry about opportunity by asking about the role of place. Fiscal crises among local governments often reflect a legacy of rules about the local control of places—or "localism"—in two important ways. First, these deficits represent the unbudgeted costs of paradise, a grand reckoning for past excesses that are now visible in bloated pension obligations, staff layoffs, and threatened bankruptcies *within* the finances of towns and cities across the country. They diminish the quality of life and eventually the opportunities of residents. Second, and less known, is how localism exacerbates disparities in opportunity *between* places, too. Generations of inequitable localist policies have favored the places currently occupied by a fortunate few over those of the emerging majority. This distribution of public resources is unfair, unreasonable, and unsustainable.

Yet balkanized local realities obscure linkages among localities. It turns out that *most* municipalities are battling fiscal distress or rapid demographic change; many are battling both. They're just too fragmented to know much about the others' plight or how one's policies can affect others. For too long we have ignored causal dynamics in the conditions between places that we always assumed were independent. For just as long we have ignored regional interests. Meanwhile localism has driven up costs for all but the wealthiest municipalities and neighborhoods. Revealing the interdependent relationship among towns and cities, then, suggests an essential *mutuality*, as Dr. King said in the fifty-year-old quote above. Of the many reasons to address inequities now, the best is that, more than we ever knew, *we need each other's success*. The alternative is for the nation to become something we don't want it to be.

This book is a long, sometimes difficult conversation about the social and fiscal consequences of residential life as we've chosen to organize it in much of the United States. Common to our communities are the assumptions that built them—some well-intentioned, some not. Examining assumptions allows us to ask frank questions of empirical evidence, like who really gets the most government subsidies, or why should I live near poor people? We will travel throughout the nation and investigate whether racism really limits people's options anymore, or whether blacks and Latinos have any good reason to get along. Throughout, we must question how we have used place to condition access to middle-class opportunities and whether there is common ground for reform. I think there is, in a framework called metropolitan equity, with which I conclude the book.

In this overview chapter, we examine relationships among place, equity, and mutuality as illustrated in a story about rogue parenting. Then we look at how our system of local control may have forced the rogue parent's hand. Next, we discover that this unwelcome rogue may really be us—or most of us—merely disguised as a rogue, who comes from stressed-out places like our own. Colorblindness—the idea that race is irrelevant and its mention is bad news—enters late as necessary backstory, so much of the work of race and class differences having long been mediated through rules about place. At that point, I introduce the remaining structure of the book along the six common assumptions about residential life that have configured most American communities. Though understandable for the paradise they once brought, I maintain that those assumptions are now wrong, unsustainable, or both. In what threatens to be the denouement of the American Dream, I offer equity as a second-act principle for remaking opportunity. Because there is harm, there should be accountability; but instead of blame, I suggest we think about principles from the law of negligence. Mutuality of a progressive kind, I argue, can make for happy endings.

## The Thief Who Stole School

This is a crime story. Our felon is a forty-year-old single mother from Akron, Ohio, named Kelley Williams-Bolar. A jury convicted her of criminal "deception" after prosecutors proved she had falsified residency records that purported to show that her two daughters—aged twelve and sixteen—lived with their grandfather in the Copley–Fairlawn school district in the Akron suburbs. The Copley–Fairlawn schools are good schools, rated among the very best in the state. Apparently, the schools in the district that services the public housing project where Ms. Williams-Bolar lives are not so good. Ms. Williams-Bolar knows something about the value of education, because she was a few credits shy of receiving her teaching degree at the University of Akron. Now as a felon her ability to get a license to teach in the state is in serious doubt. She already served nine days in jail, must do eighty hours of community service, and will be on probation for two years. Her sixty-four-year-old father, who was sick and under her care, was also charged with tampering with records and stealing money from the Copley–Fairlawn school district. For the two years they got away with it, they must now pay about $30,000 in tuition restitution.[2]

I did not attend the trial, but I have some idea of what the prosecution was thinking. First of all, they were thinking that this mother and her dad were stealing from the district by way of fraud, both very bad things. Second, they wanted to make an example of this mom as a deterrent to others. And third, they understand that nearly *all* school districts, municipalities, counties, states, and, of course, the federal government, are now contending with seismic budget shortfalls. This is no time for charity to district outsiders when district taxpayers are being squeezed. For every student like the Williams-Bolar girls, there's little or no state money. Locals must pay twice—for their own kids and to subsidize boundary jumpers. In many states, more affluent taxpayers would pay a third time—in state and county income taxes that disproportionately become state aid grants to make up property tax shortfalls in the school districts of central cities and poor suburbs.

I only read the reporting of Ms. Williams-Bolar's testimony, but I have some idea of what she was probably thinking, too. First, she really seems to believe that she had been cleared of wrongdoing in an earlier investigation conducted by the school. Second, she did not want her daughters to be statistics about loss and failure. She was afraid for them in their neighborhood—the apartment had been burglarized and she frequently filed police reports of dangerous activity afoot. She was also living proof (until her conviction) of the mobility a good education provides. She wanted her girls to have the same or better opportunities to succeed as she was having later in life. And third, she may even have had some sense that their ability to compete in school would affect their ability to one day enjoy better jobs, financial security, a longer, healthier life, a more stable mate, less stress, assets for retirement, and all kinds of middle-class benefits.

There's a lot about this story to mine, and I'll return to the questions of why local government entities are so cash-strapped, or why the prosecution baffled the judge by pursuing the case to the fullest, or the morality of Ms. Williams-Bolar's act. But what's most interesting about this story is the importance of place. What this mom really tried to do was transcend the boundaries of place to get her daughters to the greener pastures on the other side. It's like a prison break. This book is about why she would try and why she was denied.[3] Let's assume for a moment that this mom is truly guilty—she and her dad conspired to fool the district into thinking visits to grandpa really amounted to residency. If she had instead stolen food for her daughters, the sympathy would have been overwhelming. But rather than the proverbial theft of a fish dinner, she was stealing the ability to teach her children to fish—in fact, to fish really well, as other kids who go to fine schools can do. And for her it all turned on the vagaries of where she lived versus where the good schools are. It all turned on place. Isn't getting your children to a safe and nurturing place so their future will be brighter than yours what most parents in the United States try to do?

The story also raises concerns about the predictable consequences of Ms. Williams-Bolar not staying in her place. Whatever real or perceived disadvantages that motivated her to deceive the school district are now much greater. As we'll learn more in chapter 5, bad things multiply for felons *and their families*, including the loss of her job as a teaching assistant to special-needs high schoolers, her new career, possibly her apartment in public housing, her ability to vote in elections, and, of course, the negative way she is regarded by anyone who learns of her criminal record. All these affect her children and her father in direct and substantial ways.

Why would she put so much at risk? I would speculate that, like the Rational Dad in the introduction, Ms. Williams-Bolar was appraising the risks and benefits like a Rational Mom and aiming for at least a piece of paradise. She probably wanted more than Copley–Fairlawn's schools, which represent only one ingredient of a stable life there. She may have wanted to live on its safer streets, to enjoy the towns' public services and quality stores. If she could afford it and could still make it to her job in Akron, she may have wanted Copley or Fairlawn's reputation for good doctors and strong civic organizations and recreational facilities. Nice towns like these have even become job centers in the last two decades; companies like them as much as their employees do. Most of all, Ms. Williams-Bolar might have wanted to live among the heightened expectations and sense of well-being that accompany life in a place where local institutions work to support a family's basic needs, a place of potential growth. This is what place can buy, if you can afford the price of entry.

The battle between this mom and the school district that convicted her reveals how each is a symbol of much more. Just as Copley–Fairlawn's successful schools represent the cumulative advantages of many policy and market factors in some towns, so does Ms. Williams-Bolar's crime mirror the aspirations and frustrations of those locked out of them.

Solving the crime does not end its consequences. Indirect economic consequences affect the winners and neutral players in this story, too. The public court system, our laws, and the school district all saw their rules vindicated. The effect was exclusion of outsiders. That "victory" assumes that those institutions and perhaps a few others can keep life stable for the good folks inside the boundaries. Nevertheless, we will *all* pay for what Ms. Williams-Bolar's daughters do with their lives. If they succeed to independence, we will tax their contributions, count their votes, and learn from their experiences. But if they struggle to make do, we may spend tax dollars to incarcerate them, disability payments to sustain them, or some other expensive public intervention. One way or another, many of the lost opportunity costs to young people like them will come back to the towns, the county, and the state. As more struggling households fan out in search of jobs, safe schools, and affordable housing, regional taxpayers may encounter the myriad disadvantages that come from living in a fiscally stressed, growth-challenged part of the country. Repeating the pattern across the nation's metropolitan landscapes, U.S. competitiveness suffers globally. Thus, keeping lower-income but Rational Moms out is a costly undertaking all around. This is mutuality.

However, there's another reason why the quandary of Kelly Williams-Bolar symbolizes mutuality: she is us. It's no longer a question of whether we *want* this mom and her daughters to succeed; as a society, we *need* them to succeed. Perhaps you sympathized with her but identified with the neighboring school district. Chances are, if you're "middle class," you are now closer to Ms. Williams-Bolar's position than to her distant neighbors in Copley–Fairlawn. The inequitable structure of our residential lives is catching up to more Americans, producing a lot of middle-class instability. According to the Institute on Assets and Social Policy at Brandeis University,[4] a closer look at the conditions necessary to be securely in the middle class showed that only 31 percent of "middle-class" families were squarely middle class—and that was in 2008, the year the status of those families would be severely tested by the onset of the Great Recession. The rest were a layoff or a sick relative away from falling out. Results differ by race. While a mere third of white families were securely middle class, only a quarter of black families and less than a fifth of Latino families could confidently claim that status. The Institute's indices take account of a family's ability to pay their basic living expenses for nine months in the event of a sudden loss of income. In 2008, only 13 percent could do that. That year, over half were completely without financial assets in excess of their liabilities. In all, the numbers show that *most* "middle-class" families live on the financial edge rather than the good life.

## Localism and the Price of Paradise

So far the main forces preventing Ms. Williams-Bolar's girls from attending the Copley–Fairlawn district were a zealous prosecutor and her lack of financial means. But something else kept out her and others like her: localism.

What I call localism others call local control (or more formally, home rule), but it comes down to many of the basic policies Americans take for granted. Until I lived outside New York City (and, some would say, moved to America), I did not fully grasp how important it is for residents of a town to feel like they have some say and control over what occurs there. In big cities, things seem to magically happen without a lot of citizen input. Not so in the small towns and suburbs that are still home for a majority of metropolitan America. People covet a sense of participation. They dislike surprise expenditures of their property tax dollars. They vehemently protest major changes. And they take loud exception to outsiders and newcomers whom they perceive as a threat to their stability and welfare. Localism is the expression of this ethos in formal rules about local control. (It is *not* the same thing as informal local networks that, through religious affiliation, block associations, or knitting circles, provide essential glue in our personal lives.) Formal localism is the rough-and-tumble, fiercely literal, punctilious, unglamorous, hyper-technical system of jurisdictional governance beneath our most cherished metaphor, the American Dream.

You can recognize it by its attention to boundary lines. Under localism, the white picket fence of lore holds more than azaleas in place, "that Obama thing" hanging from a pole in the background. As we see in the next chapter, the fence is an aesthetic of order and privacy reflecting the formal trappings of collective protection. Whether visible or not, the fence is, like lanes on a highway, a repeating boundary line of amenities, tax base capacity, zoning rules, street pickup, police surveillance, school buses, and stability—most of all stability—protecting family life from disorder and family assets from depreciation. In this fashion, localism reinforced the norm of middle-class life in much of the United States. In the sediment below its white picket fences lies a middle-class bedrock serving millions of our great grandparents and attracting millions more the world over. The process was neither dream nor accident. Since the New Deal, it was a public–private partnership of policies for the people—or at least most of them. Since World War II, it was an engine of opportunity, mainly for whites. The Civil Rights Movement tried to extend this beautiful, bountiful vehicle to minorities. With that power, anybody's dream of a protective fence might be realized.

As a legal matter, these ideas are codified in local government as state delegations of home rule authority and the exercise of police powers. It is a form of decentralized decision making that allows variations in styles and preferences among towns. It may even foster a diversity of municipal personalities. Where localism has taken hold—across the Northeast and Midwest especially—it has resulted in much fragmentation (New Jersey, for instance, has 565 municipalities; New York has more than a thousand towns and cities and Ohio has more than two thousand). In the legal theory of courts following the lead of the Supreme Court during the 1970s, localism provides the philosophical groundwork for cohesive, self-determined communities.[5]

So what could be wrong with localism? In practice, localism is expensive, chronically exclusionary, fragmented, insular, and heavily subsidized. Most of all, it is inequitable. It's logic demands so. Suburbs, small towns, and small cities, built on the questionable assumption of self-sufficient communities, disproportionately rely on property taxes for their fiscal needs. Because they wish to control everything—police, fire, schools, zoning—and keep them attractive to residents and desired newcomers, they must maintain high levels of services. Which means they must always compete with their neighbors for the people and land uses that bolster, not hinder, the tax base. They must also exclude anything and anyone that risks increasing the costs of services. Freeloaders (and renters) beware. Still, as we'll see in subsequent chapters, this system of quality services, inter-local competition, and rampant exclusion could never be as self-sufficient as it claimed. It has relied heavily on government subsidy in myriad forms (though it no longer can).

Because interdependence requires recognizing some connection between Rational Moms like Kelly Williams-Bolar and nice towns like Copley, Ohio, it's easy to see why localism is at odds with any notion of interdependence. Localism teaches a reluctance to share unless it is directly in the self-interest of the municipality. Localism leaves equitable considerations out of most decision making. Like a corporation pursuing shareholder gains, individual municipalities ignore the regional effects of their internal decisions.[6] When we think about such common suburban equity conflicts as opposition to affordable housing, interdistrict choice for school children, or the siting of environmental hazards, the fundamental battle is almost always about localism. Stronger municipalities usually object, leaving the distribution of things nobody else wants unfairly concentrated in the places too weak to deny them.

By the end of this book I hope to demonstrate that the result of this zero-sum game is inefficiency, fiscal stress, segregation, and gross inequity. If you were designing a system of local government under today's economic conditions, you probably would not build in the need for more than two thousand police departments (as Pennsylvania has) or a zoning board for virtually every incorporated area (as New York State has) or 590 school districts (as New Jersey has). The costs for basic services duplicate across Miami–Dade County. Planning for the welfare of families in Los Angeles County is complicated by the many jurisdictional differences. You would be embarrassed to reproduce a system of residential and school segregation that rivals the numbers *before* the Civil Rights Movement. The waste from this is nearly as great as the inequities that result. It's hard to explain why, for example, the benefits of large public-sector economic development investments are not typically shared by regional neighbors. Localism's political fragmentation promotes the balkanization of interests as well as identities. In the inefficiency that results, losers outnumber winners more and more. This arrangement will inevitably reduce opportunity for my daughter's generation to the vanishing point.

This is why recognizing mutuality is so important. Let's see it in demographic patterns first, then move on to the mutuality of place.


## The Mutuality of People and Groups

Consider how demographic changes reveal growing mutuality. In 2011, a majority of all babies born in the United States were not white.[7] This means that the variable most responsible for our rules about community life and welfare for over a century—families with children—is now nearly as nonwhite as white. This is almost the same as saying that the very idea of the American family—that dreamy visual from Norman Rockwell, the scratchy sounds of Kate Smith singing "God Bless America," and the fresh aroma of apple pie—is on the verge of being permanently colorized, at least in the nation's population centers. According to the 2010 census, in the one hundred largest metropolitan areas of the country, married couples with children continue to be a declining share of all households (just 23 percent).[8] However, among married couples with kids, almost half (47 percent) are not white. In fact, 20 percent of that number are Latino, the demographic group whose fertility rates (plus immigration) are most responsible for all the major trends in population growth over the last decade. A majority of Latino married couples (54 percent) had children. By contrast, in these same hundred metro areas, only 28 percent of non-Latino white married couples had kids. This means that as trends continue, in just a few years the majority of all married parents will be Latino, black, and Asian.[9]

With families at the center of our policies, this changing demography may alter how we look at the social capital of children. The babies now in diapers demonstrate that racial and ethnic diversity, not homogeneity or customary racial hierarchy, is the new and foreseeable normal. When we are talking about what makes for a quality preschool, the costs of achieving optimal class sizes, or what skills a college graduate needs, there will no longer be a racial presumption about whom we're talking. When we assert the need to return to traditional "family values," it will no longer be clear whose family values we're asserting. And when we question whether single motherhood is a choice or being a child born out of wedlock is a predicament, the stereotypes will have less and less resonance because no group is overrepresented. That is cultural convergence.

Because underneath the numbers is the convergence of the norm to include nearly everybody, we will be forced to think differently about race. It will undermine the stereotypes on which we rely—even if it doesn't completely change them. Think of the racial palette you might expect to see in your average central city bank branch today. The security officer may be any race, but not surprisingly a black or Latino male. The tellers will be mostly women of color—black, Latina, Indian, Korean, Filipino. Perhaps there will be more men among the loan officers, also a mix of races. But the managers—often out of sight, in back rooms or upstairs—will be mostly white. In private equity, consulting, and the executive functions of the bank across the globe, we still expect to see a professional class that is overwhelmingly white and male. They are more credentialed, make higher salaries, and hold more power. This same status-based racial spectrum of employees will repeat itself in hospitals, tech companies, and law firms. It is simply how things are, and it fuels our stereotypical expectations about who can do what well. Right now it is partly supported by sheer population numbers. But soon—in less than a generation—it won't be. Soon the persistence of racial lopsidedness will bring instability, as elites disproportionately come from white and Asian homes despite their shrinking share of the overall workforce.

Cultural convergence will be accompanied by more fiscal and political interdependency. Every family issue has a public cost component. How we pay for them reflects our governmental arrangements. The problem for localism revealed by these new demographic realities, then, is that most places in the metropolitan area where families live will *never* be able to tax their way into stable middle-class schools and services anymore. The social capital of the tax base—the middle-class home owner professionals and blue-collar workers—will be increasingly not white. That base now comprises recent immigrants and native people of color, most of whom have never lived in those protected places nor generated the assets and resources of people who have lived there. For them, the white picket fence represents no more than a Home Depot purchase. It is just a fence, with many fewer constitutional privileges and governmental subsidies than in the past. Nevertheless, they want what Kelley Williams-Bolar wanted for her children and herself: to live a life of protected potential. As a society, we need them to achieve it. And this is really the central demographic fact of our lives, demanding that we come together for a broader, cross-border notion of the common good. As Myron Orfield's research shows below, the paradise of localism is running out just when a new majority of minorities is moving into the places where it reigned.

## Mutuality and Metropolitan Places after the Dream

An affable and approachable man, Myron Orfield speaks with the unmistakable accent of a high plains midwesterner—specifically, Minnesota, where he was a state legislator until he became a law professor. For years he has been teaching state and local officials about the social and fiscal costs of regional inequity. A man possessed by data, he does most of his magic with PowerPoint and maps. Orfield performs a range of tax-base analyses that compare the relative strength of municipalities within nearly all regions of the country. His multicolored comparisons of fiscal strength show a landscape of fragility that clashes with most Americans' ideals about suburban life, because it resembles an enormous, struggling city—with a few affluent neighborhoods buffering themselves from encroachment by a great many more in decline. Like middle-class households, most middle-class towns are fighting fiscal stress.

Before looking at two of Orfield's main conclusions, it's worth noting his methodology. For many of us it represents a different way of assessing the geography of opportunity.[10] Since most people think any municipality is only as good as its revenue streams, Orfield uses three measures: tax capacity, tax capacity growth over a five-year span, and total revenue capacity (tax capacity plus state aid). These combined measures give you a pretty good idea of one town's revenue capacity versus the next. However, a full profile of health requires that you offset the revenue picture with some idea of costs. For this Orfield uses five measures: the number of children eligible for free or reduced school lunch, population density, the age of the housing stock, population growth, and the percentage of the minority population that is not Asian. These rough measures all contain some built-in assumptions, if not biases. The first is a measure of child poverty. The second gives a sense of how urbanized the place is—higher densities reflect more urban costs for services. The third complements that, because older housing stock is correlated with older infrastructure. Older infrastructure breaks down more often and costs more for towns to maintain. Population growth tells you that a place is attractive to new residents and, if so, that the town's needs for costly services will also increase (hopefully in proportion to the new revenues raised by taxes on new residents). And the extent to which the presence of minorities represents people other than Asians goes indirectly to the heart of what everybody's usually thinking about (hint: color).

What Orfield found is that suburbs can be characterized in six different ways along a spectrum of fiscal health and household opportunity. Three types of suburbs are considered financially "at risk"—that is, under severe fiscal stress, or, as one might say of a home owner facing foreclosure, underwater. These are represented by places like Irvington and East Orange outside Newark, Compton outside Los Angeles, and Opa-Locka in Miami–Dade County. Their expenses are greater than their revenues, sometimes leading to chronic deficits. They have higher rates of all the indicia of need, become poorer faster, and lose business activity more easily. These at-risk municipalities he grouped on a continuum of hardship as "at-risk, segregated," "at-risk, older," and "at-risk, low-density." Many of the at-risk suburbs are harder and more difficult places to live than anything I experienced in the part of Harlem where I grew up. And, as we'll see, the worst of the at-risk suburbs are racially and economically segregated. They have the greatest number of poor children who struggle amid many more constraints than our five indicators describe. From the standpoint of services, the families there –and they *are* mostly family households—live in places that are well underwater and filling fast.

Suburbs—like city neighborhoods—also have spatial arrangements that reflect localism's competitive instinct for middle-class survival. For instance, each of the three types of at-risk suburbs fears becoming the next place middle-class people don't want to live. They are often the older "first suburbs" around cities and in close proximity to one another. Their fates are in each other's sights, and rather than inspire a sense of common purpose, their proximity merely heightens the fear that the "at-risk, low-density" will deteriorate into the "at-risk, older," and the "at-risk, older" sees itself slipping inexorably toward the economic bottom, the "at-risk, segregated." All this is keenly watched by those suburbs we used to romanticize, the quintessential middle-class suburbs Orfield calls "bedroom-developing." These communities are growing more or less apace with their tax capacity. They are the norm. They are mostly white. And they are, according to Orfield, where local ballot initiatives often begin and exclusionary zoning measures are in common usage, because they have the most to protect. Residents of these places put a premium on fiscal and political independence (at least when it serves them) under the rubric of self-determination and local control of community character. They, too, are within sight of the at-risk suburbs, if not alongside them. They fear both the reality and the illusion of decline. Indeed, they should know it, since many of their residents knew the at-risk suburbs a couple of decades ago when they used to live there.

Here's what happened. First, the good life in suburbia is generally not so good anymore. According to Orfield's data for twenty-five different metropolitan areas (all surrounding big cities),[11] suburbs in what he calls the "at-risk" categories included 46 percent of all the suburbs in the entire sample. Conversely, the statistical good life of suburbia exists on average for only about half of a region's suburban municipalities. How are households distributed across this economic landscape? If you include the central cities' population (and you should because many suburbs are still inextricably tied to the central cities near them), *almost 70 percent of the regional population lives amid fiscal stress. Seventy percent* of the metropolitan area. If they are "middle class," they are struggling to remain so.

Second, the growing number of suburban poor live where you'd expect them to live—in the places that couldn't keep them out. Though there are important differences by region, Orfield's general analysis reveals that almost all the poor (83–89 percent) live in "at-risk communities." If one subscribes to a theory of just deserts—you get back from society roughly what you put into it—that may not seem so unfair. But when you're talking about sharing a metropolitan area, its amenities, infrastructure, and relative competitiveness, it may seem inequitable— even unwise—that the places *without* fiscal stress housed only 12 percent of the metropolitan area's poor.

This is hardly a picture of the good life or what most of us would call the American Dream. Sadly, most of these data *pre-date the recession and the rising risk of bankruptcies*, which means the situation has gotten much worse in many parts of the country. This "landscape of precariousness," as one research team calls it, is becoming more complex, less rosy, and more similar to cities than we thought just a short time ago. Orfield's analysis further demonstrates municipal interdependence. Many of us can recall how the ratio of "have" to "have-not" neighborhoods in most of America's great cities led to their steep decline from the 1970s on. Some cities have not come back. Now the same ratio of unequal resources and tax bases is threatening the structure of opportunity among have and have-not *towns* within our metropolitan regions.

## The Promise of Progressive Mutuality

Thus far I have tried to sketch how the most toxic dynamic of localism produces its own antidote—greater mutuality of circumstances. Mutuality shows that we are generally connected by our choices, even self-interested ones. Nearly every choice we make affecting opportunity—attending private instead of public school, stealing a car, demanding a re-appraisal of our property tax bill—influences the context in which other people's choices are made. So do murder, obesity, and sprawl. When the city of Oakland estimates that homicides there cost taxpayers an average of $1 million, mutuality spreads pain beyond the victims' families by diminishing what all of Alameda County can do with its resources.[12] Mayor Michael

Bloomberg noted the mutuality associated with New Yorkers' diets when he defended his unsuccessful attempt to ban large soda containers by noting how obesity links to diabetes, which links to lost productivity and higher health care costs, ultimately borne by the general public.[13] Mutuality effects show that the costs of sprawl cannot be spatially contained. In 2006, the *Orlando Sentinel* studied taxpayer costs in that sprawling part of the nation and found that, if unabated, sprawl will cost each area resident $45,000 for new infrastructure.[14] Health insurance and climate change are other areas of mutuality on which we might agree.

When it comes to opportunity and social mobility, however, our insecurities about class differences and racial meanings make it harder to acknowledge connections to one another's welfare. Mutuality becomes more than a scientific principle and instead a source of social tension. Equity is always the last voice to be heard. Therefore, mutuality needs a normative framework in order to be a useful guide for reforms.

Enter the preacher. In 1963, when Dr. King referred to "inescapable networks of mutuality" that reveal intersecting causes, costs, and outcomes, it may have been understood as mere hopefulness. In the abstract, King's notion of mutuality makes a certain intuitive and aspirational sense—but not perfect sense. There may be mutuality that merely demonstrates the many non-obvious connections between things in an endless causal stream. That would be a *neutral mutuality* that follows the laws of physics or the operations of markets to some arbitrary stopping point. Then there's the kind of mutuality that shows how my advantages help ensure your disadvantages. That might be called *zero-sum mutuality*, a competitive fact of life producing winners and losers. I prefer to think that Dr. King meant to push us toward a third kind of mutuality, one that understands the science of the first, rejects the wasteful inequity of the second, and aspires instead to use our connectedness for more inclusive upliftment. That is more consistent with Dr. King's other teachings and with his communitarian approach to social inequality. I'll call that *progressive mutuality*, because it's a kind of reality plus hope. If mutuality reveals the reasons to act in shared interest, progressive mutuality suggests a way forward.

Yet for even progressive mutuality to mean something more than shared consequences amid a divided populace, it must refer to opportunity in more specific ways. When we talk symbolically about an American Dream, we're generally thinking about the meaningful opportunity to increase what social scientists call our own *social capital*, a kind of walking personhood of potential for ourselves and our children that comes in the form of available options. This involves fair access to the tools of opportunity, tools often associated with certain environments and the personal resources that help us make use of them. But we start where we are. People, like places, are not the same. Therefore, progressive mutuality entails a focus on how we ultimately make places better environments for developing social capital whoever we may be.

We'll look at more specific approaches in the final chapter, but for starters, let's imagine the scope of reforms in three broad arenas: local government rules, labor and transportation policies, and integration strategies. First, progressive mutuality recognizes greater efficiency and fairness when municipalities share more public services; it would seek lower fiscal disparities between towns; it might even counsel more municipal consolidation. Rules following progressive mutuality would incent smarter growth by rewarding economic and racial integration of more densely planned environments.

Second, progressive mutuality reforms would make more of transportation planning and the importance of physical mobility to economic mobility. Regional wage standards could minimize wage depression in particular localities, giving workers more choice about where to work. Impediments to bringing people who are persistently poor into the middle class can be reduced by transportation initiatives that make it cheaper and easier for workers to travel to job centers—especially when those workers live in inner suburbs and must reach outer suburbs beyond the reach of mass transit systems.

Third, progressive mutuality demands more decisive integration of people and place-based resources. It encourages wider research about how populations unfamiliar with or hostile to each other can do more than co-exist at a distance. This might mean school-funding policies that untether per-pupil spending from a student's residence—so the Williams-Bolar girls can bring their own funding to Copley–Fairlawn—or county-wide school districts. Integration might involve creating greater housing choice amid truly accessible affordable housing options so their mother could actually move there. At bottom, integration has to mean less isolation—of the wealthy and their disproportionate resources and the poor with their disproportionate deficits.

All of these examples represent ways of deconcentrating both wealth and poverty, spreading resources where they can do the most good and reducing costly inequality. They also represent limitations on local control. On those issues where equity is most needed but often lacking, localism has to give way to a broader orbit of decision making.

Americans get all of these things occasionally, but it's possible to do them more often. Being progressive is not a function of party affiliation or ethnic identity. My point is that fairness, respect for differences, and efficiency is what makes mutuality progressive. Its equitable soul makes it a guidepost for policy making in the common interest. Yet two issues remain: race and blame.

## Colorblindness and the Evidence of Things Not Seen

In all the local coverage of Kelley Williams-Bolar and the mixed emotions her story stirred, rarely did anyone mention the fact that she is black. Nor for that matter was there any attention to the fact that the school district in which her children were found to be trespassing is overwhelmingly white. The usual class euphemisms were there—housing projects and single mothers, top-rated schools and suburban taxpayers—but there was the typically careful avoidance of race. Did race matter to the prosecution, whose unusual decision to criminalize the matter caused the judge to say publicly, "The state would not move, would not budge and offer Ms. Williams-Bolar to plead to a misdemeanor"?[15] Was it all pure coincidence or was it circumstantial evidence of racialized thinking? We don't know and probably won't ever find out.

All we can know, as we peel back the evidence over the next few chapters, is that a black single mom's kids living in a low-income section of a city are far more likely than most other Americans to miss out on the public educational opportunities available across a more affluent suburban border. Hers is the inequality gap obscured within the larger inequality gap. Yet colorblindness—or the more recent assertion of a "post-racial" America—practically prohibits our acknowledgment of racial disparities.

Consider racial differences in terms of the broader equities of childhood opportunity. Another racial analysis of census data reveals disturbing facts about the extent to which kids grow up in impoverished neighborhoods. Poverty and even near poverty affect opportunity in myriad ways, but particularly in the exposure to violence and fear of crime, the limited quality of recreational options, and the sheer lack of resources available to young lives discovering how to put their potential to work in the world. As we'll explore in chapter 6, poor environments are stressful—physically and mentally—and require much navigating and adapting in order to survive. According to DiversityData.org, in a dozen metro areas across the United States black children live in neighborhoods where at least a third of all people are poor (even more are nearly poor).[16] In another eighty-two metropolitan areas, black children lived in neighborhoods where at least 20 percent of people were poor. That's a lot of struggle to be exposed to, with few countervailing examples of success nearby. Yet compare that to poor white children. In the same metro areas, poor white children live in more stable middle-class neighborhoods than do black children, often by huge margins. In Chicago, for instance, the disparity in exposure to other poor people is four times greater for black children. In the Bergen–Passaic, New Jersey, area, it's 3.2 times more for black kids. As a general matter, poor white children simply do not face the same threats, stresses, and lack of collective resources as do black kids. Being poor is hard enough. It should not be much better to be white poor than black poor, but it is.

Similar racial disparities hold true when we pull up a thousand feet in the air. As we've seen, Orfield's mapping analysis of relative municipal stress can be done strictly on the basis of wealth and tax capacity—a classic example of class, not race. But when Orfield adds in race as a factor, the maps look almost exactly the same—or worse. Everything he could map about fiscal inequality could be mapped onto racial inequality. And Orfield's are not the only ones to reveal so much of our old history in our latest reality. As we'll see in chapter 5, foreclosure maps are also strongly correlated with the borrower's race (even more than class); so is concentrated poverty—the most debilitating kind of poverty and the one that costs cities, suburbs, and regions the most. School dropout rates and achievement scores can be closely tracked to race. And there is nothing so undeniable as racial factors in health data. This is not about "race cards" and other rhetorical backhands. This is quantitative racial disadvantage whose costs ripple through mutuality. Yet colorblindness renders it barely relevant.

If colorblindness is so distorting, why is it so widely embraced, even demanded, in public dialogue? A full answer probably deserves its own book, and we will spend more time in the details in chapter 7. For now, suffice it to say that colorblindness is a philosophical habit that we adapted out of our greatest national embarrassment: racism. Since its popular emergence during the Civil Rights Movement, colorblindness is a four-headed hydra—making it that much more confusing. There's the liberal, aspirational head that wishes to see beyond race to a common humanity. There's the race-neutral legal head that believes any consciousness of race is presumptively discriminatory. There's the more cynical, conservative head that uses colorblindness as a shield for very racialized—sometimes racist—policies. And there's the newest head, born of wider immigration and interracial love, which produces a welcome ambiguity of racial identity and can see little sense in drawing bright racial lines. Proponents of each may be extremely invested in their views and not open to challenge. Many of us are just tired of the whole race thing and prefer a non-racial way out. I understand that racial meanings are constantly being constructed and reconstructed; there is no reason to assume colorblindness isn't reconstructed, too. But my point in this book is that race matters when it has structural, material consequences that violate our norms and hold us all back. Colorblindness, therefore, is a compulsion we have to get over. Like "postracialism," colorblindness will be relevant when seeing color reveals nothing but genes.

## Waking from the Dream of Assumptions

Despite its distracting, often counterproductive effects, colorblindness reminds us of the root tensions underlying our patterns of residential organization, including our resistance to change. To understand that resistance we must examine our communities through the assumptions that built them, rather than by a dissection of laws. Behind the tenets of localism are assumptions about American ideals. These assumptions join other assumptions about the nature of racism, for instance, or the integrity of poor people. My own research and the findings of others across disciplines shows the presence of these controlling assumptions beneath everything from local zoning policies, Supreme Court decisions, and the mind-set of the realtor showing you homes to buy. My list is not exhaustive, but the following six in particular often flow in order and may even sound like a conversation you've recently had:

1. Middle-class life is based on self-sufficiency, not handouts.
2. Preserving the benefits of a middle-class life requires distance from the poor.
3. Segregation no longer exists unless it's merely voluntary.
4. Racism doesn't limit opportunities anymore.
5. Persistent poverty results from weak values and poor choices.
6. We're all humans, so we'd be better off if we dropped all racial labels.

Like essential vitamins, these six assumptions are key building blocks in the twentieth-century experiment with middle-class prosperity, supporting a kind of paradise to many while marginalizing many others—now to the increasing detriment of all. Until recently, the record of achievement associated with these six assumptions has obscured how erroneous they are. Yet the six are not only wrong because there are voluminous data to show that each is unsupportable and inefficient; they are normatively flawed, because, as we'll see, they promote unfairness in violation of our first principles. Therefore, the structure of the book is a traveling conversation through each assumption, chapter by chapter, testing to see whether they can withstand their own harms. Consistently, the evidence points to an inescapable network of consequence and the need for better, less costly policies. The concluding chapter is a discussion of reform strategies under the rubric of progressive mutuality and metropolitan equity.

## The Late-Night Lawyer Ad Is Not All Bad

Finally, the color-blind quandary remains thick for another reason that has divided Americans: how to manage blame for resulting inequities. An unequal system of dwindling winners and multiplying losers demands a measure of accountability. When material benefits derive partly from racial inequities, there is a perceived (and possibly real) threat that some will be asked to pay up. Most Americans feel they were never complicit in any wrong. Individual sacrifice further complicates the idea of collective responsibility for others' shortcomings. Hearing the implied accusations, the narrative in our heads usually launches into one of the six assumptions, and the circle of acrimony winds round again. My feeling is that mutuality demands responsibility, not blame. And the model could be the same one heard on late-night TV lawyer ads: negligence.

Every personal injury lawyer who clambers out of a TV screen to ask you if you've been injured in an accident is talking about the largest body of law in our system—negligence—which we inherited (then revised dramatically) from England. We revised it during the late 1800s when we were coming into our own as a global power and needed a system of laws that would regulate our basic conduct toward one another.

The quandary then was the same as the one that confronts us now—namely, how do you regulate for the greater good the activities of a free people? This is another way of framing the social contract. Negligence, I submit, is the modern-day iteration of that bargain.

*Very* briefly, negligence law achieves social balance in a dispute through the idea of the basic duties we owe to others as understood by the reasonable person within us. That's about it. Each of us is free to do as we wish (even the freaky stuff) as long as we take reasonable precautions against hurting others within the foreseeable scope of our activities and decisions. If we fail in that duty and cause them harm, then we are responsible—not "guilty," but responsible—for the resulting loss they suffer. For example, if I build a great business developing some kind of cyber solution, but fumes from my manufacturing plant sicken a few people in the area, negligence law makes me responsible to find cleaner methods and to pay the victims—even distant victims. This obligation stands despite the good jobs I bring, the taxes I pay, and the fact that I did not intend to hurt anyone. I may have to pay something even if my victims are partly at fault for their own injuries. Obviously, this idea of responsibility can get pretty big. It can grow with the kind of activity. It can grow with the scope of the people at risk. It all boils down to whether the decisions we make under all the relevant circumstances are reasonable. Who decides what's reasonable? *We* (juries, taxpayers, voters, common folk) decide what's reasonable based on whether, in our experience, the risks to others were foreseeable. This recognition of responsibility takes intention out of the equation. People who are accidentally harmed by otherwise good works need to be "made whole." Our system of laws regards this scheme as basic fairness, even justice. Within a given dispute, it produces a more equitable distribution of benefits and burdens. If we imagine it more broadly, it provides a basis for managing our responsibilities under a contemporary social contract.

Negligence, like mutuality, begins and ends with balancing, a balancing of duties, risks, and causal connections. Right now in the United States, by forgetting some of our first principles and upholding our grandparents' assumptions about place, we are weakening the basis for the middle-class that we need in order to sustain our way of life while putting millions of lower-income people at undue risk of diminished opportunity to become middle class. Yet, as the past has clearly shown, the resulting harms are foreseeable. It is unreasonable to reproduce so much inequity, because it ignores the interrelatedness of our fates. Still it happens, for many reasons, but mostly, as I explore next, as a result of the six commonly held assumptions. Because we have acted under them for so long—each of us in society—we are responsible for the consequences of our assumptions, *especially* the unintended ones. The good news? As the final chapters show, there are many good ideas occurring in laboratories across the United States that hold the promise of regional growth, racial and economic integration, and more sustainable institutions for all of us.

Ultimately, the compound rhetorical question Americans have to ask ourselves is this: Knowing that our economic position will soon rely disproportionately on people at the bottom of the opportunity ladder, and trying to dig out of a deep recession that's changed many of the economic rules, and recognizing that a persistent lack of equity contradicts some of our most basic values, what compels us to keep paying a premium for it? We'll see.

# 2

## ALL THIS I MADE MYSELF

### ASSUMING THAT MIDDLE-CLASS LIVES ARE SELF-SUFFICIENT

*We shall solve the city problem by leaving the city.*
HENRY FORD

The story of our assumptions about place begins in the suburbs, not our big cities, as you might think. For many of us, the city is a place to find yourself, to discover your identity like some unsolved mystery, and to prove yourself. But that quest is traditionally for the young. Soon enough those urges give way to a desire to complete yourself (or your family) in a place built for that purpose, one that provides the raw materials—privacy, safety, natural beauty, and control—with which to "settle down." The suburbs, unlike cities, never take credit for your completion; they merely preserve it. The assumption of self-reliance may be the foundation of how Americans think about opportunity—how it's achieved, who deserves it, where it thrives—experienced, as always, in certain places. In our cultural imagination, the suburbs became that place over others. Even today, the ideal of suburban life politically and rhetorically continues to exalt the noble self-sufficiency of American middle-class personhood against the entitled, redistributive, and morally relativist character of the city. As this chapter shows, however, this basic assumption could not be further from fiscal reality.

From its expansion in the postwar years, the suburban model of the American Dream has relied on a wise but extravagant government scheme of massive subsidization. For most, but not all of us, these unprecedented subsidies related to key ingredients of economic well-being such as mortgage financing, income tax policy, highway infrastructure, home values, and ultimately household wealth. There is nothing hidden about these subsidies, which leads us to ask not whether middle-class status is deeply subsidized, but why we assume it's not. That irony is the focus of this chapter as we examine some postwar suburbs of the East Coast, the effects of New Deal supports, the ideals that evolved alongside that material history, and finally the contradictions and consequences of ideas and policies that valued exclusion above all.

As Christina "Chrissy" Thomas relates, our assumptions about middle-class self-sufficiency came to life in the suburbs of Philadelphia where she first went with her husband in 1957, not in the teeming, corrupt, anonymous City of Brotherly Love where she grew up.

"I was so proud," she says, tugging lightly at the lapels of a black house vest and almost blushing. Her eyes sparkle with a flash of long-nurtured memory, reminding me of favorite aunts, even my own mother. The high pitch of her voice is precise, tender birdsong. We are sitting at her table, eating a delicious lunch of meatballs, salad, and quiche she has prepared in the same home she and her husband left the city for decades ago. "We had practically no furniture at all. Just a little TV and our bed."

When they first arrived in the new Concord Park subdivision, it was still winter. You could scarcely find the town of Trevose on a map, though it was not far from Pennsylvania's new Levittown development in Bristol. The drive from Philadelphia felt like forever, she recalled. The miles seemed to stretch endlessly away from the city, though her friend Evelyn had told her it wasn't a long trip. Ms. Thomas recalls how proud her husband was to choose their lot, surveying from this angle and that how the view of things would be from their windows, the fall of the sun, the trees that would grow. They were so giddy about the opportunity to live in their own house, with their own front and backyard. In no time, however, loneliness crept in. She didn't work, though her husband did, so she was home alone. Even when a moving truck appeared and deposited another couple from the city whom she befriended, the loneliness could be the one disadvantage of their new home in "the country." Otherwise, it was perfect.

"When the weather got warm, you would hear the voices of children," she recalls, smiling. "You could hear them at a distance, and then little by little you would hear them closer until they knocked on the door. 'Do you have any little children?' they would ask me. 'Can they come out to play?' It was through that, one by one, the neighbors came."

During the 1950s and early 1960s, neither the town of Trevose nor Concord Park had much in the way of amenities or services, which meant the residents had to make them—schools, parks, puppet shows, even plumbing. The new people were resourceful. "There were a lot of professional people in one way or another. Doctors, lawyers, teachers, architects, engineers, chemists." They each paid $1,000 down for their ranch-style homes. They had a public system for drinking water but not for waste. That turned out to be no small challenge.

"We had our problems with the cesspools," Ms. Thomas recalls, making the first of several increasingly sour faces. "If I had known, I would *never* have bought a house here. Finally, after much work, it took a long time, thanks mainly to one neighbor who persevered, we got the sewers in." She pauses, exhausted as if she had just finished installing the sewer lines herself. "We were *desperate*. It was horrible!"

"It was," agrees Alice Swann, Ms. Thomas's best friend and another elegant older woman full of story and quick to laughter. "I grew up with an outhouse," Ms. Swann continues from the other side of the lunch table. "This was worse than an outhouse. This was in your house. It was pretty yucky."

They dealt with each need themselves. They were a community of pioneers, and they banded together, organized, and got a sewer installed, created puppet-making activities in a neighbor's backyard that eventually became the Wonderland Puppet Theater, and even negotiated the opening of a kindergarten (where Ms. Swann worked for a time). The pride they relate as they recall these beginnings is unmistakable and infectious. It's evident all around you as you look about the smallish three-bedroom house—the orderly flow of furniture, the care with which the art is arrayed, the clean sight lines from corner to corner of an impeccably kept house. Most of us would recognize this place in an instant: it is the sweet home and the long work of honest, middle-class lives.

We typically think of the 1950s, the era when Ms. Thomas had no sewer, as the real onset of suburbanization in the United States, the time when post–World War II housing production met up with demand and cars found highways to connect them to the urban periphery. But the suburban ideal was in gestation a lot longer than that. The 1950s represents the earnest magnification for all to see of a dream dimly conceived in the eyes of the rich long before. The "suburbs"—that dangerous, un-serviced hinterland beyond the city limits—weren't thought much of until wealthy families built country estates there in the 1850s. By the late nineteenth century, "streetcar suburbs" (i.e., suburbs created by the stops street cars made) began to open up the possibility of a single-family detached home to more middle- and even working-class people.[1] Soon the romance was on, as described with some cynicism by the urban historian Lewis Mumford: "To be your own unique self; to build your unique house. . . . [I]n short, to withdraw like a monk and live like a prince—this was the purpose of the original creators of the suburb. They proposed, in effect, to create an asylum, in which they could, as individuals, overcome the chronic defects of civilization while still commanding at will the privileges and benefits of urban society."[2]

The suburban dream begins, like all dreams, with the self at the center of things. And what the self comes to possess there, the self has gotten deservingly, through one's free labor and industry. No one gave anyone a home with a yard outside the rancor of the city; it was earned and maintained by a resourceful self. As Kenneth Jackson, a great observer of suburbs, notes, the ideal coincides with a place of physical privacy impossible in cities. "[J]ust as the body is the most obvious manifestation and encloser of a person," wrote Jackson, "so also is the home itself a representation of the individual. Although it is only a box, and often unindividualized of mass production and design, it is a very particular box and almost a tangible expression of self."[3]

The mythology about what the suburbs could do for a person (and his family) found its way into many endearing narratives, both formal and informal. From advertisements in magazines to pronouncements by the Supreme Court, the American Dream of upper mobility narrowly loyal to a single-family home amid lawns and trees, animated popular conceptions of American identity. Why else would the Supreme Court say this about a dispute over a zoning law that banned unrelated graduate students from renting some rooms together in a pristine Long Island town?

> The regimes of boarding houses, fraternity houses, and the like present urban problems. More people occupy a given space; more cars rather continuously pass by; more cars are parked; noise travels with crowds.
>
> A quiet place where yards are wide, people few, and motor vehicles restricted are legitimate guidelines in a land-use project addressed to family needs. This goal is a permissible one. . . . The police power is not confined to elimination of filth, stench, and unhealthy places. It is ample to lay out zones where family values, youth values, and the blessings of quiet seclusion and clean air make the area a sanctuary for people.[4]

It's pretty clear how the Court's language easily marked multifamily housing as an official suburban nuisance in future disputes, echoing the message of another big zoning case, called *Euclid*, fifty years earlier.[5] (Certainly no realtor would mistake multifamily housing for "sanctuary" ever again.)

Jackson's *Crabgrass Frontier* is still one of the most comprehensive accounts of how we came to know "suburbs" as psychologically and economically distinct from cities. Today, the two dimensions have merged into something indistinguishable, resembling consumption more than self-sufficiency. In many established suburbs, residential life seems based on a consumer model, offering shoppers one amenity and another. But in the late nineteenth and early twentieth century, building public institutions and community resources, as Chrissy Thomas and Alice Swann did in the 1950s, was a common feature of becoming a suburbanite. Breaking from the city brought significant infrastructure challenges that, at first, only the resources of home owners establishing their community could overcome. Land at the edges was cheap and wages were relatively high. Technologies were making it possible for developers to offer housing options to a wide range of buyers. In fact, home ownership in the "suburbs" was within the reach of so many Americans that, as early as 1900, studies showed that European immigrants who had come for factory jobs and first settled in the squalid density of nearby tenements, were enjoying a rate of home ownership that was greater than that even for native-born whites. The dream made financial as well as psychological sense. Streetcars made commuting possible, but folks needed the utilities to work. Sometimes better electricity, police protection, and water services came through annexation of the subdivision by the city from which it sprang; this was how cities expanded their own geography before 1930. More often, suburbs wanted to remain independent. They began to resist annexation by appealing to state legislatures. They incorporated as separate and distinct municipalities. And suburbs figured out how to get financial assistance for their needs because, despite doing things in the name of self-autonomy, they could not do it alone—not if they were to remain affordable.

## Subsidizing Suburban "Self-Sufficiency" with Big Government

The relationship between suburbs and cities could be antagonistic in ways. A study of Newark, New Jersey's suburbs between 1874 and the Great Depression by Richardson Dilworth demonstrates how towns built infrastructure in order to secure independence.[6] Infrastructure development is what separated an urban existence from a suburban one like a bathroom from an outhouse. The big public projects were in the cities, along with all the bribes, graft, and corruption. The taxpayers were there, too, yet so were the engineers who actually designed and implemented public works. In order to avoid the corrupt political culture of the city and in an effort to be mindful of high costs, towns began hiring the engineers trained on city projects to do their infra-structure projects at lower costs. The engineers converted urban-scale techniques to town-sized projects, becoming more efficient along the way and developing lucrative side practices on behalf of young, sub-urban municipalities. Public works in the suburbs would soon match the expectations of city dwellers. Although this strategy could not have happened without the market for expertise created by urban taxpay-ers, it promoted suburban independence and advanced the cause of autonomy. The more suburbs could be autonomous, the more attractive autonomy looked. Fragmentation of the regional landscape followed, and we've been captive to it ever since.

The history of suburbanization shows that what began as a roman-tic ideal about perfecting oneself could become popular only with gov-ernment help—*massive* subsidies. The explosive growth of a suburban middle class in the United States was fueled by a critical partnership between private developer interests and Franklin Delano Roosevelt's New Deal legislation. It included local practices of charging urban taxpayers for the development of the periphery, the formalization of home-loan lending criteria, and the direct role that the federal govern-ment chose to play in changing the rules of suburban home ownership and building the highways to get folks there. Such practices started in the 1930s, but really kicked in by the time soldiers came home from World War II. If it wasn't clear before, it was certainly clear then: the suburbs were favored places. They would have the best of everything at the lowest cost. As Jackson notes, the most desirable environments were being made on the edges at city expense. Affordability unimagina-ble to us today made it a bonanza that middle-class people like Chrissy Thomas and Alice Swann could not rationally turn down.

The money was cheap and plentiful. Automobiles, delivery by truck (not by train), and architectural efficiencies all helped elongate the boundaries of suburbia, yet nothing facilitated the expansion like federally guaranteed mortgages. Out of the National Housing Act of 1934 Roosevelt created the Federal Housing Administration (FHA), primarily as an employment program for people made jobless by the Great Depression. The FHA followed the formal practices of the new Home Owners' Loan Corporation (HOLC) for determining the qualifications of borrowers. It also developed uniform, written, objective construction standards. A mortgage industry that had been the preserve of building and loan associations began to interest retail banks attracted by the underlying federal mortgage guarantee. The FHA institutionalized the mortgage that, until deregulation in the early 2000s, millions of middle-class Americans came to trust: the thirty-year, self-amortizing loan with constant monthly payments at an interest rate of about 6 percent. Down payments were lowered to about 10 percent. "Quite simply, it often became cheaper to buy than to rent," Jackson wrote.[7] Together with the Servicemen's Readjustment Act—or GI Bill—Roosevelt had launched the makings of the modern middle class.

However, cities and particular neighborhoods within them weren't likely to see this money, which is a key fact in the creation of the black ghetto (discussed in the next chapter). According to Jackson, "[T]he main beneficiary of the $119 billion in FHA mortgage insurance issued in the first four decades of FHA operation was suburbia, where almost half of all housing could claim FHA or VA financing in the 1950s and 1960s."[8] Cities were explicitly disfavored by federally insured capital, making it harder for middle-class families left behind to sell and even harder to stay. Following HOLC guidelines, lenders refused to issue mortgages in many areas. Urban home values declined along with the tax base. The postwar boom responsible for making the United States a middle-class nation effectively demanded that the middle class leave the city if they wished to remain middle class. Jobs were leaving, too. No less an industrial city than Detroit was, by the late 1950s, already experiencing the relocation of manufacturing jobs to the suburbs above Eight Mile Road. Additional federal legislation hurt cities, like urban renewal and public housing, which we'll see in the next chapter. But it is important to stop and track the money for a moment. What began as self-sufficiency gradually became commodified self-interest on the dime of what's derided today as "big government."

The next catalyst to suburbanization was the National Highway Act of 1956, which nailed shut the idea of a metropolis interconnected by streetcars, subways, and other mass transit. Those technologies were overtaxed and underfunded. States got money for highways, and the interstate highway system was built over the next two decades—changing, as President Dwight Eisenhower had hoped, "the face of America."[9] The proliferation of highways was a gift to developers and their suburban buyers, without which the periphery could not have feasibly expanded. The irony is that what connected us in new ways disconnected us in many others.

* * *

Pause for a moment before we examine the biggest subsidy of all and consider how most people (even people who study this stuff for a living) talk about the development of these areas: it's typically about "markets." If beliefs about self-sufficiency lie behind the claim of municipal autonomy, the idea that ties these beliefs together in our thinking is markets. Real estate markets, labor markets, the market for good teachers, the market for good ratables, bond markets, supermarkets—it's usually a question of how forces work within a market dynamic to produce good, bad, and indifferent places to live. Talking about neighborhoods in terms of markets, however, removes all mention of subsidies. Most of us assume that markets are driven by invisible factors, not government policies; that is, governments don't make markets, private actors do. And, of course, markets are not accountable for what they produce. Markets are neutral (though they should strive to be efficient). Obviously, as we've just seen, this is not quite so. If we're being honest, things like massive government subsidization and the encouragement of decades of deliberate discrimination are not what we would call the stuff of free markets. The critical housing markets on which so much middle-class opportunity has been made in the United States looks a lot like the public construction of a vast private sphere—which, until recently, worked pretty well for most of us. In other words, it was politics before markets.

## The Greatest Subsidy of All

Yet the biggest subsidy of all was exclusion. Exclusion completed the suburban housing market. As denial of federal loan guarantees helped decimate city housing markets, exclusion of certain people and certain activities inflated the value of the suburban enclaves. None of this was accidental. The Home Owners' Loan Corporation's rigorous and detailed scoring system for loan applicants took the measure of an applicant's race, vocation, current and future location, and housing choice. Like certain areas, certain people were denied or demoted to the third or fourth of four "grades." To make determinations of worthiness clear, realtors and lenders could rely on "secret" Residential Security Maps for guidance. The maps were foolproof: large red circles were drawn with markers around areas ineligible for loans, a process called "redlining." If you didn't like maps, there was a manual. Either way, the preferences were clear: new construction, single-family detached home, white skin. Nothing was perhaps more important than the latter, as the presence of blacks in a neighborhood—even the most token presence—could turn the area into a no-loan zone. As bad as the HOLC standards were, they were institutionalized, nationalized, and given the full faith and credit of the U.S. government when they were adopted by the Federal Housing Administration.[10]

Exclusion was Chrissy Thomas and Alice Swann's problem in 1957. They're African American.

Ms. Thomas and her husband had looked everywhere for a suburban home to raise a family, but could not find one in a community that would accept them. Their friend Evelyn had a boyfriend who was working as a realtor for Morris Milgram, a Jew turned Quaker, who was developing Concord Park as a racially integrated community in the shadow of Pennsylvania's Levittown—and using many of Levitt and Sons' innovative development principles to do it.

Levittown held a special allure for many families then, especially return-ing veterans who had fought overseas to preserve the American Dream and were anxious to live it. "Many of us wanted to live in a place like that," recalls Ms. Swann, whose husband had served in the armed forces. "We couldn't even see the model homes there. I had a friend who showed up at the front door of the place and the realtor slipped out the back door."

Evelyn encouraged the Thomases not to give up, and eventually, after that long drive from Philadelphia, they found it—right across the road from another unusual corner of Bensalem Township, the all-black neigh-borhood of Linconia. If Concord Park expressed the deliberate planning of a builder for social change, Linconia was an accident. Professional blacks had been quietly building summer homes there for years—in all shapes and sizes, with no particular zoning or building regulation to guide them, just 50' by 150' lots, often without easements where roads were sup-posed to go. By the time Concord Park came along, Linconia had become a year-round community of black people with more modest means.

"The white folks didn't know we was over here," Charles Ellzy explained to me in his living room. Mr. Ellzy is another elder, the president of the Lin–Park Civic Association, a solid, square-faced man with dark brown skin and a royal blue button-down shirt. Over the constant gurgle of a half-filled aquarium long deserted by fish, Mr. Ellzy recounted life before Concord Park, when there were no streetlights or paved streets.

"They'd come through with graters and smooth the street down. Then they came with rocks. Rocks were a big improvement." Linconia was a tiny community, and Concord Park was farmland. Mr. Ellzy had not thought much about segregation when Morris Milgram started con-struction. He was more concerned with how razing the land over there would affect the path of rainwater in Linconia. He also remembers the new residents differently. "The people who moved over there thought they were a little better. The homes were all the same. Cost $9,999. They started to do things over there that we didn't do. Puppet shows. They were on the move. They were more advanced."

The sewer lines, as needed in Linconia as they were in Concord Park, were a hardship, though. Everybody in both communities had to buy it.

There was no city to subsidize it, and the county would not help. Older Linconia residents in particular struggled, and it took years for the resentment to settle.

Back in Chrissy Thomas's house, we have moved on to homemade brownies by now. My eyes have scanned into the den Mr. Thomas added and out the window at a wide yard covered in snow. When asked, Chrissy Thomas soberly admits that she and her husband did not come to Concord Park for the idea of promoting racial integration or to live near a black suburban community. They simply wanted the experience of non-discrimination in which to raise their daughters. "It really didn't have anything to do with integration. I just liked people. And I wanted to live where I wanted to live. It turned out we became so close, and we had so many great adventures from living here that it just became overwhelming at times."

"Milgram's Dream," as it was affectionately known (or "checkerboard square," as it was locally called), was to create binding integration by insuring a racial mix of home owners, about 60–40 percent white to black, and for a time covenanting buyers to sell only to someone of their own race. When he shared his plan with his father-in-law, he was told he was crazy and that the subdivision would never work. His family supported him anyway. When he sought financing from Philadelphia-area banks, he was turned down. Finally, a New York savings and loan agreed. Many black buyers, desperate for the same suburban opportunities that whites were snapping up all over the nation, were turned away in order to maintain balance. Some buyers applied from other parts of the country sight unseen. Yet despite the restrictions to preserve racial balance, the struggle to keep Milgram's interracial dream alive, even its history, has largely failed.[11]

## The Multiples of Privilege: Wealth

Most of our grandparents would cringe politely (and say much more in their heads) at the suggestion that buying that suburban starter home in 1957 represented a token deposit on some unearned privilege, but they would undoubtedly agree that it sure was a good time to get into the housing market. For all the psychic investment many people have in their yards, their gardens, or their renovated basements, it's their financial investment that connects the dream of self-sufficiency to the reality of financial stability. It's all tied to markets, of course, and timing is always key. But suburbanization along the path described in this chapter made generations of Americans solidly middle class—and more. If you owned your suburban home in the late 1960s, you watched it appreciate approximately twenty times by the early 2000s.[12] That type of simple investment, an investment your grandparents (or great grandparents) would have been foolish not to make if they could, accounts for almost two-thirds of all the net financial worth of most Americans, according to sociologist Thomas Shapiro. Shapiro studies wealth dynamics, believing it tells a lot more about people than income does. To him wealth is "the total value of things families own minus their debts," and he refers to "transformative assets" in particular, those assets like the equity in a good home in a great location that can be leveraged into resources for a productive life.[13]

Wealth also puts the notion of a meritocracy, hard work, and self-sufficiency in another perspective. First, let's recall wealth's basic function: to become a stable economic platform. The more valuable one's assets, the more economic stability one enjoys—and the imagination runs wild as to the things that may be possible, like starting a business, buying rental property, a new smile, college funds, a child's wedding, grandchildren's down payment on their first home. Say the assets are minimal or the value is limited for some reason, wealth might still be the last resort after income has run out; it may be the difference between homelessness and home, or it might help an underinsured person survive that catastrophic illness. Income is great, but wealth is really having something to fall back on during times of hardship—like a Great Recession.

Even now wealth in a home is not increased so much by the self-sufficiency of a do-it-yourself renovation as by outside help—namely, the legacy of suburbanization that we've just discussed, the government and the market. The government helps to increase housing assets by favoring home owners with generous tax policies. American home owners can take advantage of at least five different tax breaks at the federal and state levels. The main one, the home mortgage interest deduction, simply rewards home owners for paying the interest they are already contractually bound to pay the bank each month. Another allows the federal income tax deduction for the payment of property taxes, which favors home owners—especially wealthy home owners—to the exclusion of renters. In 2010, both deductions were estimated by the Pew Charitable Trust to equal a total government subsidy of $80 billion and $25 billion, respectively.[14] The mortgage interest deduction is so regressive that the same study found that about 60 percent of the subsidy goes to households with incomes in excess of $100,000 a year.[15] Further, home owners can deduct the interest on loans they make to themselves based on the equity in their homes. And when they decide to sell their homes, home owners can enjoy substantial exemptions from capital gains taxes. (None of this generosity prevents the average middle-class voter from automatically objecting to tax increases.) Shapiro finds it odd that Americans are not outraged by the fact that most of these tax policies overwhelmingly benefit richer households: "The top 10 percent of owners receives one-third of all housing benefits and the top 25 percent receives 59 percent of all benefits."[16] I find it odd that more of us won't simply acknowledge the handout.

Then there's the market. Because exclusion has worked so effectively to produce neighborhoods free of undesirable people and uses, most of us only consider housing markets that are viable—that is, places where property values tend to increase steadily and schools vary but range from good to excellent. Unless you occupy the unfortunate status of the excluded, you typically have many choices. When you sell your home, you benefit from a market that virtually includes everyone (except some undesirables). And like you probably did, your buyers will make their first down payment with critical financial assistance from—as Shapiro's interviewees told him—"Daddy." Of course, it may not be dad, but the point is that five out of eight first-time homebuyers get significant help with their down payments in the form of family "loans"—intergenerational wealth transmission—that may never be repaid.[17] The advantage there is that better mortgages (e.g., lower interest rates, fewer points) are available to those with bigger down payments (and good credit). The informal science of down payments is a surprisingly revealing aspect of housing markets.

Let's look at some numbers. According to sociologists Lauren Krivo and Robert Kaufman, studies conducted just before the housing crash in 2008 demonstrate some basic benefits of home ownership for middle-class whites across the country.[18] In 2004, 70 percent of middle-class whites owned their own home. The median amount of equity owners had in their homes was $80,000. These are the basic facts for the white middle class, who, of course, still comprise the majority of home owners by far. The picture of benefits changes when certain factors—"payoffs" or expected gains from particular inputs like income or education—are thrown into the housing equity equation. For instance, every additional $10,000 in income lifts white home owner equity by about $18,000. Making more money has a payoff in housing wealth, as you might expect. Another four years of home owner education level increases equity by $20,000. Living in a suburb in the West or Northeast, having made a generous down payment, and owning a previous home or condo are all factors that pay off in terms of increased home equity for white home owners—the norm for all home owners. Home equity also improves the total equity picture, since the home is usually the primary asset for household wealth and embodies many of the other ways that people accumulate stocks, mutual funds, retirement accounts, business interests, and other assets. Once again, home ownership has generally proved to be an excellent way to create wealth and the long-term resources for a productive life.

## Self-Sufficiency?

This is wonderful. It is cumulative. It is an efficient way to leverage a necessary resource—your shelter—into the broader assets needed for stability, and few other nations in history have seen it happen for so many. But this is not self-sufficiency. This is an American Dream built on an interdependent network of selective generosity—much of it public, a lot of it governmental. Our national politics are often embroiled in arguments about the role of government, with many of us demanding "it" get off our backs, or "it" give less to the undeserving "special interests." Few of us would give *this* back, though, and even fewer would accept true self-sufficiency in its place. The gift of this dream came not only to us as individuals, as this analysis suggests. It came to our *families*, a few generations ago, and stays with our families through care and rational (estate) planning. When waking from a long dream, as we do in this book, it is always fun to peel back the symbols—the talking cats and endless hallways—to wonder what it really meant. The American Dream of suburban home ownership can fairly be called a dream about what we wish for families. Nobody was protecting the right to abundant trees and safer streets for single men with fast cars. The separation of cement factories from residential areas was not for the benefit of recent college grads with bad haircuts. That bucolic scene described by the Supreme Court in *Village of Belle Terre* or the concerns the same Court expressed about zoning controls in its 1932 *Euclid* decision, all of it, the whole dream, is really about what is optimal *for raising families*— a place for them to be and grow and become economically stable now and in the future. Rather than fight the city, urban taxpayers, streetcar developers, and innovative builders facilitated a gentler, safer, more stable life on the periphery. But to really make it the inexpensive family investment bonanza that most of us could never hope to afford on our own, the government insured the low-cost amortized mortgage market, nationalized lending standards that excluded people deemed a drag on property values, and built highways for us to get farther out there. These are among the many subsidies large and small we've enjoyed as increased household wealth. It was done in the name of "local control." It was through the exercise of that local sovereign's "police power" to enhance "public welfare" by land use decisions. Thus, in the consumer– citizen's language of dream fulfillment, personal autonomy could be imagined only alongside community autonomy. Subsidization was overlooked as the just deserts of the self-sufficient. But what forgives the illusory rhetoric is that all of it was done for the sake of families, millions and millions of families, like yours, who together make up the best of us.

But not all families. Recall Martin Luther King's idea of mutuality—what I revised as progressive mutuality, the kind that recognizes that interdependency is not neutral if it rests in part on exclusion and must account for our effects on others. Well, exclusion was a subsidy for many in the housing market, but a tax on others. Let's look at some more numbers. Although white home ownership is at 70 percent across the country, it's just 46 percent for blacks and 49 percent for Latinos. White home owners have over $20,000 more equity in their homes than do blacks and Latinos. And none of the payoff factors mean as much to accumulating equity for blacks and Latinos as they do for whites—not education, not years of ownership, not prior home ownership, not even income.[19] Even a Latina home owner who earns a lot, got a master's degree, and has held her home for many years sees less value in her investment than does a white woman of similar status. Perhaps this is because the Latina's loan terms were typically much worse—at a higher interest rate and with a smaller down payment. Even when you look at people struggling to be middle class, people who would enter the housing market at a clear financial disadvantage, moderate-income whites are at least twice as likely to own homes than are moderate-income people of color.[20] We'll return to some of these issues in more detail in later chapters, but the point is to appreciate what we have and not to call it what it's not. It is an imperfect dream of home ownership as a means to mobility that worked very well for millions. However, it was made with willing help from the government as well as the sacrifices of those left out.

Most of us don't spend a lot of time thinking about these factors. If we did, we would be sure to wonder if the next thing coming is an accusation of racism. It's not. I am not suggesting that people today are racists, but I am suggesting that their grandparents probably were and certainly their great grandparents. These fine people put in place a system of advantages and disadvantages—designed in part based on their firm racist beliefs—that continues to this day, distributing opportunity in most places and denying it in others through color-blind rules that have clear color-based consequences.[21] The question is not whether one is a racist, but whether one has any responsibility to transform a once racist system into a more equitable one, even if it means re-examining what your grandparents gave you. Because so far in the story, everything is structure and everyone is reasonable. Even if your grandparents were Klansmen, forces larger than their own hate made these deals too good to pass up. The most important point for now is to recognize that the vast majority of us are complicit in a wonderful scheme of benefits that looked, to most anyway, like the start of a social contract—or the aging of a New Deal.

## . . . And Then What Happened?

The leg up that fueled so much American household wealth is crippled by many factors now, the bone fractured in multiple places by the effects of economic restructuring, demographic transformations affecting education and the labor force, and perhaps the biggest rule-changer of all, the Great Recession. Demos and the Institute on Assets and Social Policy developed the "Middle-Class Security Index," which includes five areas of household financial stability—assets we can reach in a pinch, health care, education levels, housing costs, and the sufficiency of budgets to cover emergencies. The combination provides a realistic picture of middle-class capacity or vulnerability. What it showed is significant slippage between the boom years of 2000 to 2006. For all middle-class families, only 31 percent were secure in their ability to cover expenses in an emergency or ride out unexpected losses. This period, of course, was the calm before the storm; anyone insecure in 2006 was ill-prepared for the kinds of job, housing, and health shocks that would arrive two years later with the recession. As bad as that was, the profile for middle-class blacks and Latinos was worse, indicating a more tenuous hold on the things that make any family middle class. The rate of security for blacks was 26 percent during that period and for Latinos only 18 percent. The factors behind this are well-known to most of us—rising housing costs, family members without health insurance, falling incomes relative to debt, and, not so obviously, dramatic declines in the median value of liquid assets.[22] Then came recession.

The recession has revealed some hard municipal truths about the fiscal self-autonomy that follows legal self-sufficiency, and few of them are promising. In early 2011, the comfortable California suburb of Costa Mesa's city council decided to launch a pre-emptive assault on looming budget deficits. The members proactively decided to cut half the town's public employees—yes, half (preferring privately contracted services instead).[23] Rather than receive his pink slip, one worker wandered off to a fifth-floor ledge of the municipal building and jumped to his death.[24] Whether the council's unprecedented action was a Republican ploy to scare Democratic-leaning public employee unions or not, the episode illustrates the fault lines of self-sufficiency. The legal independence that helped build so many municipalities was greatly aided by subsidies from larger bodies of government—especially the U.S. government. With federal and state aid coming to a crippling halt, many local governments—even relatively wealthy ones—are facing the dire consequences of an untenable arrangement.

Or take a more modest place. Today, the Trevose subdivision looks like one of the great many close-in suburbs you see in Pennsylvania, Maryland, New Jersey, or, for that matter, Ohio or Michigan, whose heyday is long past. It is still quite nice, even in the snow, the trees are grown, and the people stay connected by church and civic associations. But it looks like an aging version of its former self, smaller now in hindsight. There are signs of new life, including modest new, two-story homes, which were not being built for many years. Trevose, you see, has become black. Nobody knows why for sure. Many remaining residents of Milgram's Dream speculated that white families in particular took advantage of the expiration of covenants and sold to the only people who would buy—blacks. White flight following the riots that occurred in cities during the 1960s, especially after Martin Luther King's assassination in 1968, continued in the 1970s and 1980s and may have induced some to move farther into Bucks County. Chrissy and Alice even wonder if rumors that some white families left when their daughters reached dating age were true. It doesn't matter. Black families shut out of the suburban dream moved in, and the two communities—Linconia and Concord Park, dubbed "Lin–Park" by many locals—remained nearly all black for decades.

The return of integration there is about eight years old. There are many Indian families. People from Northeast Philly saw the prices and the convenient location and came. My tour guides proudly pointed out the homes of a white family here, a white family there, or an interracial couple. But there are not so many professionals anymore, mostly first-time home owners as before but perhaps with a more tenuous hold on being middle class. People I talked to have concerns about the school and its ability to pass its "adequate yearly progress" goals and not be shut down; it's been designated an English-as-a-second-language and special education school, which many prospective parents avoid. The Trevose school and another are closest to a cluster of minority neighborhoods. Beyond the schools, the big issue confronting residents now is the prospect of re-zoning. The mayor of Bensalem wants to allow a developer to build the kind of large-scale gated town-house development so popular in other parts of the township. It would bring traffic right through the Trevose hamlet and change the character of the place, they believe. Yet it is another hallmark of changing times and the desire among elected officials to improve tax bases without tax increases. Charles Ellzy thinks the people who will move there, like those who have come recently, will have no idea of the area's unique history.

Chrissy stayed, but Alice left. House size was an issue for many original residents of Concord Park, but Chrissy didn't want to leave, especially after her husband died. "The girls are gone now, I'm here on one floor and I like it."

As for Alice, who visits often and lives not far away, "We moved out because I kept having one baby after another."

"Yes, you did," Chrissy nods. "I'd say, 'Alice, when are you gonna stop?'"

Five kids total and she finally stopped. The table goes quiet for a thoughtful moment, as all of us seem to ponder the uneaten brownies on the white china plate. Years seem to be spinning past their eyes.

Alice's gaze sharpens again and she smiles. "It was the one bathroom that really did it."

## Counterfactual: Amending the Social Contract

The idea of self-sufficiency embroidered suburban life with a sense of righteous can-do-ism that deserved and received formal autonomy from the government and courts. Self-sufficiency is an assumption deeply embedded in the idea of place and the American Dream, and, as this chapter has shown, it is largely fictitious. Perhaps an unusual community like Concord Park can claim some degree of self-sufficiency in its creation against all odds, but most suburbs and their residents enjoyed massive government and private market subsidies, without which they would not have expanded or remained independent for long. For many millions of American families, this was a good thing, the essence of membership in middle-class citizenship and a strong argument for our national wealth.

Yet imagine if this good idea of home ownership had not demanded the wholesale exclusion of others for fifty years? Imagine if the signature discrimination against blacks, Latinos, and recent immigrants had been rejected in, say, 1957. Would the suburban model have failed? Would the subsidies available through the FHA and GI Bill, for example, have been overtaxed and ineffective in building so much stability? Would cities have struggled to maintain a hold on the middle class, locked in a competition with suburbs for middle-class households, schoolchildren, shoppers, and taxpayers? Where would we be today?

# 3

## KEEP YOUR DISTANCE

### ASSUMING THAT MIDDLE-CLASS STATUS REQUIRES DISTANCE FROM THE POOR

The assumption that maintaining one's middle-class status requires keeping distance from the poor may be the hardest one to overcome. This was explained to me in calm and thoughtful terms by a stranger with whom I argued as we rode a train from Washington DC to New York City. We had passed some of the East Coast's most devastating ghettos in Baltimore and Philadelphia, and I had been making many of the historical and structural points you are about to read. He, a businessman in his fifties, had been dismissive and incredulous, and always responded with personal anecdotes. Just when I thought I had challenged his thinking an iota, he sighed and said this:

> All we can ever do is live in the present. Whatever happened in the past to create these bad places and all the pathologies you find there is really not my responsibility. The fact is, in the present, these are not people you want to live around. They're not like you and me. If we're talking about the poor, the ghetto–barrio poor, the gangbanger poor, no way, you don't want that kind of person watching you leave home every day

for work, you don't want him and his friends talking to your daughter, and you damned sure don't want your kids in the same class with them. You just don't. It's hard enough to try to figure out how to raise your kids safely today. The last thing you want to do is sacrifice your sense of peace and security for the good of people who are generally so far gone in their ways of thinking and handling problems—they're so *angry* and so quick to violence, so high and looking to get higher—that I don't care who you are, black, white, or purple, you don't want to be anywhere near that nonsense. Bottom line, nobody's *that* liberal unless they're stupid. Me, it's about protecting what I have. If that's selfish, I earned the right to be selfish. They can have my sympathy, but not my neighborhood.

This kind of honest candor is hard to rebut. It represents the feelings of not just rich or middle-class people, but a lot of poor people, too. That is one reason this assumption of avoidance is so difficult. Another is that most people don't talk about proximity to the poor like the man on the train did. Most people talk about the poor with unrestrained vituperation.

Suppose the issue is whether "affordable housing" will be built near you. We pay too little attention to the character of opposition to affordable housing. Even some of the most polite resistance could qualify as hate speech. For example, when the *Star Wars* movie director George Lucas decided to sell some of his prime Marin County, California land to an affordable housing developer, some of the local residents immediately objected to the prospect of "lowlifes," "drug dealers," and "criminals" moving in. Marin County is so rich that in this patch of (glorious) earth across the Golden Gate Bridge from San Francisco, an annual household income of $88,000 would qualify for "affordable housing."[1] The qualifying "lowlife" might well be a young assistant district attorney, who spends her day prosecuting actual drug dealers and other criminals. It doesn't seem to matter. There is an almost no-holds-barred negativity associated with affordable housing that defies reason or competent evidence to the contrary. Just read the anonymous online comments to any local newspaper article about a proposed affordable housing project of any kind. The vivid imagery of bad folks comes fast and furious, with a certainty that can only be refuted by "knee-jerk liberals," always blind to reality. In the Marin County case, even George Lucas's supporters assumed that property values would decline. They too are wrong. Though opponents and supporters of affordable housing assume that mere proximity to the poor will, like a status-altering communicable disease, threaten the preservation of a middle-class life, studies consistently show otherwise.[2]

There is something to the vitriol, something unexamined yet potentially revealing. My analogy to hate speech is not accidental. Remember that, although people profess a very general antipathy for having poor people occupy affordable housing near them, the reality is that poor white people somehow manage to find housing that is affordable in neighborhoods and towns that are not particularly poor. In fact, the white poor (who make up the majority of all poor people) live scattered amid the middle class. They are not shunted to special areas for the despised. This is at least circumstantial evidence that the "lowlifes" we fear are mostly black or brown. And racialized antipathy is an essential ingredient in hate speech.

I mean this as more an *aha* moment than *gotcha*. What makes it *aha* is that we have made significant strides in overcoming our conscious racism by, in fact, interrogating its irrationality, subjecting it to both morality and efficiency tests, and deciding, little by little, that that is not the way we want to construct the relations of citizenship. Unfortunately, *class* antagonism has rarely received that kind of collective introspection—much the opposite. It stews in its fears and institutionalizes its stereotypes. Not surprisingly, it has become a convenient repository for latent racism. Yet just as the United States could not remain a model of democracy while maintaining an explicit racial caste system under Jim Crow, it cannot evolve into a vibrant, pluralist economy while perpetuating gross economic inequality. It is unimaginable how one competes globally with such a non-inclusive structure in place, let alone win.

That is ultimately the argument of this chapter. But it unfolds with due respect for the assumption, because the assumption is the very heart of localism, our system of residential rules. From New Orleans to Oakland, from Miami to New Jersey, we'll follow the myriad forms of economic exclusion and its ratification in the court-sanctioned logic of *legal* localism. Then, after a look at the costs and consequences for the excluded poor and working class, we'll look at the debate today. The guy beside me on the train was good; I'll give him that. But here is a rebuttal.

## Localism and Its Discontents
### *Blood-Only Localism in New Orleans*

Hurricane Katrina, the Category 3 storm that struck the city and region of New Orleans in August 2005, left over 1,800 dead and a flood of questions about the spectacle of poverty and vulnerability. In the travesty of so many dark-skinned faces waiting hopelessly for help outside the Superdome, we recoiled at the horror of living and dying in the wrong place. It was a national study in mutuality, its zero-sum failures and its heroically compassionate triumphs. It was not, however, a time spent seriously reexamining how those people wound up at the mercy of the landscape or how to prevent the peril from recurring. Localism prevented most of the survivors from relocating anywhere near the homes they had just lost.

Several years later and New Orleans has changed a lot, but still suffers from a critical lack of housing affordable to its many lower-income residents. Given the loss of so many units, rents are very high and most of the public housing projects have been shut down in favor of mixed-income developments that have yet to be built. The city seems to have taken advantage of Katrina as an opportunity to employ the assumption for the good of its own tax base.[3] And this raises a question obvious almost everywhere else: why haven't more of New Orleans's displaced poor moved to one of the thirteen higher-ground suburban parishes since the storm? This is the clear trend across the country—migrations of low-income households to close-in suburbs. Why didn't more of them do so to begin with, rather than wait in agony to be bused or flown off to far-flung places like Houston 350 miles away?

The second assumption is the answer. For all its past glory as one of the most progressive and culturally interesting cities in the world, New

Orleans had become a repository of grinding poverty. If poverty often correlates with crime, it had become a lethal place for many. Its public institutions, like schools, police, and criminal justice system, reflected that. The economy was overly dependent on a tourism industry characterized by very low wages and little job mobility. Before the storm, the poverty rate in New Orleans was 28 percent. As of the 2010 census, it was 24.4 percent.[4] Poor and moderate-income black New Orleanians had been prevented from moving into most of the surrounding parishes by custom and local laws.

One in particular was the parish of St. Bernard, itself a hard-hit victim of Katrina. St. Bernard residents might be expected to act defensively in the face of vast changes brought on by sudden disaster. In 2000, according to the census, St. Bernard had over sixty-seven thousand residents. In 2007—two years after the storm—there were just over twenty-eight thousand. That's a big change for a relatively small city. Family poverty had also increased while median incomes dropped compared to national figures. What in 2000 was a place where three-quarters of the residents owned and lived in their homes, in 2007 almost 40 percent of residents were renters. Of course, the racial and ethnic mix changed, too. The white population dipped to 85 percent in 2007, down from 88 percent in 2000. Yet the black population had increased from 7.5 percent to 10 percent in that time, and Latinos had gone from 5 percent to 7.5 percent. Out of New Orleans's surrounding parishes, only two, St. Bernard and Jefferson, have had to contend with such influxes. The others remain virtually all white.[5]

After Hurricane Katrina, the parish adopted a blood-only zoning ordinance that limited renters to blood relatives, a move that would preserve the town's complexion. This tactic accompanied restrictive covenants that already limited to whom owners could rent. Both are among the arsenal of exclusionary practices used by generations of American towns. This time a federal judge decided that the techniques used to deny New Orleanians access to housing in St. Bernard violated federal antidiscrimination laws.[6] Sidestepping the region's torturous racial history, outraged residents employed the language of class, color-blindness, and local autonomy to express their frustration with the federal judge's ruling.

"We should have the God-given and government-given right to govern this parish to protect property values and the people for their life, and for all the values of the community," one exclaimed to a reporter. "It has nothing to do with race. It has to do with the economic stability of the people of this parish."[7]

If we're being honest, most of us hear that gentleman speaking code. Fair housing has everything to do with race, but also with the influence that race has on the economic value of a place. But let's take him at his word about race. Let's assume these decisions had nothing to do with the perceived race of the future renters, but rather their socioeconomic class. The irate St. Bernard resident might have a point if St. Bernard were singled out among non–New Orleans parishes in the region as the only place outside the city that is forced to allow multifamily rental homes. Following the example of economically integrated communities across the country, studies show that St. Bernard would probably be a financially stronger parish if it adopted by political will the very openness that the federal judge required by law—*but only if its neighboring parishes did the same.* Rather than wait for a judge to rule against the other parishes, a better course would be for all of them to act cooperatively to address regional housing needs. But that would contradict the assumption that the middle-class character and opportunities in St. Bernard depend for their continued existence on the absence of low-income households—even when those poor are returning to the region to restart upended lives. Construction has begun on the tract homes just beyond a main commercial road, not far from a little park in an ethnically diverse, moderate-income neighborhood near the parish border. But the litigation has continued for years.

## The Tail That Wagged Mount Laurel

Meanwhile in New Jersey, a reputation for making fair housing a regional reality was being unmasked. For anyone who follows the saga of fair housing—that is, housing that follows strict antidiscrimination principles like the ones spelled out in Title VIII of the Civil Rights Act of 1968 and many similar state laws—the words "Mount Laurel" are uttered with great reverence, the kind of singular admiration garnered by only the rarest act of successful social justice. New Jersey is one of the most suburban states in the country. With only the exception of Jersey City or Hoboken, its cities—Newark, Paterson, Camden, Trenton, Elizabeth—are spoken of like epithets. (During the writing of this book I lost an old friend because I referred to her town of South Orange as a suburb of adjacent Newark.) The fragmented form of government there is reflected in the fact that the country's most densely populated state has 565 municipalities. It is perhaps the legal birthplace of localism, LULUism (locally unwanted land uses), and NIMBYism (not in my backyard), too. The primary weapon of choice? Exclusionary zoning. Like some of the attempts we saw in St. Bernard Parish, exclusionary zoning is the use of neutral-sounding land use ordinances to keep out certain kinds of housing and people, such as banning multifamily homes that are affordable to low- and moderate-income households.

Back in the early 1970s, the town of Mount Laurel did just that. The developer who unsuccessfully sought a building permit sued in state court. The case went to the New Jersey Supreme Court, which in 1975 announced a decision that has been nationally renowned ever since.[8] Relying on the state, not federal, constitution, the court held that every municipality in New Jersey had a duty to build and maintain its "fair share" of the regional demand for affordable housing. This idea became known as the "*Mount Laurel* doctrine." It contemplated various legal and practical mechanisms by which housing need would be identified and housing available to low- and moderate-income households would be built. Most of these were worked out during the course of intense ongoing litigation. By 1985, the beleaguered New Jersey Supreme Court had had enough. The legislature took over and passed a fair housing law, which established a state agency to do the heavy lifting of determining need, monitoring output, and setting operational standards. The people's work was done. New Jersey had succeeded where no other state had before. It had figured out how to get beyond the hard-fought assumption that poor people and their housing were as bad for middle-class communities as were steel mills and chemical factories. How? By spreading the burdens fairly across each region, and by blending such units into a majority of market-rate units. It almost worked as well in practice as it was praised in theory.

The problem was a single loophole in the law, which undid most of the distributing in a way that reaffirms the commitment most people have to the assumption that we are better off with invisible poverty. It was called the "regional contribution agreement"—or RCA—which appeared to provide flexibility for municipalities to cooperate with one another, rather than compete (their typical posture). Under an RCA, two municipalities—one a "sender," the other a "receiver"—could trade affordable housing obligations for a sum of money deemed sufficient to pay for their construction. Say, for example, Chatham, an upper-middle-class town in Morris County, had an obligation to build ten affordable units, as determined by the state agency. It could find a recipient municipality that was willing to take up to half of those units (five), for a fixed unit price times five. But which municipalities would want money to build affordable housing in a state where the Supreme Court had to force municipalities to accept some responsibility for affordable housing? Poor ones and larger cities with lots of poor and moderate-income people trying to find housing they could afford, like Newark. The RCAs were an extraordinarily popular mechanism for un-distributing redistributed affordable housing from opportunity-rich suburbs to fiscally stressed central cities and inner-ring towns. Over many years, cities like Newark became destination hubs for spokes of sending activity from all over North and Central New Jersey. The pattern of sending and receiving was repeated for Camden, Trenton, Paterson, Elizabeth, and others—low-income places receiving the funds from high-income places to build housing for more low-income residents. The senders' taxpayers were literally paying off their desperate regional neighbors to unburden them of poor people. Any municipality that makes that cost-benefit calculation has determined that it is cheaper to be rid of the poor (even in low numbers) than to live with them.

Finally, enter the market. What about the remaining half of the sending municipality's housing obligation? And didn't the building of units in the city at least produce a net gain of affordable units in the region? Studies of how more affluent towns managed their obligations offer mixed results at best.[9] Towns tended to cherry-pick their poor. It turns out that the elderly on fixed incomes often qualified as low- and moderate-income, as did college students and divorced suburban moms with children. These were more acceptable poor people to blend into more affluent communities. Using targeted marketing of available units, the towns met their obligations with these poor—the kind my friend on the train grumbles less about, the kind with which he might even identify.

Unfortunately, the RCAs did not create the net gain of housing expected, even if it was moved back into central cities. The costs per unit rarely squared. For a long time, they were not even closely monitored. And the RCAs fostered a market for housing funds in which desperate cities competed with one another to lower the price. If Irvington, for instance, could take Chatham's five units for 10 percent less than Newark offered, well, Chatham's taxpayers would be happy and Irvington would get some, but not as much, affordable housing.[10] And so it went. Quietly, while the rest of the country was praising the *Mount Laurel* doctrine, local government officials in the state were busy undercutting its intended effects with a perfectly legal practice of exchange. In 2008, the state legislature finally repealed RCAs. But it's hard to imagine a more concerted effort to affirm the assumption that middle-class status requires distance from the poor. (As of this writing, the status of the fair share doctrine remains in legal limbo after attempts to nullify it by Governor Chris Christie.)

## Ghettos from Space

Then there's the other side of the assumption: its ghettoizing effects. And this I mean in the most generic way. If middle-class people won't live too near poor people, then poor people will generally live together.

The converse position of the man on the train is ghettos. They arise through the cause and effect of parasitic mutuality. If most of us somehow manage to avoid clouds, it is because others must live under them. Before we get to the important question of whether a different type of mutuality can be wrangled from this complicated assumption, we should imagine the landscape of concentrated poverty.

In the 1980s and 1990s, sociologists like William Julius Wilson and Paul Jargowsky taught us about the concentration of poverty, a sterile-sounding term for something much more difficult that can now even be seen from space. Our new graphic capability renders something so lousy and debilitating in a voyeuristic form that combines science with literature to reveal spatial losses and place-based costs. Go to your computer. Boot up Google Earth or some easy incarnation of a satellite GPS system. Get comfortable by doing the things you usually do on it. Travel the world. Review that visit you like to take to the Champs-Élysées in Paris; check out the exact location of beachfront hotels where you want to stay in the Dominican Republic; see inside a volcano. Do all the magical, dreamlike things that being there by satellite can do. Click on those mostly bad pictures folks were kind enough to put up of details on the ground. Then try to find those three-dimensional views that allow you to hit the street and see actual landscapes, sometimes as if you were walking down the block instead of sitting in pajamas far away. It's these that really let in the literature of a place, filling in perspectives only teased at from space. Now forget what you've heard and try Oakland, California, where I lived and worked as a young man after college. The locals call it God's country. I had never imagined that a city could have hills rising along the horizon like an antelope's back; some days you can smell the brackish waters of the bay that surrounds the region like a giant reflecting pool. All of this is clear from space, a manageable city, full of regular people of every stripe and origin. Across the Bay Bridge, the jewels of San Francisco's skyline pointing at heaven. In the East Bay, storks and pelicans sweeping over the footpaths of "Oaktown's" Lake Merritt. It's California, and all that beauty seems unreachable by the dense urban poverty I knew as a boy in New York. Which means we're ready to go to the 'hood. We'll head to East Oakland to visit forbidden blocks of concentrated poverty.

The first thing you experience on, say, the corner of MacArthur Boulevard and 83rd Avenue is what the scholars call isolation and the census maps show as no way out. This is not to cast aspersions. However, it is to say that it is almost immediately apparent that this flat, desolate streetscape is probably a bad place to be a stranger alone, even in the sunshine. The businesses still open are few and unwelcoming; for many blocks in either direction there's just a sparse monotony of hair care shops, fast food joints, liquor stores, check cashers, and more autobody establishments than anyone could seemingly need. Most of the stories of these streets reflect at least financial struggle, a basic contest for resources, broadly defined. There are people who know the area better than I do—as residents, firefighters, nonprofit workers, researchers. They are quick to warn of its seriousness, how the dangers have increased, its unpredictability, especially for people just showing up from outer space. In that sense it is like a lot of other despised places. The key to understanding it as a center of concentrated poverty is not the sense of danger, the high incidence of low-birthweight births and diabetes, or even the condition of the schools. For now, the key is to understand that walking in this direction or that, even driving, poverty around here is so concentrated that you'd have to go a long, long way past most people's comfort zones in order to feel comfortable again. It is a difficult place to leave. Fortunately for us, we can click out of there.

The aerial feel demonstrates the otherworldness about this particular type of place—what I have called "antimarkets" in earlier work.[11] Not an elegant term, I know, but antimarkets are, first and foremost, places of concentrated poverty. Concentrated poverty generally indicates a census tract of "extreme" poverty where at least 40 percent of, say, families with children under the age of eighteen have incomes below the poverty line. You can move the threshold down a bit—to 30 or 20 percent, which would give you neighborhoods of "very high" or "high" poverty. You can use households instead of families. The thresholds are somewhat arbitrary since the poverty rate is the same whether you pay the high costs of living in Oakland or the low ones of Jackson, Mississippi. Plus, our assumption has made it so that a place with so much official poverty lives beside a whole lot of unofficial poverty, or "near poverty," which in some places is as great or greater than official poverty.[12] Our intersection, for instance, shows a 2010 census tract that's about half black, half Hispanic, with very high family poverty. Only 6 percent of adults have a college degree or better, and 82 percent of home owners pay more than 30 percent of their incomes toward their mortgages. Almost all the census tracts around it have similar features, and most show declines since 2000.[13]

The East Oakland map shows what the Miami map shows, or the Houston map or the Bronx map. Census tracts with extreme or very high poverty tend to cluster together in connected neighborhoods. They may be unique in lots of ways, even vibrant and culturally rich beyond compare. But they nonetheless share the trait of very limited economic resources, and they are on the wrong end of the assumption. For that reason they cluster, with areas of extreme poverty abutting each other, connected to tracts of very high poverty, connected in turn to areas of high poverty until they reach some magical border where a strong majority of middle-class households live. You can do it by neighborhoods, as the Oakland map shows, or you can do it by whole regions, as an RCA map of northern New Jersey municipalities would show. The same assumption governs the landscape.

All the neighborhood goodies exulted in the previous chapter are negated here. The pattern of being isolated from other areas, connected only to other poor ones and largely peripheral to neighborhoods rich in commerce and civic resources, represents something of a historical land use map. That is the next feature of an antimarket. It's the place that holds all the things (and people) that middle-class areas reject. It's got waste treatment facilities, bus depots, industrial brownfields on contaminated soil, and oil refineries—a chaotic repository of the things that can and once fit into broad commercial zones except that families moved in. It is not well planned. It is not zoned to protect young children. It has very few of the amenities, public infrastructure, or

73

consumer options that are good for much business of any kind. Investment naturally goes elsewhere or comes in at inflated—or, in the case of
credit, unconscionable—prices. Public institutions dominate the lives
of residents. Private concerns are vaguely regulated; too many are criminal. If this happens long enough (and no other discernible revitalizing
force comes along like gentrification), the antimarket neighborhood
becomes an island known only to itself, an irrelevant enclave, its families spatially marginalized at best. In chapter 6, we'll examine assumptions about the poor themselves, not just the spaces they occupy. But
next we have to unravel how our assumption about social distance produced such similar results in so many different places.

## Localism and the Ghetto: Thesis and Antithesis
### Ghettos Made Easy

Ghettos were formed by the assumptions explored in this book, especially this one about preserving middle-class stability by keeping the
poor at a distance. But assumptions need agents in order to actualize
them. The primary agent here was the U.S. government. The particular tools used by the government were four: redlining, urban renewal,
public housing, and segregation. William Julius Wilson would add to
the mix deindustrialization, the market-driven process by which cities
ceased to be centers of the kind of unionized manufacturing jobs that
gave financial stability and home ownership to a breadwinner with only
a high school education. Together these forces became a public–private
partnership of marginalization.

As we saw in the last chapter, the process of circling with red markers
black and immigrant neighborhoods on a map and declining to issue
mortgages there—"redlining"—was an early public–private partnership between realtors and the Home Owners Loan Corporation in the
1930s. The immediate effect was disinvestment in racially defined neighborhoods while the long-term effect was subsidization of communities
without color. What condemned the capital-poor landscape of the urban

ghetto simultaneously enriched the artificially discounted communities of all-white suburbia after World War II. The universal practice of redlining helped to remake the landscape of opportunity from city to suburb. Deindustrialization followed, beginning in the 1950s, and either greatly reduced the size of urban manufacturing and its labor force, or moved it to the suburbs. The flight of so many middle-class taxpayers beyond the urban boundary forced cities to come up with plans to keep them or bring them back. Urban renewal was the policy brainchild of this desire and, in most cases, a devastating blow. Marshaling the sweeping power of eminent domain, it cleared whole intact neighborhoods—homes, businesses, core community organizations—and barely financed their relocation. In the name of blight, then slum clearance, it left thousands to search for alternative housing in often very tight housing markets. Nearly all of these people were black. Nearly all the people that cities hoped would return to the business parks, arenas, and museums that would be built on black people's former communities were white. They rarely ever came. Often the great edifices of rebirth remained stillborn in their grandiose plans, the large lots empty.

The survivors of these policies, however, often found apartments in public housing sites whose particular locations in every city where they were built revealed a pattern of keeping the poor out of sight, on the other side of the highway or behind a factory wall. Indeed, the other side of the highway was the modern equivalent of the proverbial "other side of the tracks." This expression is less metaphor than description. In the early part of the twentieth century, men (most of them working class and black) who worked in the jobs associated with the rail traffic into towns and cities were settled into encampments and communities away from the growing town—that is, on the other side of the train tracks. Sometimes these places, like Overtown in Miami, were literally called "Colored Town" or, in other places, "Darkietown."[14] They were the rule under early twentieth-century patterns of segregation. That rule stuck, in both southern and northern cities, sustaining segregated housing markets all the way to deindustrialization. Further into the century, highways were overtaking train tracks as the man-made markers of community identity. Inside these lines, urban renewal began a massive process of displacing functional communities into dysfunctional housing projects, inevitably isolated from the city's vitality on the other side of a highway. While the program took homes and assets away, deindustrialization took jobs away.

The pace of both worked a special torture. Urban renewal could take forever. Deindustrialization happened in fits and starts. Though the people displaced did not necessarily start out poor, they often became so. In Newark, for instance, over a dozen urban renewal projects occurred between 1952 and 1967, culminating in the clearance of about six thousand housing units.[15] Yet the designation of "blight" that began the process of condemnation was usually eight to ten years before any construction began.[16] That's a lot of limbo for people unsure of whether their neighborhood would last.

Dr. Dorothy Fields was a schoolgirl in Miami's Overtown neighborhood when urban renewal came to class. Dr. Fields is now a historian and the executive director of the Black Archives in Miami, but today I caught her speaking from experience. She remembered life in the Overtown of the late 1940s as self-contained, with what we'd now call a commercial corridor, entertainment, culture and five theaters from 6th to 20th Streets. She remembers how she might go downtown with her mother and see a beautiful dress in the window of a store they weren't permitted to enter. A dressmaker in Overtown merely had to be told about it, and a version would appear, available for sale. Even then the idea of urban renewal was already in the air. Dr. Fields's family moved out in 1948, a year before the National Housing Act that formally created urban renewal, because they had heard talk of a "relocation plan" and didn't want to lose all value in their home. It wasn't clear exactly when, but the highway was coming through. The last straw for her family was when Dr. Fields's high school teacher assigned the class to write an essay on their neighborhood to be called "The Highway in the Sky."

"They were getting us ready," she explained. To be expelled.

The displacement that dragged on over many years in Overtown ruined property values, destroyed businesses, and turned dreams to nightmares. Plans for clearance were never specific. Rumors carried for month after month. Many of the more mobile home owners who had received letters from the city went to look in what were then the suburbs—in all-white Liberty City not far away. When white residents would see Overtown blacks peering in their windows at the homes there, "they would leave with the pots still cooking on the stove," Dr. Fields laughed. Most of the memories were not so funny. Overtown became a ghost town by the time highways finally cut through it; even today, it is a strange mix of concentrated poverty, downtown sports, cultural facilities, and artist-led gentrification. (Liberty City has, at least in parts, fallen even further.) Dr. Fields laments that her high school classmates from 1960 are so scarred by the upheaval and fearful of what it became that they won't go back to visit. "They're afraid of it."

And why not? The process of dislocating unwanted communities through big, lumbering government programs like urban renewal, highway construction, and public housing development, with all their moving political parts, was frightening in its scope and awesome in its power. While the people being moved had little say at all, the people near whom they might go had plenty to say about it. The historian Thomas Sugrue describes a process in downtown Detroit that was instructive for the market forces unleashed by government action. The government's forced displacement of citizens—first for highway construction, then for urban renewal and perhaps to public housing—contributed to a sense that these people could always be moved elsewhere, even if by private force. In the 1940s, a severe housing shortage crowded black migrants from the South into just a few downtown neighborhoods soon called slums. That crisis enabled a festival of discrimination in which landlords routinely price-gouged black renters despite the substandard living conditions. The twin goals of cross-city expressway construction and inner-city slum removal cleared the Lower East Side, the Hastings Street business district, and the ironically named Paradise Valley. Despite the loss of thousands of buildings (many of whose lots remain vacant to this day), there were no plans for relocating residents.

There was no place to go, because whites steadfastly, if not violently, refused to desegregate even the edges of their neighborhoods. So, people who had lived in slums moved into worse slums. Eventually, some would move into public housing, but the momentum of voter resistance to housing for blacks prevented many projects from ever being built in Detroit. Here was the paradox, which was signaled by the assumption we examined in the last chapter. White homeowners were enjoying a culture of beneficial government assistance in the form of mortgage subsidization, yet public housing for blacks—another New Deal subsidy passed by Congress—was perceived as a threat if it was within distant sight of a white neighborhood. As Sugrue wrote, "The success of Detroit property owners in availing themselves of government assistance for private homeownership ensured that Detroit would construct little public housing, and that the projects that were built would be racially segregated."[17] Eventually, as we'll see in the next chapter, that success would give way to white abandonment of the city altogether, but not before thousands of black residents over two decades would struggle to root.

## Root Shock

The Miami and Detroit examples are what Mindy Fullilove, a psychiatrist who studies public health, calls "root shock." She wrote a book about it, chronicling from 1995 to 2003 the fraught experiences of people among the 993 cities whose communities were bulldozed by urban renewal.[18] She found that the psychological effects of displacement were still with them more than twenty years later. Her term originally comes from botany. A tree uprooted by hurricane winds or a plant grabbed up too abruptly from where it's lived both experience an immediate shock at the root, as the organism shuts down unnecessary functions in order to survive the trauma. Unless quickly restored to a nourishing place where the roots can resume and resettle, the plant will die. Humans and their collective environments are similar, but more complicated in the range of functions that either shut down, risk loss, or adapt poorly to the new state. Fullilove writes:

> Root shock, at the level of the individual, is a profound emotional upheaval that destroys the working model of the world that had existed in the individual's head. . . . Root shock at the level of the local community, be it a neighborhood or something else, ruptures bonds, dispersing people to all the directions of the compass. Even if they manage to regroup, they are not sure what to do with one another. People who were near are too far, and people who were far are too near. The elegance of the neighborhood—each person in his social and geographic slot—is destroyed, and even if a neighborhood is rebuilt exactly as it was, it won't work.[19]

Of course, the communities were never rebuilt as they had been, which was the point. Yet the idea of root shock tells us something not only about the social, emotional, and economic complexity of displacing people because they lived in areas deemed slums, but also about the power of connectedness and the powerlessness that may linger as a result of disconnectedness.

This is the soul of the problem with public housing, as it was racially reconstituted by the late 1950s and 1960s. Much has been written in recent years about the scourge of destitute and dangerous high-rises that once plagued neighborhoods like Newark's Central Ward or Chicago's South Side until they were imploded. But a little about their history is worth remembering here. Public housing was originally an effort to provide decent, temporary housing for returning veterans.[20] Although it was a federal program, it was administered through local public housing authorities, the voluntary creation of only those municipalities that wanted it.[21] Generally, they were not racially segregated—not strictly. Both New Orleans, which had some of the earliest projects, and Newark (but not Detroit) experimented with integrated public housing for a time. Then, in the late 1950s, several important changes occurred. First, housing was strictly segregated by race. Second, it became increasingly segregated by class, accommodating exclusively poorer and poorer families. Third, it disappeared to the other side of the highway.

## Persistent Distancing

From there, the places where large public housing projects were built became the full-blown antithesis of self-sufficient suburbs, landscapes of negation. I call them "antimarkets" to reflect the fact that all the markets there work in reverse. Bad, ugly housing begets abandonment and disinvestment, while single-detached homes with well-kept yards and desirable neighbors beget rising property values. Discriminatory lending policies make credit chronically tight and open the door to high-priced, unscrupulous sources of capital, while favored terms and insured mortgages make for markets of reduced risk and steady growth. A lack of supermarkets raises prices and lowers food value at the few that exist, while multiple choices create the competition necessary for lower prices and better food, to say nothing of schools, drugs, or bus schedules. Whatever the range of factors that produce (and reproduce) these results, the middle-class public's voluntary, habitual choices to maintain distance lay at the foundation. The National Housing Act contained this very provision for local control over the existence and location of public housing. Nationally, most of the hundreds of legal challenges to local rejection upheld local choice.[22] Each time, the second assumption was affirmed. And private attempts to house the poor near the middle class over their objection—as in Mount Laurel, New Jersey—met the same fate. Persistent distancing became a pillar of localist thinking.

Thus, what was happening by the 1970s was the color-blind development of two worlds, one poor and working class, the other middle class or much better. The dichotomy was played out on land, largely between the urban and suburban, a geography of opportunity with profound future effects on the children in both. That it occurred in the shadow of the recent Civil Rights Movement gains in Congress suggested a strong local role for the dynamic. In fact, the policies of the national government (urban renewal, public housing, federally insured mortgages, highway construction) in tandem with the deindustrialized job market worked *in the service of* suburban local control. This was the birth of formal localism. Naturally, the dynamic would be challenged in courts by a generation of public-interest lawyers raised on the rights-based arguments of the Civil Rights Movement. For the reasons detailed in the next section, they would fail at the hands of the highest court in the land.

## Help from Above: The Creation of Legal Localism, Part 1 (Land Use)

The character and function of localism took lasting shape under the sanction of courts precisely during the peak period of white flight from cities, the federal passage of civil rights laws aimed at frustrating formal segregation, and intense battles over school busing. Although most legal localism had been developed by state courts, several important Supreme Court decisions under Chief Justice Warren Burger during the 1970s unequivocally established the doctrine as the configuration of middle-class preferences. Further, these cases demonstrate the way local autonomy would be balanced against the constitutional arguments advanced by civil rights advocates. Specifically, the five cases discussed here and in the next chapter (*Village of Belle Terre v. Boraas*,[23] *Warth v. Seldin*,[24] *Village of Arlington Heights v. Metropolitan Housing Development Corp.*,[25] *San Antonio Independent School District v. Rodriguez*,[26] and *Milliken v. Bradley*[27]) solidified the power to exclude outsiders through zoning ordinances and other land use devices even where such localized decisions clearly and negatively affected regional housing markets. They affirmed the sanctity of jurisdictional borders within which local powers are exercised, and defended localities' presumptive power not only to retain local control of education but of school finances—even if doing so produced gross fiscal disparities among municipalities.[28]

These meanings were not always clear on the faces of the disputes facing the justices. In *Belle Terre*, as we saw earlier, the Court resolved a case brought by college-student renters in favor of the village of Belle Terre on New York's Long Island. It affirmed the town's right under the police power to zone areas exclusively for families of related persons. Race was not directly at issue in the case and, had it been, the Court indicated that the ordinance could not survive constitutional scrutiny.[29] Instead, the home owner and renters believed the village's ordinance infringed on their constitutional rights to travel and privacy.[30] In affirming the broad police powers of the suburban locality in the case, the Court referred to precedent from large cities.[31] However, in its assumptions about the need for such expansive power and the ends to which it would likely be put, *Belle Terre* is clearly a suburban case. Despite the ostensibly locality-neutral language of Justice Douglas's opinion, the city of New York (the closest large city) could not have exercised power in that way. Like most major cities, it was (and is) too large, too heterogeneous in population and neighborhoods, and has too many kinds of already permissible uses and lifestyles to impose such restrictions.[32] As we saw in chapter 2, the Court's language locates the (idealized) environment the village was trying to maintain well outside the "city": "The regimes of boarding houses, fraternity houses, and the like present *urban problems*. More people occupy a given space; more cars rather continuously pass by; more cars are parked; noise travels with crowds."[33]

By pitting the village's regulation against "urban problems," the Court assigned to the suburbs the localist power to exclude certain types of residents that urban localities couldn't. The decision, therefore, belongs among those that establish legal localism on behalf of suburbs in direct reference to the excluded uses and users common to larger cities. These were often references to blighted neighborhoods and the slum dwellers who lived there, as in *Berman v. Parker*.[34] Blight and slum removal were the cities' problem, as we saw in the last section. Redevelopment through urban renewal and public housing beautified the city, restoring it to a place that middle-class taxpayers would want to live in again, a place that had figured out its poverty problem. But by the 1970s it was clear that those public programs had not achieved that purpose. Cities were financially strapped and often dangerous places. Suburbs were not. All that remained of the urban revitalization hopes of the 1950s were legal precedents. *Belle Terre* shows how the Burger Court used them in the 1970s to insulate the suburbs from the urban poor in the name of local self-determination.

A racial subtext is also clear in the 1970s land use cases. The power to exclude categories of uses associated with urban problems unfortunately remains code for black people to this day. It is an enormous power, made greater by its capacity to preclude strict scrutiny, and allows the proliferation of racial proxies under the guise of rational planning and community self-determination.[35] This represents another constitutive part of legal localism: legal colorblindness. This key feature immunized localism from constitutional attack not a full decade after the Civil Rights Movement.

In another zoning case, *Warth v. Seldin*, plaintiffs were fair housing advocates—individuals and organizations representing the affordable housing interests of Rochester, New York's low- and moderate-income tenants—challenging neighboring Penfield's zoning ordinance for excluding people from living in the town on the basis of class status. The ordinance maintained 98 percent of the town for single-family detached residences only, a typical feature of exclusionary zoning that precluded rental apartments. Again, race was not directly in dispute. Plaintiffs' constitutional claims were dismissed by the district court and the Second Circuit on standing grounds, and the Supreme Court affirmed. The result demonstrates a less obvious dimension of localism's conservative power: the meaning of membership. Not only did the Court reject the claims that were based on economic discrimination, but the dismissal on standing grounds worked the procedural equivalent of the zoning ordinance's purpose: it defined and excluded outsiders and denied any regional responsibility a suburb might have for their housing needs. Specifically, the justices found that *nonresidents* were entitled to no say about the regional effects (or negative externalities) associated with one town's efforts to bar the entry of lower-income residents. Plaintiffs had argued, for instance, that Penfield's exclusions necessarily affected the distribution of affordable housing opportunities across the relevant metropolitan area, devaluing the city of Rochester's housing market and burdening its tax base.[36] The majority found these arguments wholly speculative as to causation, and, in sharply dismissive language, considered any economic impact on neighboring localities merely "incidental adverse effects" of the regulation.[37] In effect, when the Court found that the plaintiff–outsiders lacked standing, their claims would be orphaned, unable to be asserted by anyone without a direct interest in the opposite point of view. (No one in Penfield organized public support for such a viewpoint.)

The third and final land use case, *Arlington Heights*, involved facts where race actually was an issue in dispute. There a low-income housing development corporation was denied a variance that would have allowed it to build a complex of affordable apartments in a suburb outside Chicago. Hearings were held in which opponents of the rezoning made mixed objections, some based on the "social issue," most based on an expected drop in property values.[38] The village rested its denial on grounds of zoning integrity, given the single-family character of the area, and the expectations of resident home owners.[39] Plaintiffs sued under the discriminatory effects standard of the Fair Housing Act,[40] but lost before the Supreme Court. Using the intent standard it had just announced in another case,[41] the Court acknowledged that minorities might be disproportionately affected by the lack of affordable housing in Arlington Heights, but that the decision to deny the rezoning request was based on racially neutral land use principles.[42]

*Arlington Heights* is important to localism in demonstrating (1) its interaction with contemporary race discrimination standards (specific intent); and (2) the relative immunity enjoyed by land use decisions with segregative effects so long as a rational planning rationale is also apparent. The decision was a test case for both sides of the suburban housing integration conflict. Plaintiffs discovered the tremendous difficulty in mounting a frontal assault on local policies that had demonstrably distancing effects in terms of both class and race. Defendant–suburban municipalities learned how insulated their land use decision making could be from constitutional attack so long as a paradigm of categorical land uses (first articulated in *Village of Euclid v. Ambler Realty*)[43] was scrupulously followed. These three land use cases provided a localist manual for excluding lower-income residents and black people generally.

Certainly a lot has changed since the early 1970s when urban renewal ended and public housing construction slowed to a halt, yet only in their aftermath did the concentration effects of poverty gain recognition outside the ghetto itself. What happened to make concentrated poverty a thing to fear? In short, suburbs became much richer in opportunity and cities became much less so, especially after the emergence of crack cocaine in the early 1980s. The bet on suburban living emerged the wiser one, as jobs, the best schools, and rising home values became the stuff of the region, increasingly less dependent on the central city. With the withdrawal of federal funding and the loss of middle-class residents and employers, cities—especially those in the Northeast and Midwest—struggled mightily through fiscal crises from the late 1970s into the early 1990s. Meanwhile, most housing policies continue to concentrate poverty by, for example, establishing housing voucher programs with rules like Section 8's that limit a renter's options to other poor neighborhoods. Even transportation policies concentrate poverty by making public transportation unavailable to low-income people without cars. Most poor people work, and they have to be able to get home. These kinds of factors trap people in unwanted places, the broad, neglected neighborhoods where poverty is bound to concentrate.

But pull up again to satellite height and notice that cities suffer from their own concentration effects. That is, though people pay enormous costs for living in concentrated poverty, as we'll see in a moment, municipalities also pay dearly. The aversion to the poor at the heart of the second assumption can morph into a more global aversion to the cities in which neighborhoods of concentrated poverty are a part. This is what happened to places like Gary, Indiana, or Camden, New Jersey, known by outsiders for little but their poverty. So, before we peek at the costs associated with antimarkets, keep in mind that the last thing you want your town to have is swaths of concentrated poverty—pockets maybe, swaths never.

## The Debate Today
### The High Cost of the Wrong Place

One problem with an antimarket is figuring out where to begin counting the costs. In Oakland, for instance, the murder rate is rising again. My own nephews there mourn too often for people of such tender ages. The scars of each loss are indicated in their fears, their reduced sense of freedom, their inability to comprehend what each time looks to them like a random explosion of stupid madness. Yet a report by the Administrator's Office of Alameda County (where the city of Oakland sits) calculated that violent crimes accounted for about 25 percent of the general fund budget in 2008.[44] The city estimated that the 124 murders in 2008 cost taxpayers about $2 million in law enforcement investigation, prosecution, jails, and other administrative costs. One in particular cost more than that sum, and it began by the victim simply being in the wrong place at the wrong time.

The place was her bed. In April 2008, twenty-one-year-old Shaneice Davis was asleep around midnight when two bullets crashed through her bedroom wall and entered her brain. She lived with her mom and infant daughter at 8296 MacArthur Boulevard—yes, *that* intersection in East Oakland. She was apparently not the intended victim of the shooting outside, and no one has ever been charged in her death. But death was not immediate, and trauma care specialists and multiple surgeries tried to save her. Two days later she died. Police had little to go on, which increased the cost and time in their investigation. Her family received counseling and other public social services. Her mother regrets the fateful decision to live there and has moved to another neighborhood with

Shaneice's child. They will bear the costs of her loss forever. City and county taxpayers will pay millions for her death alone. Yet her death is connected to multiples. The shooter in the crowd outside her bedroom that night was attending a memorial for Tommiesha Jones, a teenage neighbor who had been murdered. In June, twenty-four-year-old Zaire Washington was also shot to death close by. The killing continued. A pregnant Kennah Wilson, age eighteen, was murdered within yards of that death in August. Her baby didn't survive. Five people. One spot. Just a few months.

### Small Katrinas Everywhere

Whatever the costs, they are now part of a system of compounded costs that we didn't ever expect to pay. We couldn't have. We never saw our interests converging with the objects of our dislikes. We never seriously imagined these costs as a consequence of inequitable patterns set since our grandparents' time. Instead, we pretended that this is all a matter of individual criminal behavior having nothing to do with people's distance from opportunities, and we try to lock up those individuals for their misdeeds (which, as we'll see in chapter 6, we do more than any other country in the developed world). Yet the 171,000 individual prisoners in California cost state taxpayers over $10 billion in 2009.[45] Jails tend to be county funded. In California, 80,000 individual inmates cost another $2 billion, according to the Legislative Analyst's Office. In addition to unsustainable public costs, over-incarceration has led to overcrowding, which a federal court prohibited California from doing in 2009 and the U.S. Supreme Court upheld two years later.[46] Meanwhile, Oakland, on the brink of bankruptcy in 2010, cut 10 percent of its police force.

The storm of people we wish to avoid is well upon us, at least in terms of their dollar costs. (The emotional, human, intangible costs I ignore for now.) Each prisoner is not just the sunk cost of food, shelter, and monitoring, but lost costs in what is sometimes referred to as human capital—the potential of active lives. Were the inmate number cut in half, and that half educated, working, contributing to the tax base, voting, raising children, buying school clothes and circus tickets, imagine how the budgets change. Each has neighbors to support, not threaten; each is a relative and a family resource, not a risk. To work, that number has to come from those areas of concentrated poverty. Instead, their resource-poor concentrations are spreading well into suburbia, turning the map of antimarket neighborhoods into a map of antimarket municipalities in most metropolitan areas and challenging the economic health of regions. Increasingly, for all those folks who live in the lovely parts of Oakland—those Olympian hills that overlook the flatlands and the sprawling bay's undulating blues—for all the good people of solidly middle-class neighborhoods like Rockridge and Montclair, even for residents of Piedmont and San Leandro, it's coming: the multiplying costs of hard lives over yonder.

Which goes to show how a few intersections in Oakland represent smaller Katrinas everywhere. Instead of the sudden deaths of vulnerable thousands, they are the weekly deaths of a fragile few—their common exposure a persistent lack of opportunity in the despised places where they live. The costs to Alameda County are not as shocking as the estimated $114 billion in federal funds that Hurricane Katrina cost the nation, because those annual costs are absorbed by the region. Yet they are the costs of this assumption all the same and a grim reminder of our mutuality. Ultimately, this is the rebuttal to the man who rode beside me on the train and saw no connection between his middle-class life and these. The impoverishment at the reciprocal end of middle-class localism need not be remedied with an all-or-nothing strategy like total immersion. Concentration is the primary force behind these crippling deficits, so a proportionately hewn form of *deconcentration* should direct the remedy.

We will explore fuller answers to the problem of distancing the poor in chapters ahead. But for now it's important to acknowledge two things. First, that poor places are not the same thing as poor people, so avoidance of one need not entail avoidance of the other under all circumstances. And second, that total avoidance is at least financially unsustainable.

## *Katrina West: Houston*

The second assumption does not always control. Greater New Orleans may have been surprised by Hurricane Katrina, but Houston was not. I traveled to Houston because it was an important city I didn't know—the nation's fourth largest—but mainly to see what came of the more than two hundred thousand Katrina survivors who wound up there (and where a great many remain). Houston absorbed them in two instructive ways. The first is less formal and not well publicized. New Orleans had a substantial Vietnamese community, many of them involved in fishing, whose neighborhoods near Lake Pontchartrain were among the first to be inundated. Hundreds if not thousands of Vietnamese Orleanians appeared in Southwest Houston at the Hong Kong Mall, a Chinese community center, where they were processed, fed, clothed, given housing referrals and mutual aid. Carl Lindahl, an academic at the University of Houston who passionately studies the experiences of survivors, described it to me as "an amazing underground reaction." There is very little good or bad that's written about this process of absorption, which is probably a good thing. It sounds a lot like a communal hug.

The other was more bureaucratic, for a larger population of survivors, but it seemed to work about as well. Lindahl echoed many people with whom I spoke when he called Mayor Bill White his hero. Like me, Lindahl expected Houston to re-create a ghetto of unwanted, very poor and desperate survivors, but that didn't happen. There was a "gigantic service bazaar" where people could get disaster relief and placement, he said. Settlement was "haphazard and friendly." That doesn't mean there weren't problems. Survivors came in the full range of humanity; they experienced the transition differently as a matter of age, resources, mental states. Houstonians' generosity did not preclude more mixed reactions to the newcomers over time. But the newcomers were never concentrated. In fact, Katrina survivors were deliberately placed throughout the Greater Houston area as a matter of local housing policy between the city and county. Lindahl explained, "There may have been a value on *not* ghettoizing them." Thousands have stayed in Houston.

## Counterfactual: If All Poverty Were Like White Poverty

What if poverty were rarely concentrated? It might not completely overrule the second assumption or rebut the acquaintance on the train to imagine keeping a less stringent distance from the poor. When Paul Jargowsky published *Poverty and Place* in 1998, the alarming trends from the 1980s were clear. Poverty was becoming more and more concentrated—but *especially* by race and ethnicity. The black poor were the most concentrated by far, and Latino-concentrated poverty was rising, although not always in the same places. In the early 2000s, Jargowsky and others were cautiously optimistic that concentrated poverty was declining as a result of the strengths of the Clinton-era economy. Yet the declines were not so hopeful, in my view, and at best tenuous, which is why many if not most will be undone by the Great Recession and the foreclosure crisis. Latino-concentrated poverty in particular is steadily rising in many parts of the country; their rates are surpassing black levels from the 1980s in some regions. But one exception has held constant during the whole period: *white poverty is not concentrated.*

One last examination of the poverty map by race shows that white poverty is real, it presents serious household stresses and is a struggle to overcome, but it is not spatially trapped and you can't see it from the heavens. Rarely in any of the eight primary metropolitan areas I looked at for this book could you find a single census tract in which more than 10 percent of white families with children under the age of eighteen had incomes below the poverty line. *Ten percent poverty.* We need to learn more about how white poverty may be different in terms of its duration, severity, intergenerational effects, and correlations to education outcomes. But if the ample research on the power of place to determine opportunity holds true, then poor white families illustrate the possibility of refuting the second assumption. They are inadvertent test cases that prove that the poor can attend school, shop, vote, work, and most of all live within close proximity—even the same town—with the middle class. My hunch is that they do so with, all else being equal, better results than the concentrated poor of color.

# 4

## THE PROMISE HALF EMPTY

### ASSUMING THAT SEGREGATION
### IS A THING OF THE PAST

If you took a poll to see which of three subjects Americans would prefer to have a ninety-second discussion about, and the three choices
were segregation, slavery, or irritable bowel syndrome, I'm pretty sure
irritable bowels would win going away. If the mere mention of slavery
elicits claims of African American whining, segregation beyond the
black-and-white pictured past is more than avoided—it is flatly denied.
Besides, it's over. The increasing diversity of growing inner-ring suburbs—an argument made in this very book—is proof of positive change.
The assumption, then, is that racial segregation was triumphantly overcome decades ago. Whatever remains of it is the natural consequence
of voluntary preferences. People of similar backgrounds tend to cluster
together, which is their right.

If this assumption is true and is a fair assessment of a victorious
national struggle, then we should celebrate the tangible distance we've
covered since the days of freedom marches in the South. We don't. Every
Fourth of July, we would party in neighborhood streets, parks, school
yards, and boulevards so racially mixed that they blur distinctions.

Segregation would be hard to imagine, but the collective will to overcome it would be well-known to everyone, especially immigrants and schoolchildren, a hard-fought element of their identity as Americans. If the assumption that we have overcome segregation were true, there might be no greater claim to American exceptionalism, because, as most of us really do believe, racial segregation was the spatial manifestation of our greatest hatreds and miseries, the visible landscape of a young nation's formation by racism. It wasn't a black thing then. It was an every thing.

Yet as the last chapter shows, segregation—the economic and racial condition of systematic sorting by place—is part of a far more acceptable social distancing that is routinely mediated through income and socioeconomic status. Both racial and economic separation produce unsustainable costs to all of us, with the same combination of direct and indirect effects. Racial segregation has a different heritage, though. Government at all levels fought for it, then against it, then for it again. It joined with private attitudes and the private sector to create racial maps that were hard to undo. Then with the advent of colorblindness came something most Americans probably do not recognize for what it is: *re*segregation. In housing. In schools. To explore the character of segregation today, this chapter begins by trying to *feel* segregation before we measure it, then calculating how we suffer segregation today before examining how legal localism helped to remake it. Finally, we'll look at three subjects I have long personally avoided for their complexity: returning to Detroit where I was born, examining the problem of segregated schools, and reconsidering integration as a goal.

## Feeling Segregation

I myself was ambivalent about the continued relevance of segregation. I appreciated its significance with a historical sentimentality. After all, I grew up in New York City in the 1960s and 1970s. We invented multiracialism *and* multiculturalism before Californians had even heard of it. But reading about housing lawsuits and school diversity battles, even protesting South African apartheid in the 1980s, reminded me of something my father used to like to do when I was a boy. He would take me to a particular intersection on the Upper East Side—96th Street and Park Avenue—and we would stand together on the island dividing north- and southbound traffic.

"Look downtown for a minute," my father would say, squaring my shoulders to the south. "Now look uptown for a minute. Tell me what you see."

It was a trick, a favorite one he'd play on me and anyone who visited us from out of town. Looking downtown I saw perhaps the richest avenue on earth, with beautiful gray stone and brown brick buildings, white-gloved doormen and the (then) Pan Am Building standing tall at the end of it, almost with its hands on its silver hips, a gateway to Midtown's office wealth. Everybody, *everybody* except the nannies and deliverymen there was white. Looking uptown, the avenue was immediately split down the middle by the rise of the Metro-North commuter line, the rails encased in a thick stone elevation that darkened the street around it, crowded the sidewalks except for the long waiting line of red brick high-rise housing projects on either side. Here at the edge of Spanish Harlem, everybody, yes *everybody* was either black or brown. By a mere swivel of the head you could bear witness to the difference in proverbial black and white.

"This is the most segregated street in America," Dad would say matter-of-factly. "Worse than anything I lived through in Detroit. Probably more blatant than anything your mom grew up with in the South."

Decades later the view from 96th and Park has not changed much. Letting yourself dare to recognize segregation makes for a world of trouble, because the assumption—which is important for so many of us to believe—breaks down quickly. Forget the why for a moment and focus on what you experience. What do you see when a New York City class of schoolchildren gets on a subway car for a field trip? What do you see when you ride the elevator up to one of the offices in the Pan Am—now MetLife—skyscraper? What do you see when you ride the Metro-North train to Scarsdale? What do you see when you peer into one of those Department of Corrections buses taking inmates from Rikers Island to court dates in Brooklyn? What do you see on most of the blocks where you visit friends or family? Chances are, with the exception of a very few places in this country, your eyes, if they're not lying, see strong, probably irrefutable evidence of segregation.

The difference between our cherished assumptions and what our lying eyes can't miss has fostered a certain compromise. It is that the glass on segregation is half full. Many of us readily admit we still have a way to go in order to make the American Dream consistent with Martin Luther King Jr.'s dream of racial equality, but we point to incremental progress and look forward. Because segregation is not total—the Metro-North car is not *completely* white after a certain stop, the elevator in the office building appears to have *a few* people of color wearing professional clothes— we prefer to believe that we're heading in the right direction. We're getting there by the more productive means of our attitudes about others, not because a federal court told us so. This, I suggest, is an unconscious attempt to have one's cake and eat it, too. It is the epitome of colorblindness. That is, the utter obviousness of segregation in our lives is the heart of our blindness to color. Segregation is our biggest blind spot. But it is that very contradiction between racial realities and aspirational belief that makes the *feeling* of segregation so undeniable. *If* the thought occurs to you at that intersection, *if* you wonder about it on that elevator ride, *if* you happen to start counting the number of white or Asian children among the black or brown children on the school field trip, you may feel the dull discomfort of chronic segregation in your bones.

As with most race issues today, it is tempting to pin our living patterns on class differences, which, for many of us, seems more justified by merit or rational preferences to live apart. The racial past, we rationalize, is mostly done, replaced by economic realities. It's a chicken-and-egg situation—which came first, racial segregation or economic segregation?— though we've mostly assumed the egg position. I'd like to reintroduce the chicken properly—through our gut. There we can feel how economic differences—our preferred egg—interact with old-fashioned racial segregation—that jettisoned chicken. Take New York City again, one of the most segregated cities in the United States, a fact that surprises many New Yorkers. Walk a few blocks from my father's favorite Upper East Side intersection and you'll see another example—this time not in housing but in the other major arena of segregation, public education.

Public School 198 and Public School 77 are examples of the kinds of compromises that educational innovation in New York City and other places has produced in the last decade or so: different schools in shared buildings, some of them charters. This one on 95th Street and 3rd Avenue is home to two, PS 198, a school zoned for anyone in the district, and PS 77, a gifted and talented school with selective admission based on standardized test performance. Given its location near the famous border between racial worlds, PS 198 is about half Latino and a quarter black. The gifted school, PS 77, is part of the city's attempt to lure middle-class parents back into the public schools, especially in neighborhoods like the Upper East Side where parents either put their kids in expensive private schools or leave the city for the Westchester suburbs. Not surprisingly, PS 77 is about 70 percent white, some Asian, but only a smattering of black (about 3 percent) and Hispanic students. According to an investigation by the *Village Voice*, PS 198 was there first, when the building was constructed in 1959.[1] The two schools start at different times of day—before 8:00 a.m. and after 8:30—but their classrooms are on the same floors. Nevertheless, the mostly white students and their teachers at PS 77 use the building's *front* entrance. For PS 198, the mostly Latino and black students and their teachers must enter through the *back* of the building. The dual entrances are merely the threshold in a series of disparities that include class sizes, access to laboratories, course offerings, the number of teachers per class, and the amount of money raised by the respective PTAs. In every instance, the gifted children at PS 77 experience a decisive advantage in the quality of their education. Beyond the numbers, both sets of students receive a daily message about themselves compared to the others with whom they rarely interact but cannot help seeing.

Just what is the message being communicated to children as young as four years old in such a place? That's hard to know for certain, but it must at least reflect a difference about the schools. A child cannot or should not attend one or the other for reasons that will be explained differently by the adults to whom they listen. There should be some consistent message all the kids receive. Whatever that message is, it will involve existential questions about how smart you are, how capable, deserving, or hardworking you are and, inevitably, whether the answers to these things depend on what you have inside, how you look outside, or what your parents do or don't do for you. As Justin from the introduction shows, the questions will continue for years. Most of us grown folk have short-circuited the inquiry by deciding that this particular case involves merit and little else. Sure, the children who attend PS 77 tend to be white or Asian. They also tend to be at least middle class or more, their parents spending thousands of dollars on test-taking classes and tutors for their preschoolers. Sure, there is undeniable evidence of class disparities. But they passed objective tests to get in, and it would be unfair to deny them the privileges of superior ability. Only if the merit argument fails will most of us use income justifications to explain the differences. Rarely ever do we admit what our eyes can plainly see. The numbers are too lopsided to be coincidence, and there's no scientific support for arguments about innate superiority. Well past the millennium, let's call it what it is. This is school segregation, and the children in that building can surely feel it.

Segregation has launched its longest battles in public education, as the *Brown* decision and its aftermath demonstrated. We'll return to the schools soon. Ultimately, what happens in PS 198 versus PS 77 is a question of fairness and mutuality, which we'll get to at the end of the chapter. But we don't live in a society that dictates school choice on the basis of race anymore. Since the 1970s, we've officially done it on the basis of place, so that is where we begin the measurement of just how far we've come in desegregating our relationships to one another.

## Measuring Segregation

When you break down residential segregation, you're really asking whether nonwhites live only with other nonwhites, in geographically connected neighborhoods, in a less desirable part of town that would be too far to walk to productive encounters with whites. (Obviously, an all-white neighborhood should qualify as segregated, but that's not typically how social scientists measure segregation.) Quantifying all that is a bit tricky. You could simply count the percentage of people of each race in a census tract or town. For instance, the Manhattan Community District 8, comprising many of the census tracts south of East 96th Street, was approximately 80 percent white in 2010.[2] But that snapshot doesn't convey enough about trends (in fact, it represents a slight decline since the previous census). Or you could focus on the number trends over time.

That is what Myron Orfield and Thomas Luce did in a recent census data analysis of suburban trends.[3] What they found seems at first to support the assumption about segregation disappearing. They found a steady increase in "diverse" suburbs—that is, localities where 20–60 percent of residents were nonwhite. Looking at fifty of the largest metropolitan areas (whose combined population is almost half the nation), they found that in 2000, forty-two million people lived in diverse suburbs. By 2010, that number had jumped to fifty-three million. By the same token, the number of people living in the traditional suburb— "largely white, rapidly developing places removed from the racial and economic diversity of the large central cities that they surround"[4]—was forty-seven million in 2010, down from fifty-four million in 2000. So far, this suggests American racial blending, not segregation. However, there is a rapidly growing number of predominantly nonwhite suburbs—those that are at least 60 percent nonwhite. They counted twenty million residents in 2010 compared to eleven million a decade earlier.

The problem is that these numbers also show the spacing of segregation and the fragility of diversity brought about by demographic change and continued white flight. Diverse neighborhoods tend toward the inner ring of suburbs, supplanting traditional suburbs, whose populations are moving farther from the central city. The domino effect, as we saw in chapter 1, begins with nonwhite segregated "first suburbs" that are nearly adjacent to central cities. Orfield and Luce's analysis of the

Dallas–Fort Worth suburbs illustrates the pattern. In 2000, there were five predominantly nonwhite suburbs; in 2010, there were fifteen—all on the inner ring. In 2000, there were forty-eight diverse suburbs; in 2010, there were sixty-eight—all on either the inner ring or the second ring.[5] In DeSoto, the nonwhite population grew from 55 to 83 percent of the town's total. In Cedar Hill, nonwhites increased from half to three-quarters in the same decade. Both went from diverse, to nonwhite segregated.[6]

You might argue that the overall trend favors more diversity. Perhaps, but rarely. Once communities become nonwhite, they tend to stay that way. This has been the case since at least the birth of the assumption, back in the late 1970s. According to Orfield and Luce, "Neighborhoods that were integrated in 1980 were much less stable than predominantly white or predominantly non-white neighborhoods. More than a fifth (21 percent) of the census tracts that were integrated in 1980 had crossed the 60 percent threshold into the predominantly non-white category during the 1980s."[7] By 2010, only forty of the neighborhoods that were integrated in 1980 remained so.

These measures, while very helpful, don't necessarily measure the feel of segregation on the street. For that you need intersecting measures. Let's approach it from a commonsense perspective—what you would experience in a given neighborhood and how that experience fits in the context of the wider city or town. Context matters; you can only expect people of different races to be spread around a place if they're there to be counted in the first place. Therefore, the first thing to measure is the overall population of different races in a city. Then you look census tract by census tract to see whether they're distributed evenly around town or concentrated in tracts with few white people. That's why the basic measure of segregation is called "evenness"—or, for some purely academic reason, "the index of dissimilarity"—which measures how evenly spread out the town's population of, say, people of Hispanic origin is. It shows the percentage who would have to move into other census tracts in order for them to be spread evenly across the town. Demographers call any number between 0.60 and 0.99 high to very high levels of basic segregation (moderate segregation falls between about 0.30 and 0.59), which is then expressed as a percentage. For example, New York City scored 81.7 in 2010. (It was 83.0 in 1980.)[8]

In general, segregation is highest in the Northeast and Midwest, *not* the South. Most of the metropolitan areas I studied have high to very high measures of segregation for blacks. Logan and Stults calculated that in Oakland it's 56.6; in Miami 73.0; in Newark it's 60.5 (though the *city* of Newark has one of the highest in the country at 78.0); Detroit's level of segregation is very high at 80.9.[9] Metropolitan segregation is also high for Latinos, though rarely achieving the highs found for blacks—63.4 in Los Angeles, 63.1 in the New York metro area, 62.6 in Newark, and 48.3 in Oakland–Fremont–Hayward—and highest where Latino population numbers are greatest.[10] Asians are almost never segregated from whites unless they're living in enclaves of recent immigrants where being segregated may actually help people seeking resources while they're trying to assimilate. For instance, the highest rate of Asian–white segregation of any metro area of the country is 53.7 in Edison–New Brunswick, New Jersey, an area with a rapidly growing Indian population; seventh is San Francisco–San Mateo–Redwood City, California, at 46.7.[11]

Three conclusions emerge. The first is that more than fifty years after the Supreme Court in *Brown v. Board of Education* declared that segregated schools were unconstitutional, we have managed to maintain the kinds of segregated living arrangements that sustain segregated schools. Second, the situation is stubbornly rotten for blacks. Class considerations don't alter the picture much. Even upper-income blacks experience very high levels of segregation across the nation, though not quite as high as for lower-income blacks. The third characteristic of these patterns to worry about is that Latino segregation may be following the course experienced by blacks more than the one taken by Asians. This is true despite the fact that Latinos in the United States hail from many different countries and from many different immigration profiles with vastly different resources.

The first two conclusions—persistence of racial segregation over time and its unique severity for blacks—led to critical analyses of black segregation patterns by sociologists Douglas Massey and Nancy Denton, which they called "hypersegregation." In a groundbreaking book called *American Apartheid*, Massey and Denton argued that not only were we ignoring the persistence of segregation (and this was in the mid-1990s), but we were ignoring how many different characteristics of debilitating segregation were overlapping for blacks—especially poor urban blacks (as well as darker-skinned Hispanics).[12] Hypersegregation was the condition of living in a neighborhood that scored high on not one measure of segregation, evenness, but *four out of five*. Subsequent researchers described these five dimensions this way: "Evenness refers to the differential distribution of groups across neighborhoods, exposure measures the probability of interaction between groups, concentration refers to the amount of physical space occupied by the minority group, centralization indicates the distance to the center of the urban area, and clustering indicates the degree to which minorities live in areas that adjoin one another."[13]

Hypersegregation, in other words, was the equivalent of witnessing racial isolation from space, as we did in the last chapter with East Oakland's poor neighborhoods. Its combined dimensions show you how a black person in, for example, the Lower Ninth Ward of New Orleans is likely to see only other black people all day—whether at school or the grocery store—and how far they would have to walk to find white people and, very importantly, the institutions and businesses that usually accompany those white people. When we think of racial segregation as racial isolation, it is much easier to see its connection to opportunity. When we see segregation as a limitation on opportunity, it is much easier to see why people confuse class difference (which they justify on merit) with racial differences (which they don't). We should not be confused. The two can't be untied.

Our most recent hypersegregation analyses were conducted by Rima Wilkes and John Iceland using 2000 census data. In that year, blacks were hypersegregated in twenty-nine metro areas. In several—Chicago, Cleveland, Detroit, Philadelphia, Milwaukee, and Newark—blacks were hypersegregated on five out of five dimensions. Many more metro areas were hypersegregated on four out of five measures. These included Gary, New York, Miami, LA, and Baltimore, but also fourteen southern metros, such as Mobile, Memphis, New Orleans, Houston, and St. Louis. Latinos were hypersegregated along four measures in Los Angeles and New York City.[14]

As an intuitive measure of school segregation, I prefer isolation. It's direct. An isolation index tells you the percentage of students of the same race with whom an average student attends school. In 2008–9, white students in the Portland, Maine, metropolitan area, for instance, had little to no idea what it's like to go to school with students who are not white. On average, 92 percent of their primary school classmates are white. Latino kids in the Los Angeles region attend schools that are 77 percent Latino. Black schoolchildren in Greater New Orleans and metro Detroit sit in classes that are at least three-quarters black.[15] Each percentage represents who these children know as they are introduced to the social world. It's their racial reference for intelligence as they are introduced to learning. The isolation index tends to go up as the proportion of minorities in a district rises and in areas that are fragmented into lots of school districts, like the Northeast and Midwest especially; Hispanic isolation, however, is high in those areas as well as the Southwest and California, where their numbers are greater.

These findings come from DiversityData.org, a project of the Harvard School of Public Health, which also documents the interplay of economics in school segregation. While 43 percent of white students attended schools where 20 percent or less of the kids came from impoverished families, only 7 percent of black and Hispanic students could say that. While 43 percent of black and Hispanic kids went to schools where family poverty was 80 percent of all kids, only 4 percent of white kids could say that. Often, the disparities occur in the very same region.

It's not always clear what we hope to learn from these numbers. Studies keep telling us that students who are educated in racially and economically diverse settings exhibit improved critical thinking, higher achievement, and reduced prejudice—all the salutary qualities we would want for adults navigating a more pluralistic global society. People keep saying they want these benefits—even the Supreme Court, which has not been particularly open to arguments about diversity from a social justice angle.[16] The discussion gets the most traction, then, when you talk about the benefits of exposure, not the consequences of isolation. Yet DiversityData.org also collects data that show just the opposite trends when it comes to the education of white students. The "white exposure to blacks or non-white Hispanics" index is frequently very, very low. That is, white students' isolation in a great many metro areas—even areas with only moderate levels of segregation—is extremely high. For instance, in the New York region where by all accounts people of all races publicly mix and work in high numbers, white primary school students attend classes that are, on average, just 5.8 percent black. Or consider Boston. White kids there see Hispanic classmates at a rate of just 6.7 percent; in Philadelphia it's 5.7 percent.[17] It's as if all the numerical diversity of their regions is mere background ornamentation in their lives.

This last point shows how isolation measures allow us to consider the costs of school segregation from a different angle: ignorance. The world we live in is controlled by the laws of physics, so we teach students physics. We study math, too, because it is everywhere around us. Math and physics are necessary parts of the knowledge base of an educated adult (unless that adult goes to law school). Yet nonwhite students are—or will be shortly—all around us. Children who are otherwise being assiduously prepared for the challenges life will bring are often taught in environments that pretend these other people don't exist outside some anthropological fascination, or as if the social world were flat. Learning in a segregated environment most of your life is therefore *at least* a social disadvantage. Since segregated school environments often take the histories and cultures of nonwhite students for granted, there is probably a substantive knowledge disadvantage, too.[18] This is why segregation amid the new demography changes the argument for "diversity." It is no longer simply morally attractive or even historically reparative and it certainly isn't charity. It has become basic educational necessity, like learning grammar. Those who don't get it will be doomed to retraining one day.

## Suffering Segregation's Costs; or, Having
## Their Cake and Eating It, Too

The numbers above rebut the common assumption that the United States is no longer a racially segregated society, because it is. We do segregation—persistently and effectively. But that doesn't fully reveal why it's a problem, or whether it is merely the resultant expression of a free people exercising choices and preferences. I briefly turn the conversation there now.

Remember that in chapter 2 we looked at the assumption that being middle class meant being self-sufficient, only to learn that being middle class has meant being deeply subsidized by decades of generous government policies. Those government policies (like federally insured mortgages for certain types of housing in certain types of places) also had segregative effects by creating markets of exclusion. These were later given legal support, as we'll see again momentarily, by the Supreme Court, mostly in the 1970s, and became the law of the land. Typically, we expect an "exclusive market" to command higher prices. The market for segregated housing is no different, its home values artificially increased—or subsidized—by segregation and people's preference for it. That's not to say that middle-class people who worked hard to pay their mortgages for decades didn't proudly earn the equity in their homes. It just means they got a lot of help from segregation and earned a lot more equity than they would have if they truly had to rely on hard work alone and the luck of the market. Wherever they moved, they paid a premium to live in white segregated communities, which they got back whenever they sold.

Naturally, there is an equal and opposite detriment. Middle-class black people, for instance, who bought homes in segregated communities decades ago also worked very hard for what they got, but got a lot less equity—thanks to the depressed housing values of a segregated housing market. Their investments enjoyed fewer protections against intrusion by government action or private discrimination. Racial segregation interacted with the economic separation we explored in the last chapter. In many places it produced the most disastrous community a child could ever be born into: concentrated poverty. Concentrations of minority poverty occur when racial segregation combines with class discrimination to create isolated worlds of radically diminished opportunity. How do we know? Hypersegregation is the proof. That is, compounded, multi-dimensional segregation of blacks and increasingly of Latinos is proof that concentrated poverty follows determined segregation like the tail of a dog (a rather vicious dog).

Of course these costs/consequences are not really a problem for "haves" so long as there is only token mutuality with "have-nots"—or worse, zero-sum mutuality where the haves gain at the expense of have-nots, or the majority excels at the expense of minority. If the fate of a Dominican boy in Washington Heights is not particularly linked to the fate of a Jewish girl on the Upper West Side, then his inferior prospects compared to hers may not compel much change. That has always been the bargain. Middle-class people in general and whites in particular have privately accepted that racial worlds will not collide in meaningful ways, and that their advantages are not at risk, whatever the arguments for or against them. Yet that is precisely what's changing demographically, turning segregation into a tax that more and more people and places can't afford.

## Institutionalizing Resegregation: Legal Localism, Part 2 (Education)

Jim Crow would never get a laugh nor find a welcome stage today. The black-faced minstrel character, probably the first, found fame and fortune in the 1830s by amusing white audiences with his hideous portrayals of American slaves; his name was promoted to a whole system of racial marginalization in the decades after emancipation. First in 1954, then with the civil rights legislation of the 1960s, the vulgarity of Jim Crow laws gave way to something more gentle—a legal framework committed to equality as never before, but often tentative in its terms and prone to dilution. Indeed, something so hostile to America's first principles was transformed into something quite kindred while producing similar results. The brutish amateur actor who began the first act clothed in the villainous robes of Jim Crow, returned as a thespian in the second to play the part of the hero wrapped in an exquisite core value: local democratic control. This value drives our system of localism, the idea that a municipality has sovereign rights to determine its own character through legislative action. By 1980, localism had trumped the equality principle to reproduce formal segregation but in a non-racial way. For all its benefits, localism has a fatal flaw, narrow parochialism, and this we'll see is its most destructive aspect.

Many writers have chronicled how the Supreme Court's decision in *Brown v. Board of Education* set off a panic of resistance to desegregation across the postwar South. Matthew Lassiter, for example, described how middle-class southerners gradually abandoned both cities and the truculence of "massive resistance" among working-class whites by initiating token school integration measures.[19] Those trends revamped the landscape, contributing to the suburbanization we saw in chapter 2 and insuring that desegregation would be limited by membership in smaller towns that controlled entry with local land use laws. It is not, however, a southern story. Thousands of towns across the Northeast and Midwest followed similar strategies to avoid residential and school integration beyond a very limited point. The country was no longer segregated by law; inroads had been made for some middle-class blacks. Yet the basic patterns of separation held and they stand to this day, because they were blessed in a series of cases by the Supreme Court itself. We explored some of the landmark land use cases in the last chapter. The same Burger Court authored two others in the education realm—*San Antonio Independent School District v. Rodriguez* (1973),[20] and *Milliken v. Bradley* (1974)[21]—that completed the edifice of legal localism.

In *Rodriguez*, the Court confronted a direct federal equal protection challenge to the way the majority of states allowed local control of school funding. Plaintiffs were a class of Mexican-American parents from tax-poor, urban school districts in Texas, challenging the state's method of school finance on the ground that its reliance on locally collected property taxes beyond a baseline of uniform state funding worked substantial disparities between property-rich and property-poor districts.[22] The wide differences in per-pupil expenditures helped to support smaller class sizes, higher teacher pay, and more experienced teaching for the property-rich districts.[23] The district court had ruled in favor of the plaintiffs, finding that education was a fundamental right under the Constitution, wealth was a suspect classification, and any governmental scheme that discriminated in public education on economic grounds was therefore subject to strict scrutiny.[24] The Court reversed on each, finding no fundamental right to education, denying that wealth was suspect, and upholding the importance of local autonomy over school finance on rational basis grounds. Mindful of the federalism concerns implicated in the plaintiffs' challenge,[25] the majority characterized the trial evidence as involving murky issues of social and economic policy outside the Court's expertise, and producing only an allowable and expected amount of fiscal inequality.[26]

Despite the necessary emphasis on state power relative to federally guaranteed rights, *Rodriguez* is squarely a localism decision in its substance and its narrative of local power. The majority dismissed the fiscal inequality between rich and poor districts as a compromise between local fiscal control and irreproachable statewide minimum standards. Instead, the disparities reflected differences in ingenuity and democratic priorities between localities, primarily matters of choice yielding competitive diversity. As Justice Powell stated, "[L]ocal control means . . . the freedom to devote more money to the education of one's children. Equally important, however, is the opportunity it offers for participation in the decision making process that determines how those local tax dollars will be spent. Each locality is free to tailor local programs to local needs."[27]

The argument fully ignored the relative incapacity of tax-poor districts to exercise such fiscal choices on behalf of their schoolchildren, and that, as Justice Marshall pointed out in a stinging seventy-five-page dissent, the inequality of fiscal resources resulted in denial of an equal opportunity to learn.[28] These concerns, according to the majority's narrative, were irrelevant to both local control and equal protection in the school finance context. The Court even foreshadowed the competition for "good ratables" that dictate so many local governmental decisions to this day: "Nor is local wealth a static quantity. Changes in the level of taxable wealth within any district may result from any number of events, some of which local residents can and do influence. For instance, commercial and industrial enterprises may be encouraged to locate within a district by various actions—public and private."[29] If the blueprint for sprawl and fiscal zoning was not already known to suburban communities across the United States by then, it now bore the Supreme Court's imprimatur.

The second case, *Milliken v. Bradley*, affirmed the primacy of local control over education policy in rejecting an inter-district remedy for Detroit's clear record of racial segregation in its schools. Like *Warth v. Seldin*,[30] *Milliken* is one of the few to comprehend directly the regional scope of institutional racism. The district court found that, given residential patterns at the time, no *intra*-district remedy could achieve desegregated schools within the city and, because any attempt would probably further identify particular schools (i.e., code them) as majority black, it would hasten more white flight to the suburban periphery.[31] Given where whites and blacks actually lived, only a regional or metropolitan remedy would work. Schools in suburban districts would be compelled to cooperate in the remedy. Those districts sued.

The majority per Chief Justice Burger disagreed, concerned less about the probability that serious constitutional violations would go without a meaningful remedy than with the administrative uncertainty caused by crossing admittedly arbitrary boundaries.[32] Yet the narrative of *Milliken* is not as emphatic about local control as its legacy suggests.[33] Instead, it is more meaningful as a pronouncement about community and responsibility, which resonates to this day. After all, Detroit was not always so black; its white population had been streaming out of the city for years up to and beyond 1970 when the *Milliken* case was first brought.[34] Local control of predominantly white school districts in the suburbs outside

Detroit defined and defended a sense of community for its residents. Many of them had fled Detroit and therefore rejected membership in that community. In doing so, according to the Supreme Court majority, those suburban communities and their school districts could not be asked to assume any of the responsibility for the segregative policies leading up to that point in the Detroit schools nor for the effects of such demographic shifts. What mattered from a somewhat formalist constitutional perspective was that those demographic shifts ended up in nearly all-white districts which did not and could not have engaged in segregation. An inter-district remedy would force them to accept blame for Detroit's past practices, casting serious doubt on the sanctity of jurisdictional borders.[35] In this sense, the majority's arguments are familiar to many discussions of legal remedies for past racial discrimination—colorblindness. Historical context is ignored in determining causation; upholding the non-racial design is what matters, not the results.[36]

The doctrines of legal localism illustrated by the previous sample of cases were of critical utility in institutionalizing a variety of transitions occurring around mid-century. On the one hand, the fatal contradictions of *de jure* segregation and the separate-but-equal doctrine had been exposed to the world after World War II and was jurisprudentially untenable. Here, *Brown* must be seen against the larger context of federal legislative changes, the burgeoning Civil Rights Movement, and, for many whites, unwelcome cultural confrontations.[37] Cities embodied much of the impetus for flight. On the other hand, the suburbs and a strong economy were expanding along with the role of the federal government in providing the financial and infrastructural means to a middle-class ideal for returning veterans. That the benefits of national policy would accrue on a racially discriminatory basis did not for residents of recipient communities pose a challenge to their validity. Instead, the changing landscape promoted a twentieth-century notion of rugged individualism and the welcome political moderation of colorblindness.[38]

Yet the powers of local autonomy that made suburbs safe havens from the city, the poor, and blacks were always characterized by defensiveness.

They were in many ways untried powers, not on behalf of the very afflu-ent, but for the middle-class, blue-collar ascendants to suburbia who were somewhat unaccustomed to wielding exclusionary controls. By the 1970s, as we have seen, the controls were tested by myriad legal attacks. They held. From these decisions, a jurisprudential edifice was erected that would define insiders from outsiders, draw economic meaning from jurisdictional lines, empower suburbs against the cities from which they came, and limit their responsibilities even to their regional neigh-bors—for the first time, none of it on the basis of race. Neutral rules then interacted with markets and quickly increased the value of exclusions. Suburbia's footing has not been questioned since.

Most important, the creation of legal localism effected a paradigmatic alteration of race relationships by substituting economic proxies for race that could withstand constitutional challenge. Localism is, therefore, a postwar instrument of economic segregation, and economic segregation is nearly always a post–civil rights proxy for racial segregation. Today, the doctrines that give mechanical support to these proxies are settled law. Expectations also have settled. The conjoining of legal localism and localist expectations around the economic right to exclude reflects the mind-set of privatization (another idea that has rapidly gained trac-tion in the public sphere over the last few decades). Like private clubs with unfettered rights to make their own rules and determine their own membership, the sovereignty of local governments to ignore nonresi-dents—at least where economic membership is concerned—goes mostly unquestioned.[39] Unfortunately, this idea of sovereignty, without more, facilitates continued segregation. It promotes resegregation.

Surprisingly, every one of the Detroit focus group participants I talked to who were old enough to remember *Milliken* disagreed with the Court's interpretation of people's thinking at the time. For them, the relationship between Detroit's tradition of segregated schools and white flight to its suburbs was as close as cause and effect. But legal reality and vernacular understanding are not always consistent. Another irony is inescapable: colorblindness worked to sustain the arrangements of color obsessiveness.

## Revisiting Detroit

Detroit is a very contested patch of earth. It is hard to find a city whose every line, budget item, or walk of life is so reflective of racialized decision making. Back in the day, whatever Detroit could have been—the postwar "engine of democracy," its indelible contributions to American culture in jazz and soul music during the 1950s and 1960s—was subject to an extreme type of racial determinism. That is, a strange combination of racism and economic opportunity built and dismantled this once-proud city. Since its heyday, many of its struggles (but not all) show what a poor planning tool racism is. Imagine a kind of war against shared opportunity, where the weapons are formal laws and the laws of force racial covenants, "blight" clearance, highway construction, urban renewal, school segregation, home owners' associations, mob intimidation, police brutality. Eventually, a sad new strategy won out: retreat and relocation.

There is a little bit of me here, too, I realized as I conducted my research. I was born in Detroit. My father was a native Detroiter of both Jewish and gentile immigrant extraction. At Wayne State University, he met my mother, a black fugitive from Kentucky, who had followed her favorite uncle and other family members to the city's jobs in our version of the great black migration north. As soon as they married, his family abandoned him to his unpardonable choice. As soon as I was born, we left Detroit. As a result, my parents' reactions to changes to the city where they both came of age have always seemed prescient to me, meaningful beyond my own family history.

There are many amazing things about the city of Detroit. Take, for instance, the pervasiveness of its single-family homes, which is probably unknown beyond its boundaries. Or that so much incredibly good music—anthems to many lives around the world—was born there. But the most amazing thing to reckon with is well-known about Detroit: its white people have virtually disappeared. This old fact seems to require little reflection anymore. Yet if one stops to think for a minute about their flight, it is both amazing and incredible. In 2000, just before the economic boom, the city's white population was only 12.3 percent out of a total of about 950,000, according to the census.[40] In 2006, the white population had declined to just 10.4 percent, and more than 100,000 people had left Detroit.[41] We know, of course, that they had been leaving for years, that these famous boulevards and avenues, the empty, enormous remaining factory structures, the downtown office buildings, had been abandoned by people who had made real histories here, histories that could not be reclaimed or relocated elsewhere. In 1950, the population of whites in Detroit was 84 percent, and 71 percent in 1960. By 1970, it was 56 percent, then 36 percent in 1980.[42] They took with them their identities, their labor, their loyalties, and their memory, and transplanted them elsewhere—often within a few miles to the north. This you cannot witness with a mere swivel of one's head, but if you try hard enough and put your ear to the ground, you can almost hear them go about their rituals and routines again.

Detroit is a city assiduously designed for single-family homes on elm-lined blocks, with lawns and backyards. These were nice streets back then. They are mostly nice streets now. The jokes comedians told in the 1970s and 1980s about the city as an armpit or a wasteland were not true. But as time nourished misinformation, the punch lines turned out to be prophecies. Today, none of it is funny, which is partly what made my first trips to Detroit's suburbia so surprising. Many of the neighborhoods there looked just like the neighborhoods in the city of Detroit. Many looked a little worse. In other parts of the country, one neutral explanation for flights to suburbia is the bigger-house-and-yard-for-the-buck argument. Not here. Detroit was built like a suburb, which may be why its regional geography feels like the flat, undifferentiated logic of sprawl. Originally, they came for something else. To escape blacks and black political power, for sure. But also, if not mainly, for jobs. As Orfield and Luce found, "In the last fifty years, it has not grown in population at all, but has expanded more than 60 percent in urbanized land area. Essentially, Detroit taxed itself to build new rings of predominantly white, exurban communities of escape."[43] Segregation is also the mother of sprawl.

Though it feels long ago, there are people still alive—the elderly parents of my friends, for instance—who will relate that the sense of progress in fleeing to suburbia for many whites was dampened by the frustration of surrender and retreat. Whites may have left Detroit for its suburbs because they had to. But a great many stood and fought for a segregated way of life that meant the world to them. Like both sides of my father's family, many white Detroiters in the postwar era were European ethnics not more than a generation removed from their home countries, who had relied on kinship networks to get jobs, learn valuable trades, and buy homes in Detroit's notoriously tight and expensive housing markets. The historian Thomas Sugrue suggested that the meaning of the home reflected Old and New World values and was often quite personal, a measure of community belonging, status achievement, and national citizenship. So was the neighborhood. Life was lived close to others. Privacy was diminished, and people knew and relied on information about others like themselves. Sugrue wrote about the implications for white maternal identity. If women could stay home to care for children, then their worlds were strongly defined by their relationships in the community—their sense of safety, familiarity, and self-esteem: "Women, far more than men, depended on the neighborhood networks for both economic and emotional subsistence."[44] Not surprisingly, white women held even more hostile attitudes than did white men to open housing and school integration.

One of the great ironies of suburbanization, however, is how what began as economic commonsense and racial escape for some became, over time, economic commonsense for everyone. This is Southfield today. Southfield represented the suburban desires of whites who had moved just north of Detroit's Eight Mile border to a solidly middle-class town. Jews from the city soon followed in substantial numbers. Themselves victims of racial covenants for many years in Detroit, Jewish sellers were far more willing than others to sell their Detroit homes to black buyers. Those homes and idyllic streets continue to be a miraculous beachhead of black middle-class life, but over the decades, many, many blacks followed to Southfield. Why? Because taxes are lower, insurance is cheaper and more comprehensive, schools are better, services are more regular, crime is diminished, and work is often closer. They leave not only for Southfield, a solidly middle-class place, but also for other suburbs, increasingly abandoned by whites and some more affordable in decline. This is the second story of Detroit's emptying. Since 2000, 185,000 blacks left the city. In 2010, Detroit's population declined to about 713,000, the lowest it has been in a hundred years.[45]

Contested places always seem to be full of irony, and another good one is that now, almost two generations after *Milliken*, many of Detroit's suburbs *invite* Detroit's students to attend their dwindling schools. Today, the "inter-district remedy" that was flatly rejected by the Supreme Court is a necessity to keep schools afloat. A great many white kids who grew up in the suburbia beyond Eight Mile Road and went on to college didn't want to come home to raise families, so the schools there are at risk of closing unless enrollment goes up. Enter black kids.

## Resegregating Education

My unscientific impression of Americans of every racial or ethnic group is that today, the education of one's children occupies the same psychic place that a new single-family home did fifty or a hundred years ago. The symbol representing the fruit of a well-planned private sphere is not as much the home itself as the quality of the education the children growing up there receive. Education is an opportunity equalizer. Thomas Shapiro found that it is often the main reason families make the moves they make.[46] Many parents turn the education of their children into the repository of their greatest hopes for themselves, while others can treat it as a commodity. Still, for both it's the epitome of their love. As the story of Kelley Williams-Bolar in the first chapter showed, parental autonomy is rooted in their children's learning potential, and they will risk that autonomy for their children's school chances. That emphasis on autonomy has transformed in recent years as reformers single out the one educational good on which everyone seems to agree: choice.

If you are like me, you have painstakingly avoided the complex politics of public education—at least until you had your own children. It is a quagmire wedged in a morass, then filtered through a bureaucratic kaleidoscope—to say nothing of its financing puzzles. For years I studied everything about place and equity *except* the innards of education policy, careful not to get sucked into the vortex of testing, standards, choice, vouchers, property taxes, state aid formulas, and school finance litigation.[47] Well, I'm over that now and have reached a surprisingly simple conclusion: every school policy issue is framed by racial and socioeconomic segregation. Every single one. One might even say with just a little exaggeration that the whole matter of educational excellence in the United States begins and ends with segregation.

Starting from the present and working a little ways backward, the nation's public schools are as racially segregated now as they were roughly forty years ago; they're more segregated than they were twenty-five years ago.[48] The picture is much worse for the hundreds of so-called failing public schools, located primarily in urban and rural districts whose student populations are overwhelmingly—that is, over 90 percent—black or Latino and about equally poor.[49] This is essentially the problem, today and tomorrow, because the demographic trends clearly demonstrate that these lower-income students of color from segregated schools will fast become a disproportionately large segment of the country's general population and, most especially, its labor force. When we talk about educational deficits, we are largely talking about them and the tremendously expensive challenges they pose for the public fisc. After all, education spending is typically one of the very largest parts of any local or state governmental budget. In the almost sixty years since *Brown*, the nation still maintains a system of education with a pronounced achievement gap between those poor students of color and the middle class. However, every single remedy that's gotten any traction since *Brown* has assumed that nothing—*nothing*—can challenge the geographic sanctity of our socioeconomic (and usually racial) divide between students. We have collectively decided that whatever remedies we can think of—adequacy litigation, school choice, teacher incentives, teacher evaluation, teacher discipline, charter schools, vouchers—nothing will call for integration ever again.

There are many reasons for our resistance—politics, culture, fear, and combinations of all three. But two facts remain in front of us. One is that the present system in both its status quo state and its reformist mode is incredibly expensive, despite extremely limited improvement. As rampant cuts in local education budgets make clear, it is almost certainly unaffordable. The second is that *integrating low-income students with middle-class students in predominantly middle-class schools is the only thing that consistently alters the achievement gap.*[50] Other ideas work in very small quantities in particular places at particular times, but none is consistent or reliable or affordable. None.

James Ryan demonstrates how the roots of our segregated schools began through token desegregation efforts designed by and for middle-class white families avoiding the dictates of the Supreme Court's decision in *Brown*. What's most interesting about the process he describes is not that white middle-class parents raised on the idea of segregated schools would mount such strenuous and prolonged resistance to integration. Of course they would. Nor should it come as much of a surprise to learn that their interests ultimately prevailed. No, probably the most intriguing aspect of the process Ryan describes is how, as in housing desegregation, the possibility of creating integrated environments was frustrated by the resistance to *metropolitan* solutions like the one sought by the *Milliken* plaintiffs. As long as district or municipal boundaries were deemed sacred, people could take cover behind them—always protected by the principle of local control. No remedy for segregated schools could ever overcome the presumption of political validity that decisions made in accordance with localism enjoyed. What killed the promise of school integration, therefore, were rules about place. This is why analysts like David Rusk (whom we met in chapter 1) say with confidence today that school policy *is* housing policy and vice versa.

This may be a good time to recall the meaning of *Brown v. Board of Education*. That decision overturned the "separate but equal" doctrine of *Plessy v. Ferguson*. It called for an end to school segregation—or desegregation. But the opinion said nothing about integration. To this day, the people most intended to benefit from integration—black parents of school-age children—often wince when the term is mentioned as a goal. They object to the implied stigma that blacks need white students present in order to succeed academically (as do I). But this has little to do with the real theory of *Brown* or the value of school integration. The real theory of integrated schools is very expeditious: more educational dollars, better resources, and greater accountability follow white students—especially middle-class white students (and their parents). Pair one with the other, and all who participate enjoy the benefits of an educational system in which fates are, as Ryan puts it, tied. *Brown*, in other words, was one of the earliest efforts at achieving the promise of a social goal—a well-educated public—through the principle of mutuality. It didn't work, which is a large part of why we have the current crisis of failing, segregated schools in segregated black and brown neighborhoods. And that remains the heart of it, really: neighborhood schools. Since parents want their children in neighborhood schools, and neighborhood schools are located in the middle (as opposed to the border) of neighborhoods, and neighborhoods remain in too many cases segregated, then it's not hard to see David Rusk's point about school and housing policy being one and the same.

There is a continuing history of educational reform that goes beyond the constitutional fights of the 1970s, but it remains locked in its segregated terms. We saw (until recently) litigation around state constitutional rights to adequate schools, fiscal neutrality (or equality), and needs-based funding. These are not irrelevant to the process of trying to improve education in the hardest places to find it: high-poverty schools. Yet all these result from a compromise that Ryan and others say originated with President Richard Nixon in 1972 and his Equal Educational Opportunities Act.[51] In exchange for keeping poor black students out of white suburban schools, poor black schools would get more funding in order to improve education there.[52] Ryan neatly refers to this principle as "save the urban schools, but spare the suburbs." This would appear to solve all problems, and it is the path we have pursued ever since—except that the outcomes have not met expectations. It turns out that the problems of learning in environments of high poverty are so great that, as studies show, even middle-class kids from homes with educated parents perform worse in such places. Increasing funding cannot seem to overcome this reality.[53] "There is something about the school itself that depresses achievement," writes Ryan.[54] Even the annual reports of America's children falling behind students from other countries are skewed by this reality, because American students perform on average much better compared to other countries *if you take out the weakest schools.* "The real problem is the performance of high-poverty schools, especially those in urban areas," Ryan continues. "That is where the real crisis lies."[55]

It is difficult to calculate the costs of these failures in terms of life chances and social capital. It takes only a little empathy and a knowledge of the challenges faced by young people starting out to imagine how the deficits pile up for kids who, by the accident of birth, are so obviously separated from opportunity. The challenges of a scientific life, the netherworlds of other languages and cultures, the power of reading for fun, information, and analysis, writing one's thoughts—all these basics of being a capable, independent adult citizen are exchanged for frustration, boredom, fear, embarrassment, and a sense of inadequacy, which is hard not to pass on to one's child.

But let's reduce the costs to money. We can imagine what attending poor schools and doing badly means for the economic future of a young person; they earn tens of thousands less over a lifetime and live shorter, more unstable lives. Let's instead think about what all that limited opportunity is costing *us.* The trade-off between integration and attempting to buy better schools is extraordinarily costly. When lawyers argued *Brown,* per-pupil expenditures for white schoolchildren dwarfed the money spent to educate black kids. Much of that disparity still exists. Yet even in those few states like New Jersey that have seen school finance litigation intended to benefit low-income students of color, studies show that more money—in some cases substantially more money than even wealthy white schools get—does not produce much school improvement.[56] Why would strapped taxpayers agree to keep paying such a premium to educate unwanted children? Trends suggest, if given the chance, they may not.

Are these kids really unwanted? Well, yes, in the sense that nobody wants them under any circumstance. Even our most popular reforms such as charter schools, vouchers, and other "school choice" programs establish rules that allow strong school districts to decline to participate. Nearly all these ideas are *intra*-district ideas. Poor students typically do not have the option to choose schools outside their districts or "megazones." The reality is that informal school choice is already the dominant program for sorting educational opportunity: by purchasing a home in a community known for good schools. That's the "choice" followed by as many as 25 percent of all American parents, according to Ryan's research.[57] Since that choice is bound up in financial and psychological investments about "quality" and "property values" in addition to attitudes about race and class, it is not surprising that taxpayers continue to pay more to keep out children they deem threats. In larger school districts like New York City's, choice models are tied to competition. Academic "merit" decides who gets into the better programs. The segregation we saw between PS 77 and PS 198 results primarily from disparate economic resources, as wealthier students test into stronger schools.[58]

Because this is not a book about education, we don't have to reach a definitive conclusion about whether more money or more choice is the final answer to the problem of unequal educational outcomes. Both have obvious appeal depending on a range of different factors. At this point, all we really need to know is whether integration—the lost piece—is simply misplaced or rightly discarded as part of the solution. We deal in probabilities. If Ryan is right about learning environments, it proves three likelihoods. One is that segregating poor students of color into majority-poor public schools has damaged them, a separation they neither invented nor chose. Another is that children who have been fortunate to go to public school in predominantly middle-class settings have enjoyed a privilege at the expense of poor kids, a benefit they neither chose nor earned. And the final likelihood is, based on the evidence, a near certainty: the most direct and cost-effective way of producing educational excellence and a return to our equitable principles is to get these two sets of students together in the same classrooms somehow.

## Reconsidering Integration

So far, I seem to be advocating integration in both our living arrangements and our schools as the antidote to the segregation that's costing us so much. This may be why I, too, was ambivalent about examining segregation for a long time. A more resolute integrationist, legal scholar john a. powell, suggests that much of the hostility toward integration among nonwhites (at the least) reflects an association with assimilation. They are not the same thing. Nor is integration the same as desegregation, as Martin Luther King explained: "Although the terms desegregation and integration are often used interchangeably, there is a great deal of difference between the two. In the context of what our national community needs, desegregation alone is empty and shallow. We must always be aware of the fact that our ultimate goal is integration, and that desegregation is only a first step on the road to the good society."[59]

But there is another rebuttal to integration that has little to do with assimilation. It is that you can only push people so far beyond the comfort of their strongest preferences. What we have now, even if it is regrettable in a philosophical way, is the practical, though imperfect, configuration of people's wishes. This is what they want. This is what they have freely chosen. This is the fair exercise of their autonomy. And most of it is perfectly legal. In this context, integration is truly—and only—a dream, and wasteful to pursue.

This is a powerful line of argument, I believe, and I once subscribed to it. It led me to the more pragmatic goal of desegregation (primarily through the active enforcement of existing laws that prohibit discrimination) and an abandonment of integration. That is the position john powell would say that most liberal education reformers have taken—that is, that parity of resources and testable outcomes is the goal, some of which will happen in less segregated, if not desegregated, environments. Following that thread, we now cast everything in terms of "choice" and try hard to improve the choices available to all people.

The problem is that choice is not the golden egg we say it is. The capacity for choice may be golden, yet the available choices are rotten. This is so because choice, as we all know already, occurs only within a set of attainable alternatives. It's never "free" in the sense that it can be whatever one hopes or expects. If it were, Kelley Williams-Bolar would never have been prosecuted for choosing to send her daughters to the wrong Ohio school. Choice is also suspicious because it was the same vehicle used by middle-class white families to avoid integration after *Brown*.[60] School choice sounds terrific until one starts scrutinizing the framework in which options appear, or the history from which patterns emerge. Something more deliberate seems necessary.

Which is probably why john powell—who just as deliberately goes by lowercase letters—calls himself a "radical integrationist." Through conferences, I have known and listened to him for years, and he even looks and sounds like a radical integrationist. A tall, dark man with a long salt-and-pepper beard and soft engaging eyes, he speaks as you'd like to hear the evening news, with a calm and clarity totally lacking in panic or sensationalism. Radical integration, he says, understands education to be much more than inputs, outputs, and outcomes; it is the broader process of citizenship development. Radical integrationists, he's written, "believe that education, and particularly an integrated education, has intrinsic value and is constitutive of who we are, individually and socially."[61] Education is preparation for active participation in a multi-racial, multi-ethnic society. This is not possible in a segregated school. What's needed, then, is integration at multiple levels—in the places where opportunity concentrates and in the classrooms where it's nourished.

As a starting point, we must have *integrated resources*—that is, shared, jointly accountable, qualitatively similar, equitably governed in common places.

120

## Counterfactual: What Bronxville Knows

Even wealthy Bronxville, one of Westchester County's richest towns, is concerned about rising school taxes.[62] Localism has winners and losers on a municipal continuum, and towns like Bronxville are the clear winners. If Bronxville residents—90 percent white in 2010, median home value $1,000,001, and 2 percent poverty—are thinking about cutting the luxury of high teacher salaries, for instance, it seems certain that they have no interest in seeing affordable housing built there. After all, as we'll see in the next chapter, many wealthy Westchester towns avoided building affordable housing for years precisely because they saw no benefit in having poor or black people present.

Yet all of that assumes Bronxville's fate is contained within its borders. Bronxville wants the very best schools, but is weary of the rising cost in property taxes. What if rather than raising taxes yet again a little more of those costs could be shared by a larger source of funds—a bigger arm of government—on the condition that Bronxville reduce the barriers to lower-income students of color? A 15 percent increase in those students would likely have no negative impact on district achievement or resources. It would have to come, however, from a commensurate increase in those families in town (they couldn't be bused in from the Bronx, for example)—again based on incentives to build housing affordable to such families. And a marketing campaign would have to target those potential families where they are now. New York State could do that. The federal government could do that. If they did, they would have to do it equitably across the metropolitan region, spreading the opportunities and subsidies among the many Bronxvilles of Westchester and Long Island. Maybe the region could even decide to do that.

Would the good people of Bronxville make such a bargain? Indeed, Bronxville being Bronxville, their decision might have ripple effects across the towns of the region. What would they have to lose?

If we're being honest, they would risk the myth of their own exceptionalism (an affliction from which many of us suffer). They would lose not just the sense of material superiority any exclusive community has, but some of the psychic supremacy that goes with elite status. Yet here's the rub. As Justin Hudson, the young Hunter High School valedictorian from the introduction, observed, there are great minds in *every* community—as well as very good minds, average minds, and so-so minds, too. We all start with the raw intelligence, nerve, and stamina to learn. Belonging by race or ethnicity to the class of unwanted minds obscures that basic fact. But out of that fact comes the reality that *if* more of those minds received the collective resources to develop to capacity, *all* of our communities would be smarter, more resourceful, and more stable. We who come from those lesser places—and I count myself among them— have known this forever. If anyone else should understand this simple fact about human potential, it ought to be Bronxville, where the successful nourishment of even average minds is taken for granted. Being wealthy does not make one smart. Students struggle to learn in every kind of community and in every kind of home, but the ultimate outcomes depend on the resources available to address shortcomings. In other words, all the Bronxvilles of the United States know what the un-Bronxvilles know, because they have achieved it by nurturing all the capacity with which their children were born. They don't leave it to chance in those places, which is precisely why they should be in the best position to recognize that need for other people's children—especially when they, too, will one day depend on them.

# 5

## WE RENAMED THE PROBLEM
## AND IT DISAPPEARED

### ASSUMING THAT RACISM NO LONGER
### LIMITS MINORITY CHANCES

I live in a very old house, which is a good thing (until something breaks). On the first cold days of October, when you turn on the thermostat, you must wait for the heat to slowly rise up from the basement. It seems to climb from Reconstruction through wood and coal to the Industrial Era, up past the Progressive Era to World War I, then World War II, until finally it reaches oil, gas, plastics, and perhaps one day solar. The journey of heat through my home reminds me of what happens when the word "racism" is used, how its mere mention, like the touching of a thermostat, sets off a thermodynamic impatience from the gut to the brain. Thus begins the fifth assumption, that racism no longer limits minority opportunities.

Impatience rules the dialogue between those who hold this assumption (believing that the emphasis on existing racism ignores our nation's progress for the sake of securing undeserved preferences) and those who don't (believing that the continued existence of racism retards our progress and is too obvious to be ignored by people of goodwill). We have developed the polite habit of splitting the difference in these disagreements, finding equal merit on both sides in a resolution that resolves nothing. That's disingenuous and unproductive. The truth about racism, I believe, is not merely somewhere in between opposing viewpoints. It is a matter of finding common terminology. In my experience, the idea that racism no longer acts as a serious impediment to minority chances must be based on an understanding of racism that is individual in its terms. In this view, racism, if it exists, resides in individuals and is expressed by individuals. Racism as an obstacle is refuted by examples like the popularity of a mega-rich Oprah Winfrey or the reelection of a brilliant President Obama. The absence of individuals with white hoods (notwithstanding occasional outbursts and invective from knuckleheaded outliers) is evidence that most individuals are color-blind. I agree that we have a great deal to be proud of in our effort to undo the primordial hatreds of the recent past. The transformation in individual attitudes and achievements in such a relatively short time is miraculous testament to the power of social change. But it is an unnecessarily limited framework for thinking about bias and leaves out a lot about lost opportunity.

Another way that people discount present-day racism through the focus on individuals is by requiring very strict proof of racial animosity—specifically, *conscious* racial animosity. (They don't tend to recognize the potential threat from unconscious animus.) In this view, the fact that there has been a spate of beatings and even murders of Latino workers on Long Island, New York—some of them during hunting expeditions called "beaner hopping" where the assailants admitted to preying on Latinos for sport[1]—is about the only form of racism they will admit. This is clearly intentional conduct, so much that we've called them "crimes" of "hate." They are. But this idea of racism as an obstacle to opportunity would not cover the "Bamboo Ceiling" limiting the managerial and executive aspirations of qualified Asian workers in, say, the technology sector. Wesley Yang wrote about these struggles in *New York* magazine, describing the effects of stereotypes that Asians endure as proficient workers but deficient leaders, routinely passed over by and for white men who understand the subtle loopholes in strict meritocracy. Yang writes, "This idea of a kind of rule-governed rule-breaking—where the rule book was unwritten but passed along in an innate cultural sense—is perhaps the best explanation I have heard of how the Bamboo Ceiling functions in practice."[2] Under our current legal standards, however, Asians seeking to sue to remove barriers created by unconscious, unspoken, and unwritten workplace norms would have great difficulty proving their case.

Race—in this book anyway—is mainly important for its material implications. Anything else is what my uncles used to call the okey doke—nonsensical swindle, clever surplusage, distracting jive, tactical pablum. If we define racism in terms of its material consequences and call it the power to subordinate members of a distinctive group to inferior opportunities based on their membership, then it's possible to see other kinds of racist practices despite the absence of invective-spewing antagonists. It's even possible, perhaps likely, to see it in areas where the discriminating party's intent is virtually impossible to prove. Policies that overwhelmingly tend to marginalize nonwhites can be racist. Practices that reflect unconscious understandings and stereotypes to the clear detriment of nonwhites can be racist. And policies or practices that exploit existing patterns of long-standing racism—like segregation—can often produce racially specific harms. All three types of racism do their harms through disparate treatment, disparate effects, or disparate impact, all necessitating evidence of racial disparity to prove in a court of law. Unfortunately, our federal courts have turned away from just this form of proof, invoking the language of colorblindness to demand specific evidence of conscious intent to discriminate. The question we have to ask ourselves is whether the more conservative constitutional definition of racism adopted by the federal courts (and many people) is consistent with our own sense of what constitutes racism. I don't believe it is. In fact, the recent history of race relations has been dictated by color-blind social norms in which everybody knows better than to express their conscious (let alone unconscious) prejudice. Being racist is simply unacceptable. So, racism, if it endures, tends to proceed covertly, structurally, and, to do real material damage to many, institutionally.

Therefore, I will illustrate three important examples of contemporary racism that do just that—in the health-diminishing effects of environmental racism, the wealth-diminishing effects of predatory mortgage lending, and the self- and community-diminishing effects of our criminal justice policies. Note that all three have the potential for serious, life-changing material harm. Following the theme so far, all three are also linked in varying degrees to place. Yet before we get to the examples, let me lay some important political groundwork about how racism came to this point.

## The "Reagan Revolution" Still with Us . . .

The impatience that characterizes discussions of race and racism in our so-called color-blind society has its roots in the momentous legislative changes of the 1960s. The Civil Rights Acts of 1964, 1965, and 1968 reached into nearly every aspect of daily life—from segregated facilities to voting to housing—and represented a long overdue re-installation of the equality principle in our social compact. The question was what it would take—and from whom—to get to equality. Was racial equality something that could be had without sacrifice? If not, then who would be forced to participate and who would be exempt? As implementation of the laws engendered a far-reaching bureaucracy of agencies, rules, and programs for everything from affirmative action hiring goals to federal contracting formula, the commitment was quickly tested. For a great many who already opposed the changes, patience was quickly exhausted. As welfare rolls rapidly increased, crime surged, and the real and perceived burdens of busing took their toll, many voters pointed to the apparent failure of a growing federal government to fix the problems it was essentially paid to cure. Among Democratic voters this made for unsteady alliances and vulnerable anxieties. People don't live in policy and statistics as much as they do through anecdote and personal burdens. A riot here, a horrific crime there, a job loss or perhaps the fiery oratory of a public personality could tip a liberal-leaning person's thinking toward more conservative conclusions—or at least fuel her impatience. Impatience would ossify into anger, turning everything into monetary costs, and making these costs the basis for political opposition to a liberal state. As it happened, this process moves the date of our supposed final triumph over racism from the mid-1960s to at least the mid-1980s. In the end, impatience won.

What I call impatience, others have characterized as a simmering voter ambivalence—even antagonism, in the case of working-class whites—to civil rights remedies, one that was susceptible to the peculiar backlash politics that elected both Ronald Reagan and George Herbert Walker Bush president. Language was central to this strategy, and the language that stuck was colorblindness. As Thomas Byrne Edsall and Mary Edsall wrote in *Chain Reaction: The Impact of Race, Rights, and Taxes on American Politics*, "In facing an electorate with sharply divided commitments on race—theoretically in favor of egalitarian principle but hostile to many forms of implementation—the use of a race-free political language proved crucial to building a broad-based, center-right coalition."[3] Ronald Reagan managed to communicate a message that embodied all the racial resentments around poverty programs, affirmative action, minority set-asides, busing, crime, and the Supreme Court without mentioning race, something his conservative forebears—Barry Goldwater, George Wallace, and Richard Nixon—could not quite do. The linchpin was "costs" and "values." Whenever "racism" was raised, it became an issue of "reverse racism" against whites. The effect was the conversion of millions of once fiscally liberal, middle-class suburban Democrats to the Republican Party. Issues identified with race—the "costs of liberalism"—fractured the very base of the Democratic Party. In the 1980 presidential election, for example, 22 percent of Democrats voted Republican.[4]

By 1984, when Ronald Reagan and George Bush beat Walter Mondale and Geraldine Ferraro in the presidential election, many white Democratic voters had come to read their own party's messages through what Edsall calls a "racial filter." In their minds, higher taxes were directly attributable to policies of a growing federal government;

they were footing the bill for minority preference programs. If the public argument was cast as wasteful spending on people of weak values, the private discussions were explicitly racial. For instance, Edsall quotes polling studies of "Reagan Democrats" in Macomb County—the union-friendly Detroit suburbs that won the battle to prevent cross-district school desegregation plans in 1973—that presents poignant evidence of voter anger: "These white Democratic defectors express a profound distaste for blacks, a sentiment that pervades almost everything they think about government and politics. . . . Blacks constitute the explanation for their [white defectors'] vulnerability and for almost everything that has gone wrong in their lives; not being black is what constitutes being middle class; not living with blacks is what makes a neighborhood a decent place to live. These sentiments have important implications for Democrats, as virtually all progressive symbols and themes have been redefined in racial and pejorative terms."[5]

By 1988, these same voters had endorsed tax revolts across the country and had become steadfast suburbanites, drawing clearer lines between a suburban good life and the crime- and crack-infested city. Still they were angry, as magazine articles chronicled the rising political significance of what would be known as the "Angry White Male" voter. George Bush, down seventeen points in the presidential election polls during midsummer, overcame that deficit with TV ads about murderous black convicts raping white women while on furlough. That and a pledge never to raise taxes seemed to be enough to vanquish Bush's liberal challenger, Michael Dukakis of Massachusetts. What's important to recognize in this transition is how as recently as twenty years ago, Americans' social lives were very much embroiled in racial controversy—despite the obfuscatory veneer of color-blind language to the contrary. Our politics followed. The election of Bill Clinton represented a distinct centrist turn among Democrats toward Republican language and themes and away from rights, the "liberal" label, and the federal safety net. The question we might ask about our current race relations is, only a couple of decades removed from this political history, what would compel us to assume that we are beyond the legacy of our racial conflicts?

## . . . And the Okey Doke That Followed It

The racial polarization that connected these political outcomes was deliberately fed by national Republican candidates in order to do more than roll back civil rights. It also served to install "supply-side economics," a system of regressive tax-based reforms that contributed mightily to the costs of income inequality we currently face. That era—which arguably ended with the election of President Barack Obama—illustrates two points central to my examination of civic connectivity. The first is that the economic underside of racial polarization proved no more than the old okey doke. The second is that localism contains its own contradictions, which have come due in our time. Let me explain.

Only racism could achieve the ideological union of the Republican rich with the working man (and woman). Nothing else could fuse their naturally opposed interests.[6] The essence of supply-side economics was its belief in the importance of liberating the affluent from tax and regulatory burdens, a faith not typically shared by lower-income households who might at best see benefits "trickle down" to them. In fact, they often paid *more* under tax-reform schemes of the 1980s.[7] Edsall provides data on the combined federal tax rate that include all taxes—income, Social Security, and so forth. Between 1980 and 1990, families in the bottom fifth of all earners saw their rates *increase* by 16.1 percent; it increased by 6 percent for those in the second-lowest fifth (the lower middle class); and it increased by 1.2 percent for those in the middle fifth (the middle middle class). But those in the second-highest fifth of all income earners saw a *cut* in their tax rate by 2.2 percent during that decade; and those in the top fifth got a 5.5 percent decrease in their rate. Overall, the richest 10 percent of American earners received a 7.3 percent decrease in their combined federal tax rate. The top 1 percent? A 14.4 percent cut during the 1980s.[8] Clearly this hurt the middle class, as the vaunted trickle down never arrived. But it was working-class whites who bought the message that this model of fiscal conservatism, married to social conservatism in the form of a rollback of redistributive programs they perceived to favor blacks, would benefit them. It did not. Yet it established a popular political rhetoric by which lower-income whites can be counted on to take up *against* "liberal" policies that may actually serve their interests as long as opposition can be wrapped in the trappings of "traditional values," "law and order," "special interests," "reverse racism," and "smaller government." This was pure okey doke based on an erroneous notion of zero-sum mutuality—that is, that whatever "the blacks" get hurts me.

Which also demonstrates the contradictions of localism. Remember my earlier argument that localism—or local control expressed formally through home rule grants, as it's sometimes known—became the spatial successor to Jim Crow segregation. Through racially "neutral" land use and housing policy, it kept white communities white after the fall of legal segregation in the late 1950s and mid-1960s. Yet here's the contradiction. While voters opposed to civil rights remedies and Great Society programs followed Republican leadership toward fiscal conservatism at the *national* level, they maintained their fiscal liberalism at the *local* level. The tax base they created for themselves through property taxes in suburbia could be contained and spent locally. Edsall describes the irony this way: "Suburbanization has permitted whites to satisfy liberal ideals revolving around activist government, while keeping to a minimum the number of blacks and the poor who share in government largess."[9] Of course, all of this worked best when "suburbs" meant middle-class white people and "cities" (or today's "urban" areas) always signaled black and brown people. There was no mutuality of interests between the two kinds of places. It also worked when low property taxes—together with generous state aid—could reliably pay for great local public services like schools, libraries, and fire protection. It was a terrific deal. But that was then. Now, neither is true. The line between cities and suburbs has blurred into regions, and minorities and whites are busy crossing back and forth to work, live, and shop. Most of the fragmented municipalities that sprawled across suburbia are no longer able to sustain their own budgets, threatening the quality of their services, despite unimaginably high property taxes. The assumptions have not held.

Perhaps now we should consider the racially polarizing policies that became the norm under Reagan a failed experiment. We tried them. Some believed fervently in them. But it is clear that they didn't work and are not in our long-term national or local interest. There remains a legacy of racism, however, that continues to harm some of us disproportionately and all of us eventually. It's to those three examples that I now turn.

## Environmental Racism

If I'm right that the kind of racism that still works to seriously limit minority lives is more structural than intentional, and that much of it works its harm by the dynamics of place, then the first example of racism has to be environmental racism. This is little more than the straightforward fear of being killed *by* your neighborhood. It can happen in a number of ways.

There is a stretch of road in Brooklyn that demonstrates how urban design can kill some more probably than others. Along Brooklyn's Park Avenue, a grim street cast in shadows beneath the elevated Brooklyn–Queens Expressway, lie several blocks of dense, high-rise housing projects built in the 1950s, the Ingersoll Houses and the Walt Whitman Houses. Cars on Park Avenue drive fast. But on the end of Park Avenue where I lived, they are slowed down by streetlights that occur at crosswalks almost every block. My end is low density and people can rarely be seen crossing the wide street. However, alongside the projects there are no streetlights and no crosswalks. Yet there are two schools on the other side of the road, a huge ball field, and beyond that some truly out-of-the-way playgrounds, abutting parts of the old Brooklyn Navy Yard. Drivers like me routinely dodge pedestrians as we make our way up Park—especially children, who often stand on the sliver of median waiting for traffic to clear so that they can dart home. Each year, some are struck by cars driving in excess of forty-five miles per hour.[10] Every one of them is black or Hispanic. I often wondered why parents would let their children cross so dangerously, until it occurred to me. Decades ago, New York City designed its housing for the poor on the edges of city life, in undesirable, dangerous places beside highways. The city located neighborhood schools and playgrounds nearby, but across obviously dangerous crossings. Why not also install curbs, streetlights, and clear crosswalks—maybe even some crossing guards? The number of families with kids in the projects dwarfs those in the part of the neighborhood that has such basic safety measures. Why should these kids' physical environment be so reckless as to require them to dodge traffic every day? It seems either cruel or stupid, yet it's continued for years.

Or maybe you're not killed right away, but debilitated by the diseases associated with the air, water, or soil in your neighborhood. Or just the higher risk that it will happen there and not somewhere nicer. Few of us know this as racism. Most of us think of this as NIMBYism and we're all for it. If you tell a skeptic that Latinos tend to live in areas where people are at greater risk for cancer or asthma and that there might be some ethnic discrimination behind that, they will let you have it pretty good for stretching the idea of racism into mere ambient risks. They'll break you down with reasonable arguments about cause and effect, the lack of clear agency (Was it genetics? Diet? How come everybody didn't get sick?), and the old moving-to-the-nuisance idea of free will (if it was so bad, why'd they move there?). The problem is, the minute you turn it around and ask the same skeptic, "OK, how 'bout we move the same concentration of toxins or trucks or medical waste near where you're raising kids?"—after all, these are just by-products of the stuff we all need—well, now you're really talking crazy. And that seems to be exactly how environmental racism works. People who can't or don't politically organize their incredulity about living amid the terrible environmental dangers we all produce wind up disproportionately bearing everybody else's burden. Those people tend to be black, brown, Native American, and the white poor.

Take Chester, Pennsylvania, about fifteen miles outside of Philadelphia in Delaware County. Chester is home to most of the county's toxic chemical air pollutants, its solid and medical waste. According to the Delco

Alliance,[11] Chester in the 1990s had all of the county's municipal solid waste and the imported medical waste from several states. In fact, eight waste facilities process over two million tons of waste a year in Chester, compared to just 1,400 tons in facilities across the rest of the entire county. More than ten thousand people live within a mile radius of multiple industrial facilities, with some homes as close as one hundred feet away. In this city of thirty-eight thousand, about a third of the families with children are poor, according to 2008 census data. Nine percent of Chester residents were Latino in 2010 (up from 6 percent a few years before), about 15 percent were white, and approximately 75 percent of Chester's population was black (compared to only 6 percent in the rest of Delaware County). But there's not a single supermarket in Chester to serve them.

However, what Chester lacks in racial diversity and shopping it more than makes up for in public health pathologies. People here get really, really sick. The city has the highest mortality rate and highest lung cancer rate in the county. Its moms give birth to the highest percentage of low-weight babies in the state, and their infants die at twice the rate of other infants in Delaware County.[12] Everything with environmental racism is scientific correlation—the relationship between risk factors and known outcomes. Nearly all harm must be proved by the circumstances. This is part of the problem with environmental racism in the age of colorblindness. As a matter of law, it's hard to prove the intent to bring about horrible truths that most of us can easily infer from the facts. Still, a group in the city was able to fight off an attempt to build yet another waste facility in town—but only when they committed to taking their case all the way to the Supreme Court.[13] They sued on civil rights grounds, because environmental laws have not caught up to the problem. In fact, many lawyers now attempt to use international human rights law to secure environmental protection for minorities in a country that rightly professes great concern for the environment.

There is law at the state and federal level that recognizes the problem of disproportionately burdened communities and the peculiar racial skew of the environmental hit. The inequities are as obvious as any random zip code search on any one of the numerous websites that test the environmental harms around your child's school (the EPA has one, for example). Responding to a few national studies of environmental inequity, President Bill Clinton in 1994 issued Executive Order 12898.[14] The order, titled "Federal Actions to Address Environmental Justice in Minority Populations and Low-Income Populations," is less about action than declaring priorities for federal agencies. It addresses the need for communities to have a say in the procedures by which dangerous facilities locate near them as well as the need to monitor the substance of dangerous uses. In the parlance of 1994 and since, it broadly, but not boldly, seeks "economic justice." As Carleton Waterhouse says, "In the environmental context, justice can be viewed as a process and a means of distribution as well. As a process, environmental justice relates to the procedures used to decide how and when the risks of environmental harms will be distributed. . . . As a concern about distribution, environmental justice relates to the distribution of environmental harms and risks across communities and the larger society."[15]

There is some risk in calling something that behaves just like racism something else. After all, places like Cancer Alley between New Orleans and Baton Rouge, Louisiana, have the highest concentration of petrochemical plants in the nation, strewn along roughly ninety miles of land first settled by freed slaves.[16] Even in New Orleans after Hurricane Katrina, the focus of Waterhouse's research, it was the blatant failures of the Army Corps of Engineers to maintain the flood-protection system around predominantly black neighborhoods of the city that caused so much death and destruction in August 2005. The risks were known, but the political will and the funding were lacking. Surely, this is not just environmental injustice but environmental racism. Yet we are connected, never so much so than by our natural environment.

## Predatory Lending

Perhaps the roots of our mutuality lay in the ruins of our housing markets. It's there we're told that the American Dream of hard work and home ownership may have died in or about late 2008, depending on where you live. If so, there are multiple ground zeros, places where financial devastation—aided and abetted by Wall Street—took particular aim at middle-class households and wiped them out from the roof down before ravaging the rest of the economy. One of those places is Vailsburg, a solidly middle-class neighborhood in Newark, New Jersey. It is mostly black, with an increasing number of Latinos. I saw it as I never have before on my first foreclosure tour with Kathe Newman, a Rutgers political scientist, back on a mild, sunny day in the early summer of 2009. The Great Recession had officially ended, but the specter of loss here was perhaps the most vivid reminder of our economic mutuality as a nation.

We packed into a car littered with large, unwieldy maps. Kathe is a white woman with brown hair, all business, with a hint of humor and a slightly curious, somewhat skeptical demeanor. Under contract with cities trying to get a handle on the tax-base impact of neighborhood abandonment, she produces foreclosure maps full of pins and colorful highlights as a prelude to tables, charts, and eventually damage assessments. As in most of Newark, foreclosures were already very high in Vailsburg, and the foreclosure peak was still two years away. We rolled by each block at the cruising speed of gangbangers, looking for telltale signs. The easiest is the newly invented gray grates that cover whole windows snug enough to keep out a pipe thief's crowbar or a squatter's screwdriver. The hardest is when the homeowner has left but returns periodically to pick up junk mail, prune a hedge, or clear some debris. It's like divining the difference between a home's deep sleep and its death. Kathe is checking pulses. We look for dates on supermarket circulars, healthy plants inside windows, footprints on porches; we listen for sounds—a foreclosed house is quieter than one whose occupants are simply out for the day.

Kathe is an unwitting coroner of American Dreams, come to identify the dead. The colored pins multiply everywhere across her Newark map. Kathe explains more with her exasperated looks than she does with her words. She's been monitoring this neighborhood and others for a while. What was special about Vailsburg was its succession by middle-class black households after decades of blacks being kept out by racism. When white families left in the 1960s and 1970s, black ones moved in. In a twist on common histories, many of those black families could have gone a little farther out—to the Oranges, perhaps—but chose to stay in the city. They were a quiet, middle-class anchor in a working-class town. But the houses were old, aging like their residents. They needed expensive maintenance like roofs, foundation support, new stairs. Owners began subdividing for rental income. Then came the direct marketing by home repair contractors, nonbank lenders, and mortgage brokers—often door to door. Offering equity lines and refinancing against the inflated value of the house, the now-familiar practice became routine. The offers contained either terms too good to be true or fees, charges, and accelerators that were not disclosed to the borrower. Sometimes the roofs got fixed. Often they did not. But the refinancing contained usurious interest rates, unexplained balloon payments, surprise fees, and the prospect of either speedy default or expensive litigation.

Kathe Newman calls the easy mortgages that became ubiquitous in the late 1990s to mid-2000s "post-industrial widgets."[17] They were the new and improved, must-have invention, capable of lifting entire economies, if not the world, through "financialization." Financialization was the process of expanding Vailsburg's small-time transactions into the vast unregulated, high-gain, low-risk investments of a global secondary market. Of course, a sad wade through the ruins of this once-proud neighborhood reveals the downside. We know by now that millions of Americans of all stripes fell (or marched greedily) for this good life. The subprime mortgages that swamped Vailsburg and thousands like it affected most of us. But it was the dream of minority home ownership and opportunity that died first.[18]

This, too, is the story of an okey doke. The sale of mortgage instruments at rates the customer could not hope to afford over time is a classic example of swindling the gullible. The mass suckering of so many produced the potential for more suckering, as home buying became the investment rage across the globe. Banks dropped their lending standards and oversight. First and second mortgages like those written in Vailsburg were bundled and securitized into shares, sold and traded by equity investors like, well, widgets. But that doesn't make it racism.

So, let's pause to consider what made some of the most gullible such suckers in the first place. The other side of racial segregation is economic segregation, which, in spatial terms, means that the vulnerable are never hard to find. For decades before the housing bubble, legitimate credit lenders redlined black communities, as we discussed in chapter 3. The resulting credit vacuum was filled by shady, expensive, offshore, and fly-by-night lending for everything from furniture to homes to burial insurance. That often-unregulated antimarket is what's known today as "reverse redlining." Nobody who lends in such areas has to target overtly black borrowers in a way that would make them liable in a race discrimination lawsuit because one need only go where only blacks live and sell subprime loans. This form of race-neutral discrimination is also known as "predatory lending." Before this century's subprime loans, predatory lending was the late last century's crisis point, leading to huge lawsuits in Atlanta, Boston, and New York and critical investigative reporting like the *Atlanta Journal-Constitution*'s 1988 series called "The Color of Money." Ironically, the rash of private predatory lending in the 1990s got a boost from government policies initiated by both President Clinton and George W. Bush to promote home ownership in "underserved" communities—that is, black and Hispanic neighborhoods.[19] The federal government expanded the secondary mortgage market and reduced investor risk directly through government-sponsored enterprises. In short order, the predatory nature of lending there returned with fresh intentions under the guise of bad, subprime loans.[20] Only a handful of cases have produced evidence of a conscious desire to defraud minority buyers, of course. Yet despite the lack of smoking racist guns, there are ways to unearth the clear racial dimensions of the fraud. The key evidence they reveal is racial targeting.

Subprime lenders specifically targeted minorities not because they were unsophisticated or earned a lower income. They were marked for their race and ethnicity. All else being equal, black and Hispanic loan applicants got bad loans relative to their white counterparts in the mortgage market—something people like Kathe Newman knew years before the housing crash.[21] In 2000, the Department of Housing and Urban Development released a study that showed that black borrowers were *five times* more likely than white borrowers *of the same household income* to receive subprime loans.[22] Even controlling for median *neighborhood* income, the disparity held. More incomprehensible was the difference between wealthy blacks and poor whites. "Borrowers in *upper-income* black neighborhoods were twice as likely as homeowners in *low-income* white neighborhoods to refinance with a subprime loan," according to the report's authors.[23] "In 1998, 18 percent of borrowers living in low-income white neighborhoods relied upon a subprime loan, compared with 39 percent of borrowers living in upper-income black neighborhoods."[24] Four years later, a study by the Association of Community Organizations for Reform Now (ACORN) confirmed HUD's findings, showing that by then subprime lenders accounted for more than half of all refinance loans made in predominantly black neighborhoods, compared to just 9 percent in white ones.[25] The ACORN study showed that middle-income minority home owners like those in Newark's Vailsburg neighborhood were especially targeted for risky loans. Almost 28 percent of refinance loans made to middle-income blacks originated with subprime lenders and nearly 20 percent for Latinos; only 7.6 percent of middle-income whites held such loans. Finally, New York University's Furman Center reported in 2009 that racial targeting by subprime lenders can be tracked by levels of neighborhood segregation.[26] For example, a Hispanic borrower seeking a mortgage in a neighborhood with a low percentage of nonwhite residents had a 14 percent chance of receiving a subprime loan, while that probability more than doubled to 31 percent in a neighborhood with a high concentration of nonwhites. How did the lenders know their targets were black and Hispanic? They probably used the same data available to researchers under the federal Home Mortgage Disclosure Act, which tracks mortgages by borrower ethnicity and census tract. In any event, the strategy of racial targeting in the lending industry systematically exploited the proxy of place for the reality of a borrower's race, producing acts of financial racism that victimized both individual home owners and the entire neighborhood around them. The result was one of the most devastating assaults on the structure and content of black and Latino mobility since Jim Crow.

## Criminal Justice

The third example of contemporary racism is about the near-permanent limitation on life chances for some that is caused by our country's rules about criminal justice. These rules and practices—from police behavior and incentives to prosecutorial power and on through the policies behind our criminal laws—have also come a long way since the 1960s. But the clear direction has been toward mass incarceration of human beings who, upon release, re-enter a society that despises those who have been incarcerated. The vast majority of these people are young black and brown men. When I first discovered the patterns of our criminal justice system, I was reminded of the absurdist bureaucracy that condemns the character Josef K. in Franz Kafka's book *The Trial*. Josef is a working man suddenly arrested and charged with an unknown crime and forced into the impossible dilemma of defending his life amid a system of justice with no known logic, rules, or fairness. Frustrated and broken, Josef eventually dies without ever knowing why the state wanted to discipline him.

That's pretty awful stuff. But our system of justice—leading inexorably to confinement for so many people—differs from Kafka's in one frightening sense. It appears to have a purpose. The point is to marginalize a certain proportion of the population. Why would a free society encourage marginalization through the power of its government? According to some scholars and advocacy institutions that follow crime policy, the system for fighting crime has become a politically profitable, financially lucrative, self-perpetuating *business*—the business of mass incarceration. The main proponent of this view is Michelle Alexander, who argues in her book *The New Jim Crow: Mass Incarceration in the Age of Colorblindness* that the goal of our laws since about 1980 has been to substitute a new system of social control on black and Latino communities after the fall of the Jim Crow system. Whether she is right or whether the case can be made that the justice system is at least rigged against black and brown people demands a review of circumstantial evidence. Circumstantial evidence is often used in the absence of direct evidence—smoking guns, eyewitnesses, taped confessions of racial animus—and is accepted all the time in criminal cases. Circumstantial evidence raises inferences that something is true; the stronger the evidence, the more compelling the inference. Before we get to it, however, let's look at the facts of the "crime" itself, the disproportionate targeting and incarceration of black and brown men, their families, and, once again, the places where they tend to live.

According to Alexander and others, the facts begin in 1980, the year Ronald Reagan was elected. Crime had been rising during the 1970s, but the epidemic of crack cocaine that transformed the public's idea of criminal behavior did not actually occur until about 1984. (I happened to grow up in one of the earliest crack neighborhoods in Upper Manhattan and saw it engulf some of my best friends.) Nevertheless, as Alexander points out, President Ronald Reagan declared a "War on Drugs" in 1982, a full two years before we knew what crack was. The statistics begin from about there, when fighting crime went from being a local police activity to a coordinated approach involving the FBI, CIA, Pentagon, new laws about drug offenses, mandatory sentencing, constitutional guarantees, and a whole lot of media coverage.[27]

Incarceration rates exploded in the early 1980s and have only recently begun to trail off.[28] Between 1980 and 2000, the prison and jail inmate population increased three hundred thousand to over two million; by 2007, *seven million* people were either locked up, on probation, or on parole. For blacks, the drug-related incarceration rates quadrupled in just three years, then began a steady but precipitous increase. In 2000, black incarceration rates were twenty-six times what they were in 1983. Latino incarceration rates for drug-related offenses were twenty-two times their 1983 levels. Whites, too, experienced an increase of eight times the rate of drug-related incarceration during the same period. Put another way, in 2006, one out of every fourteen black men was locked up compared to one in 106 white men. No other country imprisons its people as frequently or for as long as does the United States. Nobody. It was not always this way. What changed was the conservative backlash on drugs, part of what Thomas Edsall referred to as the coded call by Barry Goldwater, George Wallace, and Richard Nixon for "law and order." As Alexander writes:

> Convictions for drug offenses are the single most important cause of the explosion in incarceration rates in the United States. Drug offenses alone account for two-thirds of the rise in the federal inmate popula-tion and more than half of the rise in state prisoners between 1985 and 2000. Approximately half a million are in prison or jail for a drug offense today, compared to an estimated 41,100 in 1980—an increase of 1,100 percent. Drug arrests have tripled since 1980. As a result, more than 31 million people have been arrested for drug offenses since the drug war began. . . . The vast majority of those arrested are *not* charged with seri-ous offenses.[29]

### Circumstantial Evidence of a Racist System

What the larger national statistics on racial disparities in crime fight-ing mean is that, because of the correspondence between race and economic status, black and brown men in poor communities have an entirely different experience of constitutional freedom than do the rest of us. Thanks to racial and economic segregation, we already know that they are not hard for the police to find. In ghettos and barrios across the nation, much higher proportions of young men are routinely stopped and searched by police, arrested or detained, released or charged, and if charged, then usually pleading to something that stands as a conviction on their records. A great many are then incarcerated. The cycle then starts over as they become unemployable, uneducated, and part of an insidious interdependency on one of the best-financed arms of government—law enforcement and the courts. Once they have served time for a felony conviction, they are persona non grata in most job settings, denied housing benefits and student loans, disallowed on juries, and, in many states, even lose the right to vote. Many states have elaborate laws that make the ex-offender a debtor responsible for paying many of the costs of his legal assistance, jail book-in fees, court costs, and child-support enforcement—all on penalty of being returned to jail if he doesn't pay.[30] The pariah status of ex-offenders ripples out in permanent multiples as these are the sons, husbands, and fathers of whole communities. This draconian state of affairs ought to be justified. The first question we should ask is whether the focus on people from these areas and not others is supported by facts on the ground.

The answer seems to be not at all. Crack had not even appeared in U.S. cities when President Reagan declared war on drugs, but what followed was an unprecedented federal commitment to funding drug-related crime. Almost immediately crime budgets rose, creating incentives to use the money in order to keep getting it. For instance, Alexander reports that FBI antidrug funding jumped from $8 million to $95 million between 1980 and 1984, the Department of Defense antidrug budget jumped from $33 million to $1.042 million between 1981 and 1991, and Drug Enforcement Administration spending rose from $86 million to $1.026 million during the same decade.[31] Meanwhile, crack hysteria became ubiquitous in media accounts, the scourge of a generation that had to be stopped at all costs. However, it was not a scourge everywhere, only among ghetto communities. This can be seen in the disparate treatment for cocaine-related crimes that was legislated by Congress as part of the $2 billion crime bill in 1986. That law and the 1988 Anti-Drug Abuse Act authorized new mandatory minimums for first-time offenders, revoked benefits for people connected with drug busts, and added the death penalty for some federal drug offenses.[32] Yet the focus was always on crack cocaine, not powder cocaine. Of course, crack was the cheap, rock-based ghetto alternative to the expensive powder snorted disproportionately by whites. The difference in mandatory penalties? You'd get the same prison time for one gram of crack as you would for one hundred grams of powder. The former essentially punished users and small-time dealers, while the latter only dealers.

Studies of police practices demonstrate a tendency to focus on not where the drugs are as much as where the drugs are easiest to find. For example, a Seattle University study published in 2001 found that racial stereotypes permeated Seattle policing and explained high rates of black drug arrests, not offending behavior. In fact, Seattle police followed their stereotypes even when actual tips directed them elsewhere. "Seattle residents were far more likely to report suspected narcotics activities in residences—not outdoors—but police devoted their resources to open-air drug markets and to the one precinct that was *least* likely to be identified as the site of suspected drug activity in citizen complaints," according to Alexander. "In fact, although hundreds of outdoor drug transactions were recorded in predominantly white areas of Seattle, police concentrated their drug enforcement efforts in one downtown drug market where the frequency of drug transactions was much lower."[33]

Well, given the huge disparity between the arrest, charging, and incarceration rates by race, were black and brown drug offenders and dealers more numerous than whites? Again the answer seems to be not at all. A 2000 study showed that white youth were a third more likely to sell drugs than were blacks. Government data show that "blacks were no more likely to be guilty of drug crimes than whites and that white youth were actually the *most likely* of any racial or ethnic group to be guilty of illegal drug possession or sales," Alexander writes.[34] White youths are also more often in emergency rooms than are blacks as a result of their drug use. And it's not like drug sales present a clandestine opportunity for racial mixing. As Alexander reminds us, "Whites tend to sell to whites; blacks to blacks. University students tend to sell to each other. Rural whites, for their part, don't make a special trip to the 'hood to purchase marijuana. They buy it from somebody down the road."[35]

The last question is the thorniest: why did we build a system that seems hell-bent on funding the complete marginalization of so many black and brown people, many of them non-dangerous drug users doing what even more whites were doing? This is difficult to answer, but any attempt has to take at least two paths, the administrative and the political. By administrative, I'm referring to the policies followed by law enforcement agencies and districts attorney together with the direction they were given by courts. After all, crime fighting may be a business, but it's a business subject to constitutional constraints. By political, I'm referring to what might have been behind all those policies—that is, what interests were served by our obsession with locking up men (and increasingly women) of color.

As for the administrative side of the criminal justice system, it seems clear that by the mid-1980s a great many financial incentives aligned to make fighting drugs in minority neighborhoods a top priority for police departments, which wanted larger budgets, and prosecutors' offices, which wanted to bolster their tough-on-crime bona fides. In this way, the momentum toward a system of mass incarceration became self-executing. Specifically, the creation of two government funding streams—the Edward Byrne Memorial State and Local Enforcement Assistance Program as well as federal forfeiture laws—launched continuous incentives to police forces to make arrest numbers regardless of the impact on crime reduction. Since 1988, according to Alexander, Byrne grants increased the funding and weaponry to localities willing (who wouldn't?) to establish specialized narcotics task forces. This is why your local police precinct now has such military hardware as M16 rifles, grenade launchers, and Black Hawk helicopters. This is also why every American now knows what a SWAT team is, even though they were originally designed to be a specialized few used for hostage situations and bank heists. Alexander writes that in the entire United States, "[b]y the early 1980s, there were three thousand annual SWAT deployments, by 1996 there were thirty thousand, and by 2001 there were forty thousand."[36] Beyond the incentives to beef up, however, were incentives to eat what you killed under forfeiture laws that allow police to keep the cash and assets seized during drug raids. These raids might be based on mere suspicion, yet the fruits of the raid could be kept unless challenged. Thanks to arcane rules that, until very recently, made it difficult and costly to get one's property back, 80–90 percent of forfeitures went unchallenged. As Eric Blumenson and Eva Nilsen demonstrated in their research, forfeitures gave police a pecuniary interest in the drug trade.[37] The more you bust, the more you keep.

Prosecutorial power has also increased dramatically since the 1980s while budgets for free legal representation for indigent defendants have shrunk. The power comes largely from the threat of harsh mandatory sentences that became vogue during the crack epidemic. Prosecutors have unreviewable discretion to charge and overcharge as they see fit, a formidable plea bargaining chip even in the absence of strong evidence of guilt. "[S]imply by charging someone with an offense carrying a mandatory sentence of ten to fifteen years or life," Alexander writes, "prosecutors are able to force people to plead guilty rather than risk a decade or more in prison. Prosecutors admit that they routinely charge people with crimes for which they technically have probable cause but which they seriously doubt they could ever win in court."[38] Given the financial costs of a capable defense, prosecutors rarely ever face that risk. Almost nobody goes to trial.

Meanwhile, the interpretation of a criminal defendant's liberty interests changed dramatically, as a much more conservative Supreme Court continues to overhaul the constitutional overhaul that occurred briefly during the 1960s and 1970s. The Court has blessed a free range of police behaviors that might surprise many Americans if they (or their sons) were affected by them. Even without probable cause to suspect that someone's doing wrong, police may now stop and detain people on the street or in their cars, frisk them, and even conduct full-fledged searches as long as they receive "consent." Yet as you may assume, people rarely tell cops no, and cops are under no legal obligation to tell them they have a right to refuse. These limitations on the Fourth Amendment have led to raids, street sweeps, and other tactics that can only be called fishing expeditions. The DEA's Operation Pipeline, for example, trained officers to do just that. According to Alexander, "It has been estimated that 95 percent of Pipeline stops yield no illegal drugs. One study found that up to 99 percent of traffic stops made by federally funded narcotics task forces result in no citation and that 98 percent of task-force searches during traffic stops are discretionary searches in which the officer searches the car with the driver's verbal 'consent' but has no other legal authority to do so."[39] These are the tools that encouraged so much racial profiling across the nation during the last decade and a half. In New York City, following the deaths of unarmed black immigrants by police, racial profiling of black and brown men under the strident leadership of Mayor Rudolph Giuliani drew national attention. However, little changed under his more moderate successor, Michael Bloomberg. "The NYPD stopped five times more people in 2005 than in 2002—the overwhelming majority of whom were African American or Latino," Alexander notes.[40] According to a study by the New York Civil Liberties Union, the New York Police Department stopped and frisked about 533,000 men in 2012, 87 percent of whom were black or Latino and 90 percent were innocent of wrongdoing. Though the program is justified as a way to find illegal guns, most of the arrests were for marijuana possession (5,000), not guns (729).[41] As a result of Supreme Court decisions since 1987, claims of racist police or prosecutorial practices are nearly impossible to prove.[42]

Why would our politics allow us to continue spending so lavishly to lock up so much human capital when the results are so racially skewed and offer so little evidence of crime-fighting success? Alexander's answer is that mass incarceration is the new Jim Crow, a deliberate form of social control over racial minorities. It may be. Certainly, the policies that gave rise to these funding priorities, exercises of discretion, and constitutional interpretations followed a clear "law and order" path that began after the 1960s urban riots, but reached full steam under Presidents Reagan, George H. W. Bush, and Bill Clinton. For politicians everywhere, presenting oneself as tough on crime has been a cherished virtue among voters for decades now, a sure way to prevent us from slipping into lawlessness. What is odd, however, is the concentration of crime. Here again, segregation plays a hand. Since crime is concentrated in areas of concentrated poverty, the broader public's willingness to fund tough and expensive policing seems irrational. That same public expresses no such desire to fund schools in areas of concentrated poverty at higher levels, for instance. Maybe Alexander asserts too much intention on the part of the myriad forces of social control, a coordination of efforts that seems too perfect for the government we know. Yet *something* is clearly wrong with a criminal justice system that produces so much injustice. And now that crack has at least subsided as an epidemic and prison costs are crushing state and local budgets, people are rethinking our incarceration policies. But are they doing so for the right reasons?

## Counterfactual: The Remedy for Collective Negligence and "the Race Card"

I began this chapter by suggesting that impatience is the enemy of racial progress. Impatience often provokes virulence or irritated distraction. The first is associated with the hatred of conscious racists. The latter is reserved for the rest of us, who cannot bother to know what is happening in our name or refuse to see past our ingrained doubts. Yet the evidence of environmental racism is very, very strong. We don't have great legal tools to do much about it, but we've got plenty to allow a curious public to find out for themselves. (Try it.) Or the financial crisis that largely (but not exclusively) started in already hard-hit minority communities—*middle-class* communities of hard-working, home-owning, responsible, lawn-mowing, tax-paying folk, whose primary fault was their segregated zip code. Or the lengthy evidence here of a criminal justice system that robs young minority men and the people who need them from a chance to redeem a mistake while draining the rest of us through expensive law enforcement bills and prisons. Take a few hours to visit your local courthouse during criminal arraignments and look for the kind of people you know. If you stay long enough, the pattern will repeat itself into an absurdity only Kafka could explain. Or you may simply leave shaken about the true meaning of justice.

This is not a counterfactual in which we can merely imagine having more inclusive attitudes about people of other races. We have done that much yet still wound up here. We have to be more specific in our thoughts and much less impatient. We have to think about systemic effects through the prism of mutuality. But how do we do that about racism, where everything always has demanded some idea of blame and accountability? My imperfect answer from chapter 1 is that we begin by acknowledging our negligence for what we've wrought. Somehow we produced disproportionate environmental dangers in the age of environmentalism. We reproduced the financial marginalization of minorities while extending home ownership to minorities. We've institutionalized racial injustice through our laws about criminal justice. Our priorities may be right, yet our implementation is all wrong. Sure, someone is to blame for some of these specific examples. But we are collectively at fault for being either too distracted, too ill-informed, or too gullible to demand a closer connection between our goals and the means we allow others—petrochemical producers, mortgage lenders, our legislators and police—to use. Negligence is a breach of a duty to someone. As I noted in chapter 1, the duty here is to one another as representatives of a social compact and to our children. In other words, we have done this to ourselves. The damages for negligence are often money damages. These we are already paying, though when it comes to racism, disproportionately by segregated minorities. Another remedy, however, is equitable relief— that is, injunctions for fairness. In this counterfactual, the remedy for our collective negligence about structural racism is to imagine putting a stop to what we've been doing to our own.

And there is one small, symbolic step we could take to reverse course against racism. We could burn "the race card" reference once and for all. Ever since the 1995 O. J. Simpson murder verdict revealed the diametrically opposed attitudes whites and blacks have about the criminal process, people have enjoyed describing any discussion of racism as playing "the race card," as if race and racism were but jokers in a parlor game. We could agree never to use the phrase again unless we're referring to someone who is truly exploiting our racial fears for some less obvious gain to themselves. By small steps like this we might discourage the okey doke that prevents us from taking racism seriously.

# 6

## ISLANDS WITHOUT PARADISE

### ASSUMING THAT POVERTY RESULTS FROM WEAK VALUES AND POOR DECISIONS

Most Americans have ambivalent feelings about poverty in our country, their views teetering somewhere between the folkloric formative poverty of the past and the gangster-rapping underclass of the present. For policy folks this fulcrum distinguishes deserving from undeserving poor. The first is largely historical, talked about by older family members as a necessary step in their social mobility and personal maturity, stories of sacrifice, outhouses, and mile-long walks to school in deep snow. The hardship in their words is real, but what accounts for the fond remembrance is the happy middle-class ending, always made possible by hard work and disciplined self-respect. Many of us know this story. It is that of an immigrant nation whose arrivals came with nothing. In a rich country, people do not forget their poverty. Without it there could be no American Dream.

Then there are the poor for whom ambivalence shades to hostility. Whether we describe them by the places they live, the clothes they wear, or their unpronounceable names, they are always an unwanted Other, known—if at all—only because we have to. Even President

Obama, a former community organizer, omitted public references to the poor in a first term mired in recession and deepening poverty. This distance makes the details of their lives even more mythical. Unless we are cops, emergency room doctors, teachers, or social workers, we rarely see them going about the minefields of their often public lives in courts, hospitals, schools, or the offices of public agencies. We don't read their records or make sense of the byzantine networks they often must navigate for financial assistance, bail, medical testing, or to regain custody of a child. Yet it's not hard for most of us to identify with the impatience and barely hidden scorn of the person on the other side of encounters with them. As persistently poor people, they lead difficult, problematic lives because, we assume, they consistently make poor decisions born of weak values. Except during holiday giving time, we mostly suffer the poor and their antisocial ways.

This chapter examines the hostile end of a spectrum of ambivalence toward poverty, exploring evidence of how decisions are made and the values they reflect, mainly from the perspective of the greatest number of poor people—children and young women. It is not intended as a complete picture of persistent poverty but a discussion of salient issues through important, but limited, examples. In particular, the chapter looks at decisions to have babies, what happens to many of those babies and girls in typical settings, and the stresses those environments generally impose on minds and bodies in poverty. I focus on constraints versus capacities—a lens through which all our lives might be viewed—in order to test the assumption. We'll look in Camden and Philadelphia and Houston. We'll take a public health tour and find shocking behaviors and disproportionate traumas. All of the previous assumptions in this book will coalesce to produce another picture of place-based opportunities: a stultifying culture of isolation. The story suggests that containment comes at great cost—directly for the poor themselves and indirectly for the regions around them. But first, we need more clarity about the difference between the poverty we're proud of versus the kind many of us scorn.

## Officially Poor, Right beside the Rest of Us

Poverty is measured by a federal definition that fits a single poverty line onto all states, regardless of disparate costs of living (currently $19,530 for a family of three). The uniformity allows us a window into its incidence at any given time. In 2011, according to the census, U.S. poverty had reached a rate of 15 percent, representing 46.2 million people, most of them children. We used to think of poverty as an "inner city" or rural phenomenon, but suburban poverty recently eclipsed all other places as the home to the most U.S. poverty.[1] Over ten million of these people worked (7.2 percent of all people in the labor force).[2] Growth in the millions of working poor adults reflects the realities of a low-wage service-based economy that contrasts sharply with historical accounts of poverty. These poor and near-poor people live and work all around us—as cashiers, waitresses, child-care workers, stock clerks, gas station attendants—but struggle to make ends meet, to keep jobs or simply to work as many hours as they would like.

The working poor complicate our view of U.S. poverty principally because they upend common assumptions about what it means to be poor. People struggling hard to do the right thing with their lives are a counterweight to claims that poverty reflects poor decision making and weak values. The assumption is challenged even further by more granular analyses of who is in fact poor. For example, in 2012 the United Way of Northern New Jersey released a study of a group whose numbers outstrip both poor and working poor alike—"Asset Limited, Income Constrained, Employed," or ALICE.[3] By calculating what a household actually needs to sustain its basic needs within the area where it lives, researchers were able to determine shortfalls among families with incomes above poverty but significantly struggling nonetheless. They found the median costs necessary for basic essentials such as housing, child care, food, transportation, and health care, totaled both a "sustainable budget" and a "survival budget," and figured out how many households were caught short. They found 1.149 million households in New Jersey (36 percent of all households) that fell below the ALICE threshold, of which 829,001 (26 percent of all households) were not officially "poor." There were almost three times as many ALICE households in New Jersey as poor households. Across one of the richest states in the country, more than a third of households had incomes below the ALICE threshold.

Whether we call this poverty, near poverty, or symptoms of growing inequality, this is known in the households living through it as *stress*—chronic, distracting, often disabling stress—as they worry about covering unexpected calamities, routine financial surprises, and daily life expenses. This idea of stressful resource deprivation represents a condition of hardship with which most of us are familiar—and sympathetic. Rather than abstraction, this is actually what most of us know intimately, either because we've been through it or inevitably have family members, neighbors, or good friends struggling through it. It is also understandable as part of the continuum of financial stress I described earlier in chapter 1, a growing feature of middle-class life in the United States. In fact, it is changing the whole notion of middle-class stability, as families once securely middle class anxiously realize that their hold on that status is slipping toward ALICE. All this could undermine the assumption about poverty by suggesting that a lot of poverty is not something unto itself with its own rules, attitudes, and behaviors. Rather, poverty may be primarily the inability to make it to a middle-class life despite much uphill effort.

If that were true, then poverty might be less about culture and more about opportunity. It might be less about individual deficits like laziness and more about exogenous constraints like wage growth or health benefits. Yet that's not what most of us really mean when we embrace the idea that poor people—at least persistently poor people—are the undeserving product of their own weak values influencing their own bad decisions. We assume that they (like us) should be responsible for the consequences of their own lack of personal responsibility, which may justify sometimes-punitive public policies. The assumption clearly influenced the overhaul of the federal Aid to Families with Dependent Children in the 1990s when President Bill Clinton promised to "end welfare as we know it." The consequences of these policies can be objectively severe. The poor will have to work in often menial, public jobs as a condition of time-limited benefits;[4] they may pay disproportionately more in local taxes;[5] they often pay more for lesser-quality food and other consumer essentials;[6] and they live shorter lives.[7] Policies that allow these types of ironic disparities—expecting those with the fewest resources to pay more for less—must be built on some assumption of just deserts. That assumption, I argue, is that weak values and chronically bad decisions require harsh incentives to undo.

This is really no different than the culture of poverty thesis, a view of poverty that was reflected in social science in the 1970s,[8] influenced conservative public policy in the 1980s[9] and 1990s, lost favor around the turn of the century as more structuralist accounts held sway,[10] and has recently enjoyed a liberal comeback of sorts.[11] The culture of poverty thesis holds that poor people operate according to a separate and distinct set of norms, values, and beliefs that constitute what Oscar Lewis called "a design for living."[12] Behavior that would be soundly criticized as aberrant in middle-class communities is perceived as normal in poor ones. This amounts to a claim that the poor have an alternative mindset that governs the meaning of key life ingredients, such as the role of hard work and responsibility, the approach one takes toward schooling, the appropriateness of certain sexual behavior, and basic moral understandings about an individual's connection to those around him or her. What culture of poverty theorists often found is deviance, immediate gratification, and counterproductive behaviors—just the kind of outcomes that support many people's assumptions that poverty results from poor decisions and weak values. Mostly, they find a distinct lack of personal responsibility. The thesis, like the assumption, is big (and vague) enough to weather a lot of skepticism. For every hole poked in it, a shred of truth seems to appear. I have always found that the assumption raises more questions about how we develop social capital in this society than it answers. Mutuality suggests that the inquiry may even be beside the point.

However, because this idea continues to resonate not just among scholars and policy makers but also among folks of all incomes, it's important to examine some of the evidence around it, which is mixed. On decisions like having children out of wedlock, poor women are probably more traditional than their middle-class peers. In other respects, studies show that not enough value is placed on children's freedom from abuse or girls' safety from violence in many poor neighborhoods. Yet the overall picture shows a tragic collision of constraints and capacity. Like the communities they live in, poor people face constraints on opportunity that cannot hope to be matched by their capacity to withstand them. The results include biosocial reactions that have short-term adaptive benefits but long-term disabilities. While everything does not boil down to geography (if it did ALICE households in middle-income areas might not struggle so much), place matters a lot. Whatever persistent poverty is, it is consistently characterized by public policies that once again define place in ways that help to determine access to opportunity or deny it. As we have seen so far, our assumptions have insisted on rules that effectively concentrate poverty. More than anything else, concentrated poverty produces a culture of negation and isolation and some psychological stressors that would challenge the resources of the strongest among us.

## Making Babies

We'll start with babies. Not babies themselves, rather our beliefs about when to have them, how to raise them, and whether to marry before or after they meet their parents. This troika of subjects has a rich moral history in the United States and everywhere else. It says a lot about whether yours is a puritan culture, a loose culture, a conservative culture, or a more liberal one. It contains a million policy choices about how to regulate individual behavior. It determines law. And it is probably the biggest set of factors describing a household's financial capacity. For instance, researchers of every stripe assert that two-parent families are much less likely than single-parent families are to have incomes below the poverty line. In fact, children from two-parent families typically enjoy a host of advantages that their single-parent peers don't have, such as lower rates of incarceration, and higher rates of high school graduation and college attendance, better-paying jobs, and longer lives.[13] On the other hand, a hallmark of poor neighborhoods is the incredibly high proportion—sometimes over 75 percent—of families headed by unmarried women. This particular dichotomy is often the starting point for conversations that begin as follows: "I think the poor are not victims of discrimination or stingy government policies. The poor suffer from weak values and poor decisions, like having unprotected sex too young and not valuing marriage before deciding to have babies."

## Edin and Kefalas: Giving Birth to Oneself

This is precisely the set of beliefs that sociologists Kathryn Edin and Maria Kefalas set out to test in their five-year study of poor mothers in some of the hardest neighborhoods of Philadelphia, Pennsylvania, and Camden, New Jersey. In *Promises I Can Keep: Why Poor Women Put Motherhood before Marriage*, Edin and Kefalas describe some surprising findings based on hundreds of hours of interviews with the 162 black, Puerto Rican, and white moms whose trust they earned while living alongside them. The mothers' average age was twenty-five, and they had an average of two kids. Half the moms had not finished high school, and most had their first child before they were out of their teens. Some lived with a father of at least one of their children, though most lived with family or friends. Though many received public assistance at some point, those who worked—usually in low-wage jobs—made less than $10,000 in the year prior to the birth of their first child. When you add in the profiles of the children's fathers, the basic statistics about financial opportunity hold up: before the child was born, 40 percent of dads had been to jail or prison, half had finished high school, and a quarter had no job. This is exactly contrary to what middle-class norms recommend, and middle-class women are likely to make the opposite decisions.

Middle-class women (and men) delay childbirth until their educational and economic picture improves—although many more increasingly have children outside of marriage, and about a third of all unwed parents cohabitate with the realistic intention of marrying one day.[14]

Edin and Kefalas found that poor women in fact often do it backward, but not in a sense that rejects marriage as an ideal or out of a cavalier attitude about motherhood. Just the opposite has happened. While middle-class mothers have tended to value marriage later—after their independence is sealed by professional success, with children a valuable but by no means indispensable part of that life journey—poor women view the same things through a different, more traditional lens. Specifically, Edin and Kefalas found that *poor women put a greater value on motherhood than do middle-class women and want it earlier.*[15] They see mothering as the valiant beginning of responsible life, and want marriage only when it can be all that it should be—that is, later, when both they and a potential mate are financially ready to commit to each other and make it last. "While the poor women we interviewed saw marriage as a luxury, something they aspired to but feared they might never achieve, they judged children to be a necessity, an absolutely essential part of a young woman's life, the chief source of identity and meaning."[16]

One overlooked social benefit of poor women's desire to have children earlier than middle-class women is also at the core of family values: grandparenting. If poor women have children in their late teens, twenties, and early thirties (and if their children follow the pattern), they will almost certainly experience a long stretch of life as grandparents. Middle-class people who don't parent until their mid-thirties to early forties quietly give up on grandparenting as a norm and a value—even if they enjoy greater life expectancy. From the perspective of three-generation family norms, poor parents seem far more traditional than does the modern middle-class.

The early parenting ideal among the poor cuts across gender, according to the authors. "[T]alk of shared children is part of the romantic dialogue poor young couples engage in from the earliest days of courtship."[17] Regardless of whether the father remains committed emotionally, contributes financially, becomes abusive, or changes his mind and denies paternity, the moms see motherhood as the formative event in their own identity, the birth of a constant, trusting love in a harsh environment of uncertainty and distrust. That environment is also bereft of the opportunities that middle-class women take for granted, making the decision to have children a much weaker factor than others in precluding other advantages. Edin and Kefalas assert that many poor women suffer no distinct economic disadvantage from their decision to become unwed mothers (and a significant portion reject marriage proposals from men, including fathers, they deem unworthy). In particular, poor women lose more opportunities as a result of the schools they attend, their family background, their cognitive capacity, and their mental health than they might from bearing children outside of marriage or before graduating college, according to the authors.[18] That suggests that more than acting out of skewed values, they are weighing opportunity costs differently from middle-class women based on sound information about predictable risks and making decisions accordingly. In a word, they're acting rationally amid the constraints they face and the capacity at their disposal.

Poor women's beliefs were fairly united across race and ethnicity, which suggests that Edin and Kefalas tapped into experiences that can only be explained in terms of socioeconomic class. For instance, although women of different races experienced a different frequency of specific problems with fathers, they agreed on the four or five factors that routinely disqualify men for marriage: criminal behavior and incarceration, physical abusiveness, drug and alcohol addiction, repeated infidelity. The lack of jobs—though a common feature of men's lives in these neighborhoods—was not listed as a reason to be "unmarriageable."

Then what does marriage mean if not the opportunity to build a foundation for children, an emotional bedrock for each other, and a partnership against challenges? "For most," Edin and Kefalas write, "giving up on the possibility of marriage means abandoning the hope that their difficult economic and social situation will get better in time." They cling to that hope, with different, racially correlated odds of fulfillment, yet for all of them the probability is that it won't come until most consider themselves past childbearing years. The authors conclude, "Marriage is the prize at the end of the race. Because these women live in circumstances that are often too bleak to endure without hope that someday, in some way, they can make it, they still hope for marriage. But 'getting themselves together' while trying to redeem the fathers of their children is hard work, and failure is more common than success. Yet the fact that some succeed is enough cause for hope."[19]

As compelling a case as *Promises I Can Keep* offers, there still seems to be more to the question of whether decisions to have children before one can support them are not ill-considered, and whether the whole approach to family stability does not reflect at least some counterproductive beliefs, if not values. I wondered about the men, who are on the periphery of Edin and Kefalas's study. I worried whether the mom's early and earnest identification with having an innocent baby was not a singular act of insecurity that had both material and psychological repercussions for children in impoverished environments. And most of all, I thought about poor folks in other places I have studied—New Orleans, Newark, Oakland, and Los Angeles, for instance—and questioned the truth of one key assertion the authors make: that poor women believe in a two-word tenet of good mothering, "being there."

## Traumas of Life and the Long Life of Traumas

I went back to Philadelphia to learn more about the context for decisions and values among people who could be called the persistently poor. I went straight into the 'hood—Southwest Philly—where some of Edin and Kefalas's subjects live, in order to talk to experienced social workers, who deal with the more tragic patterns of family life among the clients who come voluntarily to see them. One senior supervising social worker spoke for the record on the condition that I not use her real name or the name of her counseling organization. Others, concerned with patient confidentiality, wanted no identifying attribution.

I drove into the area on a Friday evening in early November, as dusk fell on the narrow groove of Woodland Avenue. Single-lane traffic caught up to and crept behind the SEPTA trolley cars, the evening rays of sunset occasionally glinting off their silver rails in the asphalt. Southwest is the absolute nowhere in the middle of the fifth-largest city in the United States. It is not a conduit to anywhere you need to go. The skyline is always present in the distance, but the neighborhood feels disconnected from the city's energy. The facts on the ground are the usual monotony of chicken joints with bulletproof glass, hair-care outlets once called wig stores, auto-body shops and check-cashing places. Every soul is black except the police, who peek out every now and then from cruisers. Like a lot of Philadelphia's toughest neighborhoods, the side streets are foreboding, stuck in an era decades gone, sunken row houses pockmarked by abandonment. To people who know it, Southwest is not even a little bit safe to walk around. My hosts asked me if I wanted a security escort from my car, at a distance of maybe sixty feet.

In the movie *"Collateral"* of a few years back, the lead character is a cabdriver in LA who winds up chauffeuring a contract killer's homicidal spree. A somewhat simple man in a boring life, the cabdriver clips a postcard of a beautiful sun-drenched island to the visor just above his head. He stows the verdant piece of paradise amid the aquamarine waves as a ready reminder of what he is working for, a peaceful source of perseverance, a daydream on demand. The caseworkers at Community Health are involved in anything but boring work, but they need a postcard of such sanctuary just as much. Connie Sewell,[20] the site director for behavioral health there and a social worker since 1972, believes that what she does with her caseload is "holy work." Yet her immaculate office overlooking the Woodland Plaza parking lot belies dreams of Jamaica, with pictures and artwork from the sunny island haven.

Where the sociologists illustrate the cultural flavor of poor mothers' decision making, the social workers can detail where it hurts—particularly for the children. For starters, single motherhood makes actually "being there" extremely difficult, because moms are either working and relying on others to care for their kids much of the day, or they're struggling with other habits that take them away physically and psychologically. Her clients arrive through the randomness of primary care visits down the hall. The nurse–practitioners hear of the depression, see signs of abuse, or respond to a request for medication and send them to Sewell and her staff. These clients are very poor—perhaps poorer than Edin and Kefalas's subjects—nearly all black or African, and often in more crisis than they know. Sewell is a black woman of elegance and stature. With a round face and kind eyes, she came from a small town near Camden, New Jersey, where she was the only black in everything, a strong but lonely student who emerged from her education a survivor and a champion of underdogs.

Two issues come to dominate her work. The first is developing productive parenting skills. This among a population of parents for whom "the thought of doing anything other than beating their kids or yelling at them has never occurred to them," Sewell explained in the corner of a nearby soul food restaurant as we talked over a colossal collection of crab claws. The parents she deals with have trouble seeing the child's behavior as age appropriate, rather than a deliberate act of aggression or a bother. "Patience gets missed." Although Sewell sees some of these patterns rooted in a history of disruptions to black families that goes back to enslavement, she believes that caseworkers in other parts of the city find the same issues with their clients of other races. "There's something that stands in the way of parents showing children loveliness, their innate sense of worth," Sewell says. She struggles to eat her meal after a long week of stories she won't share in detail. "But you can't give what you haven't gotten."

"A lot of parents don't know how to talk to their children," Sewell asserts. They may even see speaking gently or patiently as being inappropriately "white"—and therefore ineffectual. But she doesn't judge or reprimand parents for their approaches to their children, nor does she see these patterns as a reflection of weak values. "If I see it that way, I'm not going to be with them as they are, and I'm going to miss them the same way they are missing their kids."

One of the themes that begins to emerge in conversations like this, as well as the psychological research on which professionals like Sewell

rely, is fear. At least since psychiatrist Robert Coles's pathbreaking studies of the untreated crises facing many children, the psychological toll
that poverty takes has been part of a discussion of stress and economic
disadvantage that few policy makers care to enter.[21] Poverty brings a lot
to be stressed about, but perhaps more to be feared. Sewell hears fear in
the angry voices of frustrated parents and sees fear in the eyes of their
children. Down to the caseworkers' offer of security as I left my car,
there is a constant aura that something bad can happen at any moment.

Before we get to the second, more troubling issue Sewell and her
staff confront, I am already back to thinking about the physiological
concept of "allostatic load"—a function of too many fight-or-flight
stress reactions on the body. The term reflects an overload of the normal processes by which our minds and bodies adapt to dangerous
stimuli. From the concept comes a theory that an abundance of threats
to one's survival demands too much from the hippocampus and pituitary glands, producing excesses of cortisol and adrenaline that trigger
a range of chronic health and learning deficits. The social stratification
theorist Douglas Massey, whom we met in chapter 1, introduced me to
the research of neuroendocrinologist Bruce McEwen.[22] Massey, as I'll
detail a little later, believes the biosocial effects of segregated poverty
deserve more attention, especially the problems associated with young
bodies formed amid allostatic load. A conversation with another social
worker, Margaret, who works with poor clients illustrated how it devel-
ops in a child in Southwest Philadelphia.

First you see a very little kid—we'll call him Jared—maybe four or
five years old, standing near a bus stop on the street and you wonder
incredulously to yourself, "Is that child alone?" Margaret the caseworker stares out the window as she speaks, as if she can actually see
the child, and maybe she can, because this scene recurs all the time
in Southwest. These streets are unsafe for a child so young alone. *Any*
street is unsafe for a child that age, but especially here. Jared thinks so,
too, says the caseworker. He has fear on his face. As time passes, inside
his chest his little heart is racing. A man approaches and walks on. Then
comes a group of big kids. The small child maneuvers out of the way,

quietly trying to figure out what to do. This time, Jared is not touched, he is not spoken to. It turns out, the caseworker says, he's not alone. Jared's mother told him to stay there while she went into a store nearby—though not close enough to save him from an immediate threat and not even visible to him. She, too, knows this is a dangerous neighborhood for such a small child alone. Like most people here, she has very little trust for others, especially strangers. Then why does she let Jared experience this anxiety? The caseworker's not sure. She suspects it's out of a belief that her child must learn to navigate these dangers for himself. Even at four, Jared must steel himself against fearsome threats. The caseworker calls it "parentifying" the child. However, the lesson will come through prolonged threat reactions—complicated chemical fight-or-flight responses—which challenge the body to defend itself more often than it is designed safely to do. The boy may even learn to react with hypervigilance at the slightest threat, seeking to overcome it with aggression or violence before it gets him. He may read threat too often, too quickly, and requiring too great a response, which may eventually get him killed or imprisoned. But the whole street scene is a microcosm of allostatic load in its infancy. Mom is that island paradise, but mom isn't there. Jared's body is training for fear.

The second set of issues Sewell and her staff confront relate to conditions that are even more immediate to a child's well-being and to a mother's claim of being there: sexual abuse and post-traumatic stress disorder, or PTSD. I am shocked to hear about both, and Connie Sewell can see it on my face. She acknowledges that our society suffers from a tremendous amount of untreated, unprosecuted sexual molestation of minors, but calls the proportions epidemic among the poor families she sees. How prevalent? I ask. "I would be hard-pressed to point to anyone in my caseload of thirty-two who has not been sexually abused—men and women." The abusers are usually men in the family, boyfriends or stepfathers. Sewell describes many as "serial perpetrators." And the worst thing may be that "once a child is abused," Sewell suggests, "it's as if she's marked."

This is a particularly hard issue to present because every community of every race and class is affected by child abuse yet differences in their public exposure can make comparisons about concealed facts unreliable. My many friends and students who either work or have performed clinic placements in family or juvenile court have lamented the frequency with which child abuse—verbal, sexual, physical, and neglect—are part of the picture of a case involving indigent clients. These anecdotal work reports support Sewell's work experience. However, it's not clear whether the sample would be similar if the traumas of more affluent families' lives were revealed by public agencies. Authoritative research about the relationship between poverty and increased levels of abuse is scarce.[23]

However, one notable exception is the "Fourth National Incidence Study of Child Abuse and Neglect" (NIS-4) by the U.S. Department of Health and Human Services, a report mandated by Congress. It represents a national needs assessment on child abuse and neglect, based on 122 counties and using "sentinel" reporting (e.g., schoolteachers, day care center staff, cops, public health providers) from more than ten thousand professionals and one thousand agencies. This still represents, in my view, a very public context, with fewer opportunities for middle-class and affluent families to be counted than the poor, but it is comprehensive nonetheless. The NIS-4 covers the years 2005–6. The results are startling. Abuse is defined by either a harm or an endangerment standard. Under either one, children in low-income households have greater incidence of abuse. Having no parent in the labor force or an unemployed parent, for instance, significantly increased both the incidence and the severity of mistreatment compared to homes where parents worked.[24] Class was a clear factor. "Children in low socioeconomic status households had significantly higher rates of maltreatment in all categories and across both definitional standards. They experienced some type of maltreatment at more than 5 times the rate of other children; they were more than 3 times as likely to be abused and about 7 times as likely to be neglected."[25] Race, too, was a factor, with black children experiencing more maltreatment than whites or Hispanics.[26] The report defends itself against the criticism that its results skew against the poor.[27]

I worry that sexuality itself is being redefined in settings where sexual abuse is common. It is hard to see how a healthy sexual self-image can grow and flourish in an environment where so many people carry such pain, shame, and anger about how their bodies have been mistreated. The fact that so little of it is prosecuted means it continues outside of norms of accountability. The fact that so much of it occurs under the influence of drugs and alcohol in environments where drugs and alcohol have an outsized presence means it is a chronic risk associated with a common state of mind. And at the heart of it all is a young person and his or her body in the process of becoming an independent sexual agent for life. Most of all, I know that child abuse is rarely the only threat condition an abused child typically faces. It is a seminal trauma, no doubt, but often multiplied by others amid traumatic lives. At the very least, pervasive sexual abuse among poor children represents an under-attended entry point into understanding their larger social marginalization.

Let's turn next to imagining cumulative effects of disproportionate trauma—sexual and otherwise. Just as most Americans know stress, most will experience significant trauma in their lives—50 to 90 percent of us.[28] According to a comprehensive review of the clinical literature on stress and inner-city poverty, children in these environments have rates of exposure to trauma in the range of 70 to 100 percent, and 83 percent have experienced multiple traumatic events. These adverse stressors include violent crime in schools or the neighborhood, domestic violence, the victimization, incarceration, or death of a family member, fires, homelessness, and gang or drug activity.[29] Margaret, the social worker, described the challenges involved in working with a family in which one sibling stood next to another who was shot and seriously wounded by a stray bullet as they witnessed an altercation on the street in front of their home. In his mind, the little boy cannot escape the moment when the calm suddenly went horribly wrong, from child's play to a loud, angry adult presence. The gun. Cussing and commotion. Gunshots. His brother screaming, fallen, bloody, eyes closing. The eternity before his mother returned from upstairs, then her screams. Sirens, flashing lights, crowds, waiting in tears.

Like many children growing up in such stressful environments, they display distress. "Reactions to trauma include increased monitoring of their environment for dangers, anxiety when separated from trusted adults, irritability and aggression, or increased need for affection, support, and reassurance."[30] One of the unique characteristics about human trauma compared to that of animals is that our minds can trigger the stress response by merely anticipating or thinking about it. We can naturally compound our own traumas by reliving them in our heads.

Dealing with a single trauma is a difficult emotional journey for anyone, and it requires a coping capacity made up of many resources—internal, familial, environmental. Yet it's the cumulative effects of multiple traumas that Sewell and her staff treat, a condition in both adults and children called PTSD. Most of us associate PTSD with the problems of soldiers returning from combat in Iraq and Afghanistan. Clinically speaking, PTSD symptoms include "feelings of intense fear, helplessness, or horror; reexperiencing of a traumatic event through dreams, flashbacks, or dissociative experiences . . . sleep disturbances, irritability, or concentration difficulties."[31] Of course, our urban poor are not soldiers. They're merely embedded veterans of concentrated poverty, living like refugees from peace in places where a large number of the random adults they will meet are contending with some degree of PTSD-related depression or anxiety and where many children are developing the same.

Especially girls. While urban males experience much higher exposure to trauma, particularly violence-related trauma, females are four times more likely to experience PTSD symptoms.[32] Part of this, according to criminologist Jody Miller, is a reflection of the ways women are targeted in very poor, highly segregated neighborhoods by men acting out aggressively masculinized roles. The public community space in poor urban neighborhoods tends to be *male* space where women can quickly become unsafe.[33] This can often include schools where violence against girls by boys, especially low-level violence, can go unchecked. Miller studied very poor adolescents (average age sixteen) in St. Louis, using a sample that was extreme in the degree of both poverty and delinquency. Over half of her subjects reported some form of sexual victimization; almost a third had been raped; a third had been sexually victimized multiple times.[34] These figures are higher than some other studies, but not by a lot. Given norms against "snitching" to police, many crimes against women go unpunished despite the presence of witnesses. Not surprisingly, many women in poor neighborhoods feel trapped indoors. In Miller's study, the prevalence of male sexual entitlement "supported negative gender stereotypes that encouraged and validated the mistreatment of young women."[35]

\* \* \*

I mean none of this to pathologize persistently poor people, or to suggest that, like the culture of poverty thesis, poor people think and act fundamentally differently from the rest of us. Rather they are just like us, only more so for the disproportionate stresses they face. Within every community are people suffering abuse, mental illness, and self-medicating with drugs that can contribute to violence and antisocial behavior. But for certain communities to have its members experience too many stresses too often makes these especially tough places in which to develop the critical social capital each of us requires for growth and dignity. Social capital is another way of describing the capacity for a middle-class life; the stresses of poverty produce a condition of potentially overwhelming constraints. Separation intensifies these constraints, sacrificing social capital development. In a sense, this is the island without a clear route to paradise.

Acknowledging that there's still a lot we can't conclude about behavioral motivations in high-poverty areas, what do these data say about the culture of poverty idea? Only that poor children are exposed to or victimized by the traumas of violence, sexual abuse, neglect, and rape at rates that put them at heightened risk of emotional crises for which there are inadequate resources—internally and externally. Their capacity for decision making and value judgments occurs in this spatially isolated context in which awful things risk being commonplace. The assumption about how and why very poor people think like they do is generally aimed at an assessment of their personal economic agency—a picture of why they stay poor. So far, we are examining here their decision making from the more threshold question of how people—any people—sustain the capacity to cope. It is difficult to have a meaningful discussion about personal responsibility and making the most of opportunities without an understanding of the emotional, cognitive, *and* economic contexts in which people make choices.

## Allostatic Load

To this spatial–psychological dimension of the discussion we can now add a biosocial component. Massey makes the connection between segregated poverty and allostatic loads to show how our environments actually transform our capacities from the inside—mind and body—to devastating effects. Remember Jared, the fictional four-year-old whom Margaret the social worker described waiting in fear outside the store for his mother to return him to a sense of safety. Over time in the 'hood (i.e., an area of concentrated poverty), and after experiencing enough traumas (or witnessing them), Jared's hormones may become dangerously conditioned to stress, especially violence. A threat triggers the hypothalamus to produce adrenaline, setting off a chain reaction in the vascular system and signaling the brain to prepare the body to deal with it. Simultaneously, the pituitary gland secretes cortisol, which sets off a chain reaction to produce energy. This "allostatic response" is the body's way of sacrificing long-term functions such as bone, muscle, and brain building in order to adequately meet the short-term needs of a physical threat.[36] These are the miracles of human biology, the complex systems at work inside us that promote survival.

The problem is what happens when too-frequent allostatic responses lead to allostatic load. The physiological triggers constitute a who's who of personality traits and health issues associated with poor folk. Chronically elevated adrenaline levels are associated with cardiovascular disease and hypertension. Frequent, sudden escalations in blood pressure take their toll on blood vessels in the arteries and may produce a sticky buildup that is a precursor of atherosclerosis.[37] Elevated adrenaline is also—not surprisingly—linked to so-called type A personality traits, such as quick tempers, impulsiveness, and aggressiveness.[38] Long-term elevations of cortisol may seriously compromise the immune system, contributing to inflammatory conditions like asthma, arthritis, and type 1 diabetes.[39] The wear on the hippocampus may produce atrophy, leading to memory loss and inability to concentrate—an acute problem of brain development and learning capacity among children.[40] "Simply put, people who are exposed to high levels of stress over a prolonged period of time are at risk of having their brains re-wired in a way that leaves them with fewer cognitive resources to work."[41]

The intersection of physiological, psychological, and social stratification research suggests that neighborhoods of isolated, concentrated poverty create the conditions for being clinically "stressed out" in ways that contribute to poor school performance, depression and withdrawal, attention deficits, aggressiveness, self-medication, lowered future expectations, and increased risk of debilitating, chronic diseases. Consider also that we haven't even discussed the salient material aspects of persistent poverty that affect children's cognition and health, such as hunger, transient housing situations, environmental hazards, and a chronic lack of essentials.[42] Contrary to the culture of poverty thesis, which implies certain bad choices by poor people, much of this picture seems like a nightmarish social experiment that proves what happens to human beings when they are trapped long enough in overwhelming conditions—like civilians in a war.

Even as civilians using our safety net, very poor people do another kind of battle that brings stresses unrecorded by public health measures. Recall that I mentioned how public poor people's lives are—how they routinely encounter the bureaucracy of social service and housing agencies, underachieving schools, the raw side of criminal justice (including suspicious, tough-minded cops), and hospital emergency care— each encounter beginning with a demand for proper identification. As caseworkers and lawyers for the poor will universally attest, these are encounters not of helpfulness and courtesy but more often of distinct mutual distrust. People in bureaucracies do not want to see poor people coming, and poor people know it. So they spend all day trying to meet demands for documentation and regulatory requirements designed to prevent fraud. They wait on lines; they're sent here, then there. Tempers rise. Bus fare runs out. Stress. (This is one reason poor people disproportionately rely on emergency room care; all the tests and specialists are generally in one place at one time.) As angry as middle-class people get about government bureaucracy, we would *never* tolerate what the poor routinely face. We would vote out the bums, demand reform for our tax dollars, and, whenever possible, privatize our options. We would spring the trap.

And this problem of being trapped—being absolutely separated—may be the fundamental problem with most antipoverty policies.[43] Isolation reveals a link between people with limited capacity and places with limited capacity. An obvious consequence of policies that consistently assume that very poor people should be physically separated from middle-class people is that they will not participate in life as middle-class people know it. They will not see and expect the same attitude from the same doctors, school officials, receptionists, dental hygienists, landlords, psychiatrists, and pharmacists on which we rely. Excluded from the resources that allow middle-class people to buffer themselves against the constraints of life, they will just have to make do in places with much more limited capacities. It's not surprising, then, that their personal capacities to withstand constraints—much more severe constraints, it turns out—would be overwhelmed.

This reality seems more ecological than cultural. In other words, if mutuality of interests and resources is the key to maintaining middle-class capacities, then a mutuality of deficits would naturally conspire to sustain a very high level of constraints in poor communities. Progressive mutuality, like the kind we hope to find in middle-class communities, simply acknowledges that we need other people's resources to build up our own capacities against constraints. Zero-sum mutuality, like the kind we find in very low-income areas, shows how the collective difficulties of meeting basic needs compounds constraints and diminishes individual capacity. In short, poor people are tapped out and adapting to deficits, as are the places they inhabit.

## The Culture of Poverty Revisited

Let's return to the question of whether persistent poverty—at least ghetto poverty among segregated blacks—represents something so different as to be its own culture. Could it be that the findings above, when combined with social behaviors, drug and gang norms, shopping habits, and educational tendencies, combine to make what can fairly be called a distinct culture within our larger culture? Perhaps. I have heard similar ideas implied by experts in and from the 'hood. In Houston, for example, I learned about the city's forgotten Fifth Ward by a generous man named Xavier Burke—officially the district coordinator for an alternative charter school, unofficially the lifeline and big brother to countless teens in or near trouble. Known as "X," he believes certain mind-sets in ghetto communities can be an obstacle to positive growth.

"The only thing that saved my own life was relocation," he explains in a deep baritone to match his six-foot five-inch frame. He came here from Alabama when he was a kid, and you can still hear his birthplace in his accent. "Same environment, same people and nobody has a positive outlook." X received a basketball scholarship to college. He coaches local kids now.

We drive at dusk to a community center to meet some of the young men he works with. This neighborhood northeast of downtown sits mostly on the other side of railroad tracks and highways. It strikes me as a vast expanse of absolutely nothing doing, strikingly gray and missing much that a neighborhood would want, like stores, strips of commercial life, a library. More than half the shotgun shacks I see are unoccupied, rundown, or burned up. All look decrepit. People occasionally appear, but for this time of day there's a distinct lack of drivers returning home from work or pedestrians walking back from bus stops. Here a string of old factories, there another railroad crossing, a few automobiles stuck waiting for an endless train of freight cars to pass. The three boys meet us in the parking lot of a windowless building that could pass for an airplane hanger. They're long, lanky, sweet-faced sixteen- and seventeen-year-olds who speak in single-word answers. We talk about how they're doing in school, their plans, what it takes to find a job. The horizon is mostly retail positions a few bus rides to downtown, at fast food chains. I hear that many of their peers are struggling with drug use, either drinking pharmaceutical mixes like "Purple City" (codeine and fruit juice in paper cups some bring to school) or smoking "Fry" (a mixture of marijuana cigarettes dipped in embalming fluid). After we talk, I learn from X that the boys are struggling in school and that the youngest is about to go on trial for murder.

Like so many who care about impoverished communities, X is concerned about their attitudes. "People in the Fifth Ward communities have been there forever. From the jump, a lot of those attitudes have been negative. So, it's hard to come in and build with the same attitudes. When I say relocation, it's not always taking the kids out. Sometimes it's bringing different kinds of people in. Sometimes it's mixing two different types of people—people who take education seriously and people who don't—mixing them together and hoping they can rub off on each other. Because everybody can learn from everybody."

Unfortunately, that almost never happens. Of all the myriad approaches to alleviating poverty and its effects, almost none ever embrace the principle that X just expressed. Because of the assumptions we've examined so far, the unshakable premise behind nearly every policy designed for the very poor is that they will remain separated from middle-class people while the policy somehow works on them. The persistence of deep poverty is complex and vexing for policy makers. Since at least Lyndon Johnson's War on Poverty in the 1960s, hardworking, diligent minds have developed a range of approaches—from empowerment zones to community-based social service delivery, local health clinics to midnight basketball, job training to drug treatment, self-esteem workshops to limited-equity cooperatives. In my experience, serious people have spent serious years trying to make a dent and often find some success. Success, however, comes mainly by stabilizing lives in poverty, but rarely by reducing poverty itself. Every approach has in common the fundamental separateness of poor people in place. They rarely share institutional space, private conversations, or nearby homes with people who are not also poor.

In a recent example from the affordable housing context, the Poverty & Race Research Action Council studied the relationship between federally assisted housing and high-performing schools. PRRAC found that there hardly is a relationship to compare. Despite the explicit purpose of some housing programs, federally subsidized housing is rarely connected to good schools in any meaningful way. Most of us would probably assume that students who live in public housing projects attend weak-performing neighborhood schools where poverty is common to the student body. In fact they do—68.6 percent of their peers qualify for free and reduced meals (FARM) and their schools rank in only the 19th percentile on math and English standardized tests.[44] However, housing voucher programs such as Section 8 were designed to undo that concentration of poor students in poor schools by giving parents housing choices that would allow them to live near better-performing schools. To a lesser extent, the same is true of housing developed with Low-Income Housing Tax Credits (LIHTC). The PRRAC study found that neither set of tenants—vouchers nor LIHTC—attend much better schools than do kids in public housing—74 percent FARM classmates in 26th percentile schools for voucher students, 67 percent FARM and 31st percentile for LIHTC. The problem is that vouchers are not redeemable for housing in more middle-class areas, and resistance to affordable housing there is stiff. As a recent struggle to change housing mobility rules in southeastern Pennsylvania showed, sometimes the government's chief housing agency—HUD—is the source of resistance.[45] One clear result is that back in Houston's Fifth Ward, X will not soon get his wish to see his kids mixing with kids from more stable educational environments.

## The Trap of Assumptions

What this chapter shows is a classic example of how the meaning of facts at the surface may be transformed by deeper scrutiny. So much of what people see—or see represented—about the very poor suggests that they operate from a mind-set that can only be considered culturally distinct and self-destructive. The assumption that the poor remain so because of their faulty decision making and weak values is one version of a culture of poverty thesis. It's not that those who believe this idea deny that persistently poor people face conditions whose chronic constraints overmatch their capacity for upliftment. It's that they believe that something internal and semipermanent is responsible for this failing, a failing that becomes infectious and socially transmissible through generations. But what if the constraints-versus-capacity mismatch occurred largely by other means? What if most of the poor actually work—or try to work, often more than one job—but still can't escape poverty because of wage and other structural constraints? What if the exacerbation of those constraints for the persistently poor results from spatially specific factors—many the product of deliberate government policies—that routinely provoke psychological and developmental responses more readily understood as biosocial rather than cultural?

Ultimately, it doesn't really matter whether we can prove empirically that the persistently poor live in a culture of poverty. *What matters is that we think they do.* Our thinking tends to reinforce our assumptions about them. Our assumptions have structured the debilitating reality of their lives, while separating that reality from more middle-class realities. Assuming that middle-class lives are self-sufficient (assumption #1) helps to establish a norm of personal responsibility for one's positive fate, even if it's only partly true. Assuming that keeping distance from the poor helps sustain those middle-class outcomes (assumption #2) supports decades of policies separating the poor from the greater resources of more affluent places, compounding the constraints with which they cope. Assuming that segregation is now merely voluntary (assumption #3) and that racism no longer limits opportunity (assumption #4) locks disadvantage in place, ignoring the clear racial patterns across social strata. The fifth assumption—that the poor bring it on themselves—closes the circle by justifying both their fate and more of the same often punitive and exclusionary policies.

This, too, is the high price of our paradise. Lost in all the assumptions is the unnecessary costs to them directly and to the rest of us indirectly that progressive mutuality seeks to reduce in the interest of a broader, stronger middle class and more beloved communities. What is difficult in achieving opportunity in poor areas today promises to remain so tomorrow, and very few will escape that struggle. We will all pay for that—in the rising costs of one bureaucracy or another, and another generation of American children wounded and unprepared. To all of us come the lost opportunity costs of people who could be greater contributors, students, taxpayers, neighbors, voters, workers, parents— more dignified and free.

## Counterfactual: Moving to Mind-Set Mobility?

Paradise may be more than what most of us want, because most of us want the same simple things for our family—beginning with safety. This facet of shared culture was demonstrated by householder follow-up studies of mobility programs that asked a question thought unthinkable since the 1960s: what would happen if families in persistent segregated poverty were given the resources to move to areas of greater opportunity? Launched in 2003 as part of the settlement in *Thompson v. HUD*, the Baltimore Housing Mobility Program provided a range of services to help more than 1,500 very low-income African American families move from inner-city Baltimore to other towns and neighborhoods in the metropolitan area.[46] Each move had to demonstrably reverse the usual numbers. Families moved from places that were 80 percent black and 33 percent poor to places that were 21 percent black and 7.5 percent poor. Most went from the city to a suburb, from schools of low achievement to better-performing schools, and from high crime and a weak consumer infrastructure to low crime and much improved stores and services. Studied four years later, the families generally reported very favorable changes in quality of life, educational outcomes, housing stability, and, of all things, less stress. Although much is presumed about the preference of poor people for poor neighborhoods, only 19 percent returned to housing in the inner city.

The Baltimore Housing Mobility Program is a rare success; the array of counseling services, support, and follow-up given to families *and* their new communities is unprecedented. We will not know all the benefits in terms of lasting economic opportunities, high school and college graduation rates, and decreased criminal involvement for some time. However, like the more recent Moving to Opportunity results from five cities,[47] mobility programs of whatever quality appear to have one critically overlooked benefit: increased mental tranquility and dramatically less trauma. This suggests that when we talk about reducing poverty, our tendency to begin and end with demands for jobs, jobs, jobs might be supplemented with greater concern for minds, minds, minds. Better health—psychological and physical—we now understand is the precursor, if not the goal, of paradise in our daily lives.

# 7

## RACELESS WONDERS

### ASSUMING THAT RACIAL LABELS NO LONGER MATTER

Mutuality would be easier to embrace if our racial identities did not routinely separate us. The sharing and trust intrinsic to the idea of linked fates and common interests would come more readily if just our humanity mattered. Racelessness, or being undefinable by race, would seem to be a crucial step in overcoming our costly divisions. Not surprisingly, we hold the popular sixth assumption—that racial labels are no longer useful or accurate—as a practical aspiration, an opportunity to live out our ideals about opportunity. Lately, we seem to exult the assumption as a foregone conclusion. Doing so prematurely turns it into a weapon against mutuality.

### Two Kinds: Colorblindness and Racial Solidarity

The assumption can be broken down in many ways, but I'll discuss just two in this chapter: colorblindness and the solidarity of nonwhites. Colorblindness is the most obvious (and powerful) form of racelessness, and we see it in three ways. First, it is expressed as a critical political reflex to slam shut a door on any mention of race in policy situations—*quick, denounce the player of "race cards"!* It reflexively prompts us to equate the influence of race with the presence of racism. Second, it's romanticized as a new ism to which we've evolved—"postracialism." For example, during the 2008 presidential election, colorblindness briefly rested on a post-racial cloud, the term used to the breaking point to explain the pundits' incredulity as a black presidential candidate gained surprising momentum week after week. A post-racial cottage industry was begat; mailboxes quickly overflowed with conference invitations, op-eds, and seminars dedicated to understanding and reifying the new post-racialism. Third, colorblindness may reflect the assertion of identities outside traditional racial or ethnic categories. In this sense colorblindness may simply be the default position in a world of truly mixed people who don't wish to claim—or be claimed by—a narrow racial identity. Defiantly blurring traditional racial categories, many people of mixed heritage claim to be "multiracial," an assertion that finds official sanction in modern census classifications.

These examples might be considered the institutionalization of the assumption, expressing it as moral reaction to distasteful race talk, a new school of cultural study or the mother of a transcendent new racial category. Yet at bottom the assumption of colorblindness, an aspiration vaguely committed to some humanistic understanding about racelessness, is distinctly powerful for the fear it strikes. Because most of us are afraid to be critical of the idea—similar to the fear of being called a racist or making a comment about race—it even constrains our private thoughts. As a result of the coercive character of colorblindness, speaking race has become taboo.[1]

Yet this fearfully color-blind way of thinking about the assumption—a fear that produced colorblindness, followed by a colorblindness that reproduces more fear—reveals a lot about the idea's weaknesses. Colorblindness is too often a forced choice. We should be suspicious of anything so silencing. As we'll see shortly, colorblindness also masks the potency of color-conscious decision making. Some of these decisions have profound material consequences that follow a predictable color hierarchy. Consciously and unconsciously, the assumption of color-blindness, as many scholars have shown,[2] assists the supremacy of "whiteness" and those susceptible to believing it. In other words, the goal of colorblindness often sustains the reality of racial privilege—the very opposite of progressive mutuality.

The other, more complicated and less discussed side of the assumption about a raceless shared humanity is well-known in the guts of people of color. It is the claim that we are naturally allied with one another in common struggle. We might call this the racial solidarity side of colorblindness. Here the assumption is important to sustaining a sense of shared suffering, especially among minorities on the political left. It's not that we're blind to color distinctions; it's that we know a basic sameness in being "of color" amid Anglo dominance. This idea gained popularity when President Obama's 2012 reelection was read as a nonwhite referendum that forcefully demonstrated how much the interests of minority voters have diverged from the white supporters of his Republican challenger. The whites who may be admitted to this new demographic fold are deemed "progressive." The position of Asian Americans (and the many differences among groups lumped into that grand category) in this alignment is still unclear.[3] Of course, this organization of nonwhite interests long pre-dates any election during this century. The common repetition of the phrase "blacks and Latinos" in social science literature, in news accounts, and in earlier chapters of this book has always implied more than a quantitative resemblance. In general, it has been used to signify deep economic, subcultural, and political affinity. We're not just like each other; we *like* each other.

Yet the basis of our bond is a sense of common "Otherness," of understanding our closeness to each other at the bottom of the social and economic hierarchy—and disliking it. This is a necessary precondition to multi-ethnic coalitions. As nonwhite people, we all experience something full, tangible, and challenging about belonging and mobility in American society. However, this factual prerequisite is fraught with psychological resistance. For one, it can consist of historically abstract memory. For another, it doesn't alter the sense that common lines of persecution are not like the heritage of unalterable genetics. We were wounded in different ways, and the differences may obscure the similarities. We forget a lot of the suffering of others, or call it something else. Behind language and culture, we've constructed disparate histories that can be reinterpreted, even changed with time. That, as the story below from Compton shows, is why the assumption is so profoundly unstable. Indeed, evidence from all over Los Angeles County illustrates what most people of color in the United States already know but rarely speak: we have as much dislike for each other as like.

I know this personally. When I was Justin Hudson's age and preparing to leave Harlem/Washington Heights for college in California, I walked around with an intuitive connection to Puerto Ricans and Dominican New Yorkers. I did not speak Spanish and our cultural differences were great, but there was something about the Afro-Caribbean connection between us that united almost instantaneously. There are so many dark-skinned Puerto Ricans and Dominicans that the phenotypic spectrum alone suggests something culturally common (I was routinely confused for both). And through living vertically in the same buildings, attending the same public schools, and sharing several hundred pertinent points of cultural connection from speech patterns to musical tastes, and, well, the binary—blacks and Latinos on one side, whites on another—the bond made a certain provincial sense.

Then I moved to California where my heart was promptly broken. Gone were Puerto Ricans and Dominicans, replaced by Mexicans/Chicanos (and increasingly other Central Americans). Almost immediately, I came to find out that blacks and Mexicans had no particular love for each other. Instead, they were regularly in conflict; no intuitive connection was felt. I wondered whether our relative intra-minority peace in New York City was spatially influenced. In contrast to the East, California communities were more horizontal and boundary lines could be more easily drawn. After college, I began a fellowship in Los Angeles (the other New York, right?) to build a model for political interethnic dialogue among the black, Latino, and Asian–Pacific Islander communities living in obvious tension. I solved nothing, but learned a lot about the fallacy of this assumption. That was in the late 1980s.

Part of this was my own naïveté about the separate cultural traditions non-white, non-American groups embrace around what might be called running from blackness. This is not just the other side of a melting pot idea of assimilation that implies becoming white. This is also the more complicated cultural traditions of animus toward dark skins and the institutionalization of racial inequality by other names. What Latino (and Asian) friends from different countries privately disclosed to me about not-so-subtle contempt for dark-skinned people and African Americans in particular has been more recently confirmed in rigorous scholarship. For instance, in a recent book the legal scholar Tanya Kateri Hernandez traces the embrace in Latin American countries of a non-racist, post-slavery idea of race that instead emphasizes national identity, multiracialism, and democracy. It denies widespread color prejudice within Latin American cultures. Nevertheless, she argues, "the all-embracing rhetoric of multiracial postracialism continues to support racial hierarchy and anti-black bias."[4] These countries did not take their cues from U.S. racial constructs, yet they have developed similar ideas about colorblindness with similar results. "Latin American postracialism has not led to a transcendence of race but instead to a reinforcement of a racial caste system in a region long touted as a racial democracy."[5]

The question is, why would we expect a radically different understanding among nonwhites in the United States?

## Compton, the Contested City

The racial history of Compton, California, a postindustrial "first suburb" of Los Angeles, is still being written. But in 1988, it would get a reputation that was hard to shake, with the release of the rap group NWA's album *Straight Outta Compton*. Niggaz Wit Attitude's title song and others like "Fuck the Police" brought through the lens and language of gangsta rap international attention to a small, predominantly black city's struggles with persistent poverty, police brutality, and ghetto isolation. Located in the southern part of Los Angeles County near the more famous Watts, Compton became synonymous with the impoverished wasteland of violent, gangbanging urban culture. Unable to physically distance themselves, neighboring cities like Paramount and Gardena instead changed the name of their sections of Compton Boulevard. As important as the new music genre was in exposing the trials of ghetto life that would explode across South–Central LA County in the civil unrest of 1992, NWA's vision of Compton obscured its past as a rare seat of black political power in Southern California. Black gangs that formed around crack cocaine in the segregated 1980s followed the black gangs that had formed to protect blacks from white mobs before white flight.[6] Blacks had migrated to the city in the 1950s as industrial workers in the Alameda corridor, but were consistently shut out of political power and ignored by white elected officials.[7] That changed gradually when, by 1969 and 1973, Compton elected black male and female mayors, respectively—the first of any metropolitan city in the country. Despite white flight, Compton was a middle-class mecca for blacks from all over the region seeking the American Dream.[8]

Fast-forward to 2008 and Barack Obama stands with his arms crossed, stern face uplifted into the horizon, the White House and a huge flag behind him, and just beyond that, Compton's municipal building. The likeness of the forty-forth president is better than many other murals, but many of Compton's current residents—two-thirds of whom are now Latino—question why it should be there at all.[9]

"It's stupid because any other president could've been painted on the wall but leave it to Compton to paint a mural of Obama 'cause he's the first black president," said a Latino high school senior. "Being the first black president has nothing to really do with Compton."

A married Mexican male in his mid-twenties echoed the perception that black interests dominate local politics at the expense of a largely Mexican Latino majority. "They [blacks] have the power. They can do whatever they want. What are we [Mexicans] going to say? They don't care what we have to say. If they cared they would have thought about it before putting [the mural] up there."

Not all the Compton respondents my research assistant interviewed in Spanish were so critical of the mural. Some were quite proud of it.[10] Yet the controversial mural of a sitting president is symbolic of a tension over what are perceived as racial spoils—that is, the racial distribution of opportunities conferred by control of local government. Many Latinos in Compton argue that they have been disenfranchised in a political process where blacks are overrepresented. The lack of Latino elected officials is evident in the makeup of the almost all-black city council and school board. As a result, Latinos feel shut out of public-sector employment. Their lack of control over education leads to a de-emphasis on resources for bilingual classrooms, curricular battles that favor Martin Luther King over Cesar Chavez, and a paucity of Latino staff and teachers.[11] Impatience with the apparent imbalance has led many Latinos in Compton to claim that it's "our turn now."

Several aspects of this growing conflict are worth pausing to note. First, the character of mutuality between blacks and Latinos in Compton is hardly progressive. In many respects (but not always) the attitude is zero-sum. There is certainly some degree of social harmony, even solidarity based on nonwhite status, socioeconomic class, and shared streets, but the underlying tensions are manifest and infect even symbolic civic matters.

Second, the last time a racial or ethnic group arrived in large numbers—blacks in the 1950s—whites left and a black majority quickly developed. Though middle-class blacks depopulated Compton as drugs and violence increased in the 1990s, the city's "new" Latino majority resulted primarily from rapid Latino immigration—with a significant percentage of undocumented people. Both transitions happened in less than a generation, but for very different reasons. Blacks have not been as willing as whites were to abandon local government.

Third, neither blacks nor Latinos seem to acknowledge the significance of each other's history.

These factors combine to create a volatile dynamic in which Latinos seem to see their interests as incapable of being represented by black leadership yet rightly subject to mathematical justice. That is, they believe that the group with the greatest numbers should control. This much is evident in the particular shape of their advocacy. Latino lawyers have brought voting rights lawsuits against the use of at-large districts that dilute Latino voting power.[12] They have brought affirmative action challenges to the city's hiring policies.[13] And Latino parents have filed complaints of mistreatment of their schoolchildren with the U.S. Department of Education.[14] These are all civil rights remedies, originating with the oppression of black minorities by white majorities and now used by a Latino majority against a black minority that (for now) has power disproportionate to its numbers. In *The Presumed Alliance*, Nicolas Vaca makes a similar case for a mathematical justice due Compton's Latinos based on their numbers. Citing the "xenophobic behavior" of Compton's "black power structure," Vaca writes, "What Latinos have learned is what their counterparts in the [neighboring] city of Lynwood have learned—wait, increase their voter rolls, and when they reach critical mass, seize power."[15] This may be a practical solution for feelings of Latino disenfranchisement, but it does not follow the traditional rationale for civil rights remedies. It is a model of identity politics based on revenge for perceived wrongs by and between subordinate groups. (Contrast how, as a constitutional matter, in civil rights contests between minority and white interests, this narrative of relief was jettisoned generations ago.)

The perception of comparative wrongs has always been a key feature of minority division. If, as I said earlier, our joint "Otherness" comes from our closeness to each other at the bottom of the social and economic hierarchy, then there is always an unstated comparison of the methods of marginalization that got us there. Latino groups in the United States have varied histories of oppression here. Some reek of national-origin discrimination as in the case of Puerto Ricans. A rare few have enjoyed a more favored status, like Cubans after Castro's revolution. The educational segregation of Mexicans, especially during the Bracero program in the 1940s and 1950s, the exploitation of itinerant labor by farm interests, and the racially charged legislative backlash against undocumented workers today have all contributed to the economic marginalization of many Mexicans.[16] And as we've seen, Latino poverty—however it occurs—is profound, debilitating, and unacceptable. The Compton example shows that many Mexican Americans deeply believe that discrimination against them may be just as easily visited on them by blacks in office than by whites; it is an ongoing malady with material consequences.

Yet, as a causal matter, it is of a very different kind than the marginalization of African Americans in the United States precisely because of the pervasive institutionalized oppression linked to dark skin. Whatever one thinks of the imbalance of racial power in Compton, it is not because blacks hate Latinos or think them incapable of governing based on their racial or ethnic identities. It appears instead as a contest of racial/ethnic spoils over a place no one else wants. This complicated dynamic, I believe, is often obscured by "diversity" as a legal rationale (although diversity has other benefits as a basis for action). The diversity debates of other, more privileged places (like university admissions, for example) have nothing to do with the contest for local control in struggling nonwhite parts of the United States. Except perhaps in the negative. Our interviews with Latinos in Compton indicated a noticeable impatience with black people's claims to a discriminatory past. This is consistent with the assumption discussed in the last chapter. Nonblacks weary quickly of the exceptionalism of black marginalization (which can compound it). As one seventy-one-year-old Compton grandmother put it, "Blacks always talk about slavery and what they went through, and they feel like people owe them things." As we've seen, the persistence of de facto racial discrimination against black Americans (and the effects of past de jure discrimination) reflects far more than slavery. If anything, the systematic use of violence against blacks is an important distinction in the annals of subjugation; it is a standing reminder of the worst that can happen to a race in a country that also promises so much. But for now the point is that there is probably a real difference in some of the modes of marginalization experienced by African Americans and Latino groups generally. Regardless of whether the difference is scrutinized, it is at least stubbornly acknowledged in a way that separates rather than unites people of color. (We'll see more of how that separation works below.)

Discrimination contests yield no medals, but it is instructive to know the source of opportunity denied. We can be cautiously hopeful that the major barriers to Latino mobility are not generally racist in nature, because if they are the remedies change. That is not the same as saying they're not substantial.[17] And, as I've tried to demonstrate thus far, the structure of limited opportunity for Latinos is often exacerbated, if not determined, by the status of the places they inhabit. Like many working-class "first suburbs," Compton represents a nominally diverse place of limited resources, stretched against significant constraints, where interests more easily clash than coalesce.

Geographers teach us that so much of the American story is migration of one kind or another. People tend to go where they can. As the Rational Dad from the introduction showed, being middle class signifies housing choice. Yet a defining characteristic of minority life in the United States—especially among blacks and American Indians, and for long stretches of time among most Latino groups, the Chinese, and Vietnamese—is going only where you are allowed to go or going only where you can afford to go on limited means. We see this in Compton and the many places like it across the country. White laborers and middle-class industrial workers settled it and tried but eventually failed to keep blacks out. The population rapidly tipped, and the new black majority tried to build a suburban life and a political base there. Structural transformations in the economy took their toll, and the forces of ghettoization set in. Blacks who could go, left. Latino immigrants, mostly Mexican, came to Compton and areas nearby because they could afford it, and because it was largely unwanted. This is both the attraction and the vulnerability of low-income places. The black people still in Compton did not choose new neighbors who did not speak their language or who cared little about their history of slavery and Jim Crow. They probably feel strongly about the citizenship gains they so recently won. Some are fearful about losing a majority. The Latinos who "chose" Compton had no say about their black neighbors either. They feel strongly about making citizenship gains, particularly in a part of the country that many feel owes them a historical debt for expropriated land and culture. Many Latinos are still surprised to learn they are a majority in Compton. As we'll see in a moment, given a choice, most blacks and Latinos probably would not have chosen each other.

If this is the basic story of difference together, then it is truly a wonder why anyone assumes that people of color—especially poor people of color in competition with each other for the most basic opportunities— would ever get along. Keep in mind that this story of a racially divided place leaves out an equitable assessment of the place itself. Though the point of this chapter is to critique assumptions about racelessness, the point of this book is to examine the role of place in determining opportunity. What if Compton cannot afford to run itself? What if there are simply too few spoils to distribute equitably among a lower-income population that happens to be Latino and black (and increasingly Filipino)? What if all the attention to racial and ethnic conflict has hidden the unfair relationship that Compton has to its regional neighbors? These are the wider questions of equity and spatial opportunity that get us beyond the racial/ethnic stalemate.

The irreducible truth, it seems to me, is that from different paths of historical marginalization too many blacks and too many Latinos in places like Compton contend with the same limited capacity for economic opportunity. They are held in place by many of the same contemporary structural barriers to mobility. As we have seen in the previous chapters, these barriers include high-poverty schools and low achievement rates, limited housing options outside of resource-poor communities, uneven rates of political participation, significant crime and safety concerns, serious barriers to stable public health outcomes, weak entry points to jobs in a low-wage economy, chronic credit vulnerability, fiscally stressed localities, inferior transportation options, and subtle and not-so-subtle forms of segregation. They are also sapped by discrimination of all kinds. Put together, these deficits make for populations that are perceived by others as more needy, less deserving, more dangerous, and less capable. Structures of separation then combine to make blacks and Latinos less protected from broader sources of economic stability in American life today. To me, these structural barriers and frailties explain better than competing claims to discrimination the sad consistency of the dyad "black and Latino" in statistics about disadvantage. Understanding these shared structural barriers, then, is no doubt the most important step in achieving progressive mutuality among the groups who most need it. As the Compton example shows, however, that understanding is clearly frustrated by an enduring sense of inter-minority inequity just when a book like this proposes equity as the superior principle for reform across society.

To explore this contradiction some more we should go beyond Compton to see whether equity has a chance to overcome entrenched racial attitudes often disguised behind colorblindness and minority group unity. We won't travel far. In the next section, we see how these two aspects of the sixth assumption merge and dissipate in the broader Los Angeles context. The evidence is sobering and the challenges great.

## The Multiracial Myth of Colorblindness

Within Compton's fraught and complicated racial transition are layers of harmony, cross-racial coping, cultural discovery, and conflict—enough evidence of conflict to undermine the assumption of inter-minority unity. Raceless it isn't; fractious it can be. But how well do we know what we perceive? What happens when we examine the racial attitudes not just of blacks and Latino groups in LA, but of whites and Asians, too? What differences might we see among Asian or Latino recent immigrant attitudes compared to those who have been in the United States for two, three, or more generations? And finally, because we are ultimately concerned with how assumptions about colorblindness create material consequences—good and bad—for people, what is the relationship between racial preferences and spatial outcomes?

These are the questions that concern my students, who come from a generation with a very different relationship to the assumption about racial labels than my own. They are decidedly ambivalent. On the one hand, they remind me that racial attitudes are at least as important as racial structures to any analysis of hoped-for reforms. While they are saddened by the persistence of negative stereotypes and what they'd call racist attitudes, they insist that "this generation" is more mixed, more accepting (not "tolerant"), and more accustomed to diversity as a way of life. They perceive negative race consciousness to be waning. On the other hand, they tend to use the phrase "black and Latino" often as almost synonymous sides of the same coin of disadvantage.

The cauldron in which to test these views and these questions is segregation. As we have seen, segregation is one of the best catchall measures of economic inequity. Unless a segregated community became so by choice (wealthy enclaves) or necessity (new immigrant arrivals), then segregation typically indicates a group that is captive to its vulnerabilities, with weak institutions, scarce political pull, and little market power in the regional context.

Specifically, we would want to learn not just whether segregation persists (as we did in chapter 4), but why. And we should view it in a twenty-first-century metropolitan area, full of nearly all relevant racial and ethnic groups, occupying every class status. LA County fits the bill as well as any other. The county may seem like an odd choice because California is unlike most of the country. Yet it represents an incredibly diverse metropolis where a large population of both indigenous folks and waves of immigrants live regionally on a politically fragmented map. It has new ethnic enclaves and postindustrial "first suburbs" like Compton. It is a cutting-edge "majority–minority" metropolis that has seen the fading of black political power in favor of Latino and increasingly Asian power. It is also one of the ten most segregated parts of the country. And this is where Camille Zubrinsky Charles conducted some of the most detailed research on inter- and intra-group attitudes of any place in the United States, looking not only at attitudes among the poor but at everybody.[18]

If the assumption of colorblindness is wrong and segregation is the proof, we might expect the case to be made in several steps. First, individuals would have to strongly identify with their own racial or ethnic group. Then they would harbor positive and negative generalizations about other groups relative to their own—that is, stereotypes. Next, they would build on these stereotypes to construct ideal places to be and places to avoid. Finally, choice—if one has much of it—would be activated in seeking out those ideal places and avoiding the others. The result, we might expect, would be segregated residential arrangements reflecting people's preferences, prejudices, and means.

Sure enough, Charles found striking evidence of the persistence, baggage, and performance of racialized thinking among all groups, helping to explain segregated living patterns. By that, I mean that all groups exhibited strong consciousness about themselves as a distinct racial or ethnic group. They held a range of stereotypes about one another, mostly negative but some positive. These views did not necessarily start in the United States, but were carried here from different cultures then modified over the time spent here. And these groups have strong corresponding preferences about whom they want to live among, which they perform through the residential choices they make whenever they can. Using an unprecedented database and a small army of interviewers matched to interviewees by language, Charles studied thousands of both native and foreign-born respondents of Mexican, Central American, Japanese, Chinese, Korean, white (Anglo), and African American origin.

## The Common Fate of the Race

If the assumption were true that people now recognize their common humanity and don't view life through the prism of their accidental race, then nearly everybody would deny that what happens to their racial or ethnic group affects them. Charles's interviewers asked that question about "common-fate racial identity" and found that majorities of all groups—between 54 and 72 percent—said yes to "some" degree. Groups certainly varied, particularly by degree. Only 6 percent of native Asians said "a lot," compared to 20 percent of whites, 37 percent of blacks, and 31 percent of foreign-born Latinos.[19] As one might expect, feelings of in-group attachment decreased for Asians and Latinos over generations—yet not for whites and blacks. Clearly, there is a lot of race-conscious thinking out there—particularly in the original binary of blacks and whites—and people's racial identities color their perceptions of well-being.

## The Persistence of Stereotype

But do those beliefs affect residential arrangements? A lot may be mediated through stereotypes. The five traits Charles asked about describe a desirable profile as someone who is intelligent, prefers self-sufficiency, speaks English well, and is not involved in drug use or gang activity. An undesirable profile has the opposite traits.[20] She found that people do indeed cling to both favorable and unfavorable stereotypes about their own group and others. While Charles found that all people tend to feel pretty good about their own group, every group ranks whites and Asians as having mostly favorable traits. As the Compton example shows, there is significant expression of negative stereotyping between Latinos and blacks in LA. Asians held the highest level of negative stereotyping about blacks and Latinos. Generally, foreign-born Asians and Latinos had the highest negatives of all about other groups.

If my students—and Charles—are right, there is a material connection between these bad attitudes and persistent residential segregation, which seriously undermines any hope of a color-blind LA. Pause to consider again how stereotypes do their work. Take the bank branch example from the first chapter. Banks are a noble but ordinary institution in our regular life, a church of money in which we expect a seriousness about resources, one that is heavily regulated by the government. In order to get a job there, you have to be intelligent, speak English well, be free of drug use and gang activity, and perhaps believe in self-sufficiency (you're certainly not there to give away money). Then recall my unscientific breakdown of employees in various roles up the bank hierarchy. The result is a racial schema—whites and Asians in the positions of greatest professional responsibility and blacks and Latinos at the lower rungs. We see this composition every day in lots of settings, and take for granted that each race is represented roughly according to its abilities. Everything about the bank implicitly reinforces our stereotypes.

Now switch to the housing context. Out in the world of neighborhoods, we have to rely more on what we think we know about our prospective neighbors. So, unless we know many different people well, we superimpose on the setting our stereotypes from the bank example plus other racial traits we've seen in movies, on the news, and in passing exchanges with others that have made an impression. Some impressions suggest suffering like the impoverished black Katrina masses, or undocumented brown women being raided from a poultry factory by armed immigration officers. Others indicate pluck and sacrifice, like the Korean or Iranian store owner, or stability, like the white soccer mom beside a minivan. They are varied and endlessly complex, but for our purposes here they boil down to just a few snap categories—efficacious or not, desirable or problematic, prospect or threat. Mostly, these impressions reinforce the idea that Asians and whites are smart and responsible, Latinos are hardworking yet caught up in poverty, and blacks, well, there are exceptions like the president but . . .

Again, Charles's work on stereotypes establishes a link between these kind of racial attitudes and residential preferences. When these same Angelenos were asked about their ideal neighborhood composition, of course diversity won—but barely. On the one hand, all nonwhite groups (native and foreign-born) desired a neighborhood that was about 40 percent populated with their own group and an average percentage of every other groups around 16 to 20 percent. All nonwhite groups expressed a desire to live among a white population that was between 20 and 30 percent of the total neighborhood. Whites, on the other hand, are less open-minded. Twelve percent of whites would prefer to live *exclusively* among other whites, a percentage much greater than even recent immigrants who have language and cultural reasons for living in homogenous enclaves. On average, whites preferred to live in a neighborhood that's over 50 percent white. Adding support for the Compton conflict, whites share with native Latinos and foreign-born Latinos and Asians a distinct antipathy for any black neighbors at all (20, 19, 38, and 44 percent, respectively).[21] Charles's findings suggest that class consciousness among Asians and Latinos is a major reason for preferring whites or people of the same race in their ideal neighborhood; they consistently identify blacks with economic failure.[22] Asians in particular report holding very durable negative stereotypes of blacks. Charles found that, even after accounting for other issues associated with being an immigrant, negative stereotypes about the economic status of blacks and Latinos contributes to Asian avoidance of these groups as neighbors. Yet in another irony of black exceptionalism, blacks do not return the animus. As Charles concludes, "Despite their status as least preferred neighbors, blacks were among the most open to integration with other groups[.]"[23]

## How to Be an American

The greater preference among nonwhite groups for living among whites is complicated; it does not represent a single-minded desire to be around them. In fact, nonwhites seek that closeness at a perceived cost: racial hostility, difficulty getting along with whites, and fear of discrimination. All the nonwhite groups Charles interviewed expressed these attitudes—negative stereotypes—about whites despite a preference for living near them. (Middle-class blacks are the one group that shows less preference for white neighbors and more suspicion of white hostility.)[24] Obviously something more than race is involved. Why would Asians and Latinos generally prefer proximity to whites if they find them difficult, while at the same time avoiding blacks?

Two currents are flowing, I think, to produce racial stratification guided by class concerns. In the first, blacks are still struggling against the old racial binary—a dual housing market—almost as old as the republic. When blacks of any particular socioeconomic level are compared with their counterparts in other groups, they live in neighborhoods that are more segregated and less affluent. When affluent blacks live with whites—at a rate of class-based integration that is lower than for any other group—they live with *less*-affluent whites. From these findings, scholars have concluded that blacks enjoy fewer advantages of home ownership than does any other group. Indeed, they are often penalized for owning a home.[25]

The other current applies generally to nonwhites who are not black. It is the old spatial assimilation model that began in the late nineteenth century with industrialization and European immigration. They are a mere generation or two away from middle-class status. The spatial assimilation model helps to explain why more recent Asian and Latino immigrants enjoy mobility patterns that generally improve with time, from new immigrant to second generation, gaining in social and economic benefits the longer they are in the country and with more educational attainment, just as European immigrants did generations before.[26] In LA, "differences among native whites and Latinos—both poor and affluent—are relatively small," Charles explains.[27] In terms of residential proximity and racial contact with one another, poor whites live near more affluent whites at similar rates as poor Latinos; as incomes rise, they share space with whites of similar status at nearly the same rates.[28] And while poor foreign-born Latinos live in neighborhoods that are less white than poor whites do, the neighborhoods are actually more affluent.[29] For Asians of all groups Charles studied, both indicators of neighborhood proximity to and racial contact with whites showed less racial closeness yet a surrounding environment of even greater affluence.[30] What these data show is less coerced racial and economic residential segregation for Latinos and Asians and greater benefits associated with choice—as both newcomers and with time. This is exactly as we would hope in a pluralist culture.

Asian and Latino immigrants, therefore, are doing what is in their clear economic interests to do, though based on a schema of instructive stereotypes. The choice they ultimately enjoy in achieving greater middle-class stability over time is the reward at the end of tough racial maneuvering. These amount to racial rules that, like our spatial rules, work against true colorblindness and, instead, in favor of more segregation of blacks. In this way, the six assumptions weave in among one another again, reflecting largely race-based, but also mobility- and class-based attitudes that—together with the other opportunity-determining factors discussed earlier—find tangible form in our residential arrangements.[31] In turn, our residential arrangements do a lot to condition opportunity—and the lack thereof.

Missed in all the attention to people of color is how these dynamics impeach white claims to colorblindness. On every measure Charles studied, whites showed the greatest overall fealty to racial rules of stereotype, preference, and place. For whites, as Charles writes, "[m]aintaining their status advantages and privilege requires a certain amount of social distance from nonwhites—particularly blacks and Latinos, the groups at the bottom of the social queue—since more than token integration would signal an unwelcome change in status relations."[32] Whites also benefit the most from Asian and Latino perceptions of their superiority. "Indeed, this racial hierarchy—in which whites occupy the top position and blacks the bottom—is so pervasive that immigrant adaptation includes the internalization and even exaggeration of it among Latinos and Asians, as seen in the patterns of preferences for both groups."[33] Asians have clearly had more success navigating this racial obstacle course. Their rates of college attendance, interracial marriage, and transracial adoption all attest to greater social acceptance by whites of a people perceived to be transcending nonwhite status—or as George Yancey and other scholars have suggested, "becoming white."[34]

## Trying Different Frameworks
### Help Blacks, Too

Of all the difficult conversations broached in this book, rebutting the assumption of shared, non-racial humanity may be the hardest. The sensitivities peak. The risk of giving short shrift to critical perspectives is great. The suspicion that any author has the ulterior motive of playing a covert blame game is real for every reader regardless of race. Most of all, the wish that the assumption be true is so crucial to our progress. The more diverse we become as a nation, the less we can rely on racial categories to distribute opportunity. What, then, can we fairly conclude from this discussion about the dynamics of colorblindness in the context of equity and progressive mutuality?

First, we must remove the obfuscation of the assumption itself. Colorblindness—either as a value or a principle of minority unity—is not only wrong, but also damaging. It captures all the errors of the previous assumptions within an aspiration that attempts dangerously to justify them. For example, in the data from Los Angeles, we see the very groups that will constitute the new majority of minorities embracing the first assumption (that the middle class are self-sufficient) and the second (that preserving that status means distance from the poor). The embrace is not wrong because the principles are bad. The embrace is problematic because it's too often made in the service of excluding others (a benefit to the excluder) based on the persistence of negative stereotyping. Further, in the color-blind context, we see the third and fourth assumptions embraced, too. Segregation is deemed a utilitarian by-product of rational mobility decisions, unmotivated by the racial animus that comes out when you ask about it. It's presumed to be voluntary and innocent, yet somehow promotes the same old inequities that hinder opportunity in segregated places. As for poverty, assuming too much similarity between black and Latino poverty precludes the closer analysis of the differences. If both are bad and increasingly concentrated (especially in Los Angeles), yet one is characterized by enduring racial discrimination and the other by more temporary labor exploitation, what do you do?

One answer is to consider place-based equity strategies, as I do in the next chapter. But here it is important to emphasize that those strategies explicitly contemplate helping blacks, too. The final chapter focuses directly on what I mean by increasing opportunity by emphasizing the importance of place through equity. For now, the crux of those varied efforts is to work first to recognize and dismantle the many inequities experienced by poorer parts of our region—a result, I have argued, of localism. Next, we should adopt reform strategies that promote a more equitable distribution of the kinds of public amenities that stimulate growth, such as transportation spending, infrastructure maintenance, affordable housing, and inter-district school enrollment. There are many creative ways to overcome the assumptions that have produced our doomed spatial rules and to broaden the middle class for generations to come. The means will vary by regional dynamics and the particular makeup of populations. Yet across the board, it is a good bet, as this chapter shows, that whatever plans are hatched should consciously help blacks, too.

Why? Because of the durability of racial segregation, place-based mobility strategies that aid blacks probably aid others; because of the spatial assimilation model, strategies that target other groups first might not wind up aiding blacks at all. So, as a practical matter, reforms must take account of the peculiar interests of blacks. This is not to say that Latinos do not experience meaningful discrimination or that blacks don't harbor hateful or demeaning stereotypes about Asians, Latinos, or whites. The reason is that the attitudes that fuel the deepest racism with a material difference still fall hardest on African Americans. Charles's work convincingly shows how this type of racist thinking is held by immigrants who come to the United States with both their own racial belief systems as well as what they've internalized about ours from American media. This thinking is then discharged in continued patterns of disadvantage across the landscape. Racial animus against blacks is the root type of racial disadvantage, the closest thing to consensus contempt we know. Deep-rooted racial animus is common to nearly every aspect of structural immobility that I discussed in the Compton analysis. Equitable solutions that don't forget that and plan for its elimination will most efficiently reduce racial barriers against *any* racial or ethnic group.

In other words, antiracism must be a an underlying component of progressive mutuality in the future just as past racism has been an underlying component of structural immobility today.

This is a default type of argument, and I can anticipate two strong rebuttals. The first is that changing demographics as a result of Latino and Asian immigration and birth rates indicate that we may well see whole new strategies to undermine opportunity for these groups that don't resemble anything African Americans have experienced. To make antiblack racism the default evil is narrow-minded and archaic. As the politics of immigration have shown nationally, even blacks can stand aside when the needs and concerns of new communities are targeted.

I can't deny any of this. Racial profiling of Latinos as threatened in recent state legislation; violent hate crimes against day laborers; high rates of subprime targeting and subsequent foreclosures among Latinos are all examples of growing animus toward Latino groups in the United States to add to a long history of labor exploitation. However, much of the anti-Latino discrimination prohibited by U.S. civil rights law is inflicted against darker-skinned Latinos.[35] Studies show that patterns of racial segregation of black and mixed-race Latinos are consistent with those for African Americans.[36] The two types of discrimination often converge somewhere at the color line. Where they don't, one hopes either that discrimination decreases over time (as it has against the Irish, Italians, and Jews) or that it is eliminated by the same sort of place-oriented policy reforms that aid blacks.

The second counterargument asks, what about Latino poverty? The very reason we tend to use "black and Latino" together in statistics about disadvantages in mobility is that Latino numbers are shockingly close to those of blacks in poverty, unemployment, lost wealth, incarceration, and poor school performance. Dominicans and Puerto Ricans in the New York City region have experienced crushing rates of poverty for decades. (For that matter, there are also pockets of persistent Asian poverty around the country, for instance among Chinese in New York City and Vietnamese in Louisiana.) Although concentrated poverty remains highest among blacks, there is increasing evidence of more concentrated poverty among Latinos—particularly in Los Angeles— where studies show that the assimilation benefits of ethnic enclaves may fall off for at least second-generation Mexican Americans.[37] To conflate the two as if they must be the same is to risk seriously ignoring important cultural, political, and systematic aspects of the poverty dynamic among Latino communities.

This too can't be dismissed out of hand. It is possible that reforms and interventions that work to empower poor blacks do not necessarily work as effectively in poor Latino communities. In some respects, the barrio and the ghetto are not the same place when it comes to the persistent lack of opportunity. They are, of course, the hardest cases. What makes them hard is the extent of their common isolation from resources, their dangers and instabilities, their geographic irrelevance from places of power. In that sense, they are the most important places in which to make equitable investments in people. Since all over the country black ghettos have remained entrenched in deep poverty the longest and they consistently vote Democratic while other groups may be perceived as potential Republican voters, I argue that their difficult transformation must not be left out of any plan—but it should not be the only plan.

## Revisiting Compton

Which brings us back to Compton. Strangely enough, Compton—urban suburb, majority–minority, postindustrial, racially tense, working class and perennially struggling to regain some semblance of its past in the blue-collar middle class—may soon represent the United States. It has characteristics in common with first suburbs outside Philadelphia and Chicago, the North Jersey towns of Roselle and East Orange, the fiercely independent way station of Miami Gardens between Miami–Dade and Broward Counties, and even Houston's Fifth Ward. Stuck within a localist framework of governance, it could go in several directions. Latinos could gradually marshal their voting strength and share local power with what might become an increasingly responsive group of black elected officials. Or blacks could draw political lines in the sand, resisting power sharing until

Vaca's revenge strategy inevitably sweeps in overwhelming Latino control. A third possibility is that blacks—as many are already doing[38]—simply go quietly, giving up a hard-won home for even less expensive places way out among the coyotes and cacti of the Antelope Valley. Compton would then convert into yet another nearly all-Latino town in Los Angeles, solidly poor and working class until time, political organization, and recovery perhaps brought more opportunity.

Only the first of these scenarios holds long-term promise for both groups. The others resign themselves to a strategy of whatever the ground will give you—if it becomes fertile, then feast, if not, then famine. Yet the first—power sharing and cultural integration—can be made better by seeking more than the ground has so far given in unwanted places like Compton and East Orange. The ground there has to be made richer by sharing more in the bounty of the region around them. They need to leverage their fair share of what wealthier communities already receive. And working-class families in search of stability and opportunity need more options than the few out-of-the-way places that will take them. It is to these particular kinds of reforms that we turn in the final chapter.

## Counterfactual: Common-Interest Politics

In contrast to our color-blind aspirations, the divisions in Compton, California, follow a long, unspoken tradition of suspicion, disparagement, and avoidance in American communities. Hostilities are often most volatile when groups feel that they're in competition with one another for scarce resources. This tradition is older than the competition among nonwhites. The Industrial Revolution is replete with examples of ethnic clashes among European immigrant minorities who would later "become white" through assimilation.[39] A similar competitive tension feels evident today in white resistance to truly embrace the colorblindness of popular rhetoric. As the white population in the

United States diminishes in relation the whole, and as the rules on mobility (e.g., going to college, buying a house, building assets through stable employment) become unstable, it's not surprising that many whites still see no reason to more thoroughly reevaluate their material relationships with blacks and other minorities.

But what if ours was a social culture in which racial and ethnic difference was merely cosmetic—interesting, expressive, and capable of producing fascinating subworlds of trends, fashions, speech patterns, and norms that enrich our lives but have little to do with our welfare? Imagine further that our *political* culture was steadfastly based on interests. Voters would think about their interests without filtering them through their cultural identities.[40] They would be less vulnerable to covert appeals to underlying racist, xenophobic, or other prejudiced beliefs by politicians. Politics (at least local politics) would revolve much more around issues affecting welfare. Voters would become even more sophisticated about evaluating policy according to their own interests and the balance of other interests. The greater good would be easier to discern.

In Compton, though tensions would not disappear, this could dramatically reconfigure politics. Integrating recent immigrants is a bona fide interest of any community that has them. Ensuring the engagement of all students, maximizing the diverse resources of the learning environment, and employing fair hiring procedures are all critical interests of a community working to promote opportunity for its families. And respecting the needs and contributions of an indigenous populace is an interest of any community committed to putting scarce energy toward growth and stability. The alternative—blocking other groups, leaving needs unattended, or working toward displacement of predecessor majorities—is time-consuming, wasteful work that takes generations to complete. Meanwhile, more cohesive communities, content with greater resources devoted to their own sphere, will advance in the current municipal competition for regional advantage. The places that have failed to coalesce socially and culturally will squander the ability to work toward broader equity. They will lose.

# 8

## THE COSTS OF INEQUALITY AND A VISION
## FOR A MORE EQUITABLE AMERICA

If the last several chapters explored the imperatives for overcoming our erroneous assumptions about place, class, and race, this chapter attempts to point the way toward beloved communities of opportunity.* Books like this one must take care not to promise too much, because the great diversity of regions and circumstances can make specific proposals sound laughable. However, certain generalizations hold. They form a basis for understanding what is a growing movement among scholars, elected officials, and advocates in a field called regional or metropolitan equity.[1] That ungainly name reflects the preceding emphasis on reaching equity through more spatial equality. Rather than simply list inequalities in the air, it asks how they occur in place. Rather than opine about have and have-not people, it documents the have and have-not

---

*I borrow the term "beloved communities" from Martin Luther King Jr., who described it throughout his writing as the ultimate goal of nonviolence and the creation of true integration and brotherhood. Putting aside King's distinct Christian overtones, I mean it here to embody many of his thoughts about the equitable end of a long process of reconciliation, an effort joined by love and a desire for justice. A beloved community is the redemption of our core values.

places in which they seek opportunity. Metropolitan equity recognizes how a norm of progressive mutuality can join law with public policy in reforming our current approaches to middle-class opportunity. And, despite great variations among thinkers, most of them target the reform of localism as the primary threat to a broader, more stable, and more inclusive middle class. Race and socioeconomic status are not ignored in this framework. However, the region is posited as an important, often overlooked ground for implementing efficient growth strategies.

With that said, we can begin to think about specific approaches along three straightforward principles of integration: mixing income, increasing equitable arrangements, and decreasing local inequities. I recognize that these three principles of integration might be considered part of first-generation strategies (or desegregation). That is, they alter ingrained structures that have separated people by race, class, and place. By contrast, second-generation strategies (true integration) would aim to improve the quality of interactions among people in more structurally integrated settings. For example, the problem of segregated schools requires first-generation strategies, while the problem of segregated classrooms within "diverse" schools requires second-generation strategies. The first is often a precondition for the second. I will join others in exploring promising second-generation strategies in subsequent work. For now, the following integration principles of metropolitan equity represent first-generation groundwork still to be laid.

*Mixed-income living.* For good reason, the mixed-income development has become the conceptual centerpiece of most government housing programs over the last twenty years. The basic idea is to integrate, say, 20 percent of units made affordable through some type of subsidy in the middle of 80 percent market-rate units.[2] Imagine, for example, a new rental building in Brooklyn, New York, with thirty-five apartments. Scattered throughout the structure with no discernible difference in quality would be seven apartments designated for people of lower income bought in under a screening program subsidized by a government agency and a local nonprofit development corporation. In theory, this not-so-new form of economic integration assuages middle-class owners' fears about living among a critical mass of poor neighbors while giving poorer residents access to all the amenities, local relationships, and wealth potential of the American Dream. It is an equitable recognition of the power of place to determine opportunities in education, peer groups, recreation, information networks, quality food access, and political representation. It is a principle closely associated with the work of Angela Glover Blackwell and PolicyLink.[3] Moreover, it builds communities by putting people in position to talk during elevator rides, arrange playdates for their children, debate local elections, borrow butter, and console about a death. It is a particularly cost-effective solution within cities, but it is not used enough. Yet for our purposes, the main problem is that the mixed-income principle is not spread to the logical ends of its potential. I mean, it is not employed regionally where the scale of the numbers could make a greater difference.

*Increasing equities.* The second principle is increasing equities—specifically, increasing equitable regionalism. This principle is kindred to much of Myron Orfield's work.[4] The root of this idea is local deconcentration in the regional context. The region is paramount because it represents the relevant fiscal universe. People live their lives regionally—schooling locally, working a county or two over, shopping somewhere else, seeing doctors and attending movies in yet another part, all the while being subject to market rates and conditions set on a regional scale. Even towns enthralled with their own local power recognize the primacy of regionalism by their constant competition for infrastructure funding, a new office park, or to beat back a proposed waste facility next door. Since the region is the real focus, it should be the measure of what is concentrated where and why. Therefore, the second principle of integration simply asks where in the region are wealth opportunities concentrated? Where is poverty concentrated? Where is the need for multilingual services greatest? Tax capacity? Tax burdens? Crime? The goal is deconcentration of any variable that significantly affects opportunity. The more disparate the distribution of benefits and burdens, the higher the costs to the region.

*Deconcentrating inequities.* The third principle is really an offshoot of the second. It has to do with deconcentration, too, but of more localized inequities and reflects some of Manuel Pastor's thinking.[5] Sometimes thinking regionally is merely a framework for seeing local unfairness that cannot be remedied by moving people to resources. Sometimes deconcentrating inequities simply means making the fortunate pay more to locate a costly regional good outside their backyards. As we saw in chapter 5, environmental harms are a good example of this. You cannot put a piece of a power plant in every community served by it, so the concentration of the hazard will remain. However, the inequity visited upon those unfortunate people who disproportionately bear its burdens can be taxed to the more fortunate remainder who are still benefiting from its presence. Those revenues can be used to help the burdened community better withstand the noxious use. Since those burdens often spread out in multiples, fairness compels us to be creative about reducing local deficits. The third principle therefore protects a relatively powerless place from being the repository of other places' negative externalities.

These three principles help erect a simple theoretical framework of metropolitan equity for some extremely complicated problems. Beyond these principles, scholars, elected officials, and advocates talk about a number of specific policies, such as inclusionary zoning, tax revenue sharing, county-wide school districts, merger and consolidation, and inter-local agreements among municipalities. I will discuss some of these and others in the scenarios that follow. But it's the principles, not the details, that matter most. The fundamental point is to see the problems of rising inequality, fiscal stress, and demographic shifts within this framework of regional equity. Doing so renders these suggestions mere guidelines about the creative ways that strapped and divided regions can work toward a more sustainable and equitable future.

Finally, what makes any of this beloved? There is regionalism and there is equitable regionalism. By itself, regionalism offers many struggling municipalities a universe of shared services agreements that will lower costs and help balance budgets. Three towns can decide on their own to consolidate into a single police or fire department, to create a joint water authority, or to share snow removal costs. These arrangements have to overcome political localism, and for that reason are most likely forged between more like-minded (and similar) localities. That would be efficient, but not equitable, regionalism. Equity enters through an appreciation of the more distant Other, the towns closer to the brink, partnering over these issues as well as the issues that divided them in the first place, like housing, revenues, social services, and education. As the next section demonstrates, this fundamental characteristic of equity stands in stark contrast to the assumptions our grandparents bequeathed us. We have done community before. Less tried are beloved communities.

## How the Assumptions Cumulatively Create Equity Imperatives

Before we apply metro equity principles to specific prescriptions, we should be clear about how this analysis got here. The book began by exploring—and debunking—two commonly held assumptions about the connection between opportunity and residential life in the United States, at least since World War II. These two—the assumption that middle-class lives are self-sufficient and that preserving that status necessarily requires a certain physical distance from the poor—are also hallmarks of localism and the frames of thinking it promotes. According to the first two assumptions, that thinking goes something like this: As a middle-class person, I should be entitled to noninterference with my hard-won status. I receive no handouts. What we as middle-class people make together through local decision making is the perfection of citizenship, the kind of stability that democratic participation justifiably produces. Outsiders are free to create their own local, self-sufficient democracies for their own welfare, which neither affects nor is particularly affected by what's done inside my own self-governing sphere—or town. The poor necessarily threaten this stasis, because they are costly takers who operate under destructive norms and do not meaningfully participate.

Hence, these assumptions are the linchpin of a system of local control, protected by courts' decades-long ratification of zoning and other police powers. The class hostility toward the poor was justified on the logic of localist economics. Since locally derived revenues pay for local expenses like schools and police, it's critical that the balance of residents can pitch in at least as much as they use up in services—that is, they should be home-owner property tax payers. These two assumptions, which are followed in some form or another across much of the country, have the further benefit of being constitutional. They manage to exclude based on race and ethnicity without ever saying so.

But they are not generally true. The middle class—especially the white middle class—has been a favorite of the law and public policies that subsidize directly (through mortgage programs and the tax code, for example) and indirectly (by excluding other people and undesirable uses that might alter the balance). We don't know for certain whether the presence of poor people will destabilize every middle-class community. Yet we do know that the white poor—who outnumber all the other poor—do in fact live among middle-class people without destabilizing local economies. From this, we learn a lot about a selective model of American opportunity that has had terrific benefits for families in terms of quality local schools, safe streets, and rising wealth (tied primarily to the home as an appreciating asset). We are left to wonder, however, whether those benefits can be extended to more of us, and if not, why not.

The why not has so far resulted from the work of the next three assumptions: that segregation no longer exists except when it's voluntary; that racism doesn't limit opportunity anymore; and that persistent poverty reflects poor choices and weak values among the poor themselves. These three assumptions embellish the first two by justifying the exclusions incident to middle-class localism. We saw that segregation is remarkably persistent, especially among blacks of all income groups and increasingly among Latinos. Economic segregation—though less severe—maps almost perfectly on racial segregation. Neither is voluntary. In fact, segregation is a by-product of the second assumption and localism's legal authority to exclude undesirable residents. In other words, segregation is often a negative externality thrown off by the defensive practices of middle-class localities. This makes minorities more concentrated in their sheer numbers and their lack of resources. In turn, concentration makes their communities more vulnerable to racially discriminatory practices, like targeted predatory subprime lending and the wealth erosion that comes from massive foreclosures. It also concentrates whatever rates of poverty they experience, while distancing them from the kinds of resources that tend to make poverty shorter and less severe.

The final assumption is the justificatory capstone on a system of hostile, balkanized interests pretending not to be the product of racialized distribution. In other words, the sixth assumption—that racial labels are no longer helpful or accurate—presents the ruse of colorblindness that can make recognition of inequity so difficult. It also makes multiracial coalitions rare. On the one hand, the assumption is the hallmark of colorblindness, a frame of thinking that too often works to justify white advantage while silencing any attention to it. On the other hand, the assumption suggests solidarity among people of color, whose interests are presumed to be allied. They might be—in some idea of diversity divorced from context—but their mutual dislike (upon which they are far more motivated to act) remains unacknowledged. This means that the assumption that we have no racial differences helps to sustain an unsustainable status quo under which the middle class is shrinking at precisely the time it needs to be growing in pace with increasing numbers of people of color.

What makes it unsustainable? Why couldn't we simply move into a new era of winners and losers—a twenty-first-century binary in which a slight minority of whites and Asians maintain middle-class status or better, and, unfortunately, a slight majority of Latinos and blacks mostly struggle in the working- and lower-middle-class that largely serves them? The answer is mutuality, the mere fact that our relative positions are now increasingly interdependent. This fact alone urges us to do more for one another, because our labor force competitiveness is at stake along with our potential as an informed democracy. Increased competition will also highlight the complexion of the conflicts, fueling a new cycle of racial hostility. Most at risk is our fiscal health. Thus, what we have seen in the last two decades are facts that compel an efficiency rationale for policies of inclusiveness and fairness. The issues now transcend our morality. Communities whose boundaries are more broadly defined and whose people and resources are arranged with greater emphasis on integration have always been called beloved communities (where they could be found). The factual analysis underlying the six assumptions demonstrates that these—ours—have also become *necessary* communities.

## How Can a Region Significantly Reduce Concentrated Poverty over a Decade?

Let's look now at two particular questions and the remedial scenarios to which they give rise. We could examine countless questions in the cauldron of unstable opportunities, but I'll choose two—concentrated poverty and fiscal disparity—as representative problems and explore their possible regional equity remedies. Keep in mind that these are mere simulations, not guaranteed fixes. Both problems are as multifaceted as their solutions, yet most of their solutions are structural. Metro equity approaches provide structural changes that facilitate the greater effectiveness of more localized strategies like smaller class sizes, drug treatment, or revising pension agreements. Following the scenarios, I will briefly discuss some of the other emerging tools of metropolitan equity reform.

As we saw in chapter 6, concentrated poverty represents the cumulative failure of many direct and indirect policies that assisted the creation of neighborhoods where opportunity is hardest to find. From a fiscal standpoint, municipalities with substantial areas of concentrated poverty suffer disproportionately low tax capacity despite disproportionately higher service needs like police and social welfare costs. Since these expenses are necessarily spread across regional taxpayers, the mutuality of limitation is clear. Poverty costs too much for all of us. For these and other reasons, the goal of reducing concentrated poverty over time is in the common interest of the city or town where it occurs as well as her regional neighbors. We might think about time frames in terms of school years in a child's life, growth opportunities in the regional economy, or development phases in housing construction. Goals should be bold yet reasonable. Many scholars think in terms of what a decade can bring.

One scholar who has spent considerable time modeling both problems and regional solutions to concentrated poverty is David Rusk, whom we met earlier. Rusk is both a regionalist and a proponent of "in-place" municipal strategies,[6] who shared a variety of original census-based simulations with me.[7] His work reveals the potential promise of regional strategies versus the more limited effects of local "empowerment" or economic development programs. In the simplified scenario that follows, Rusk alters the usual focus on census tracts showing concentrations of poverty above an arbitrary threshold. Instead, he casts the metric of concentrated poverty as a measure of economic segregation. That is, the spatially concentrated poor occupy physically segregated parts of a region. Camden, New Jersey, provides a representative example.

Camden, population 77,344 in 2011, is a small postindustrial city synonymous with crime, poverty, corruption, and relentless decline. In 2010, the poverty rate for families there was 35.4 percent, compared to 7.0 percent for its three-county region. The region's economic segregation index (or what Rusk calls "economic polarization index") was 40.3—attributable largely to both Camden and the declining suburbs near it as well as the growth of highly exclusionary outer suburbs. Even though many suburban towns in its region have thrived as growth centers in recent decades, Camden is as resource poor as they come. Because the city has ceased to be a major jobs center, it looks less like a central city and more like an impoverished suburb. Sitting on the riverfront coastline across from Philadelphia, this once-great industrial town is—like Flint, Michigan, or Gary, Indiana—one of the few places you might hear antipoverty activists call "unsaveable."

Rusk asks us to stop for a moment and think about the poverty decon-centration strategies those advocates would typically employ. Since the War on Poverty programs of the Johnson administration, the first strat-egy would be some combination of job training and targeted business development. This is what we usually think of when we are concerned about chronic poverty—overcoming local joblessness and trying to help people increase their incomes. The main problem for Camden's poor residents, however, is that even low-wage jobs have mostly disappeared and moved to places with limited access by public transportation. Poor people often lack cars. Yet even with cars, they often lack the skills to obtain more than a poverty-wage, service-sector job.

Nevertheless, the in-place deconcentration solution asks us to imag-ine residents gaining in income sufficient to lift themselves out of pov-erty. Rusk suggests a modest goal of hypothetically raising the incomes of 1,100 people there. This would lower the economic segregation index in the Camden region by a single point, from a baseline of 40.3 to 39.2. Let's call this the "income strategy."[8]

Next, Rusk suggests reducing the economic segregation index of the Camden region through a gentrification strategy. Like so many cities around the country, imagine if 1,100 nonpoor persons decided for some reason (they were attracted by older housing stock, proximity to Phila-delphia and "edginess," for example) to move into Camden from eleven surrounding "sending" municipalities that were growth centers. This seems highly unlikely and would have only a very indirect benefit—if any—to poor Camden residents. Because those people remain poor, the gentrification strategy has the least impact on deconcentrating pov-erty—from a regional economic segregation index of 40.3 to 40.1.

But a third strategy makes a difference. Rusk calls this the "growth share" approach (others call it a mobility strategy). This time he hypothetically moves 1,100 poor Camden residents in groups of one hundred to the same eleven high-growth towns he'd selected in the three-county region. Nothing else has changed. This would lower the Camden region's economic segregation index from 40.3 to 38.2—two full points and twice the benefit of the income strategy. Of course, much has changed. Camden's former poor residents now live in resource-rich communities, with better schools, lower crime, and more varied employment prospects. Economic integration has produced much greater potential for economic opportunity. Camden sees the benefit of fewer poor people. And the eleven "receiving" municipalities now experience greater diversity of people, interests, and incomes. Sharing their growth—even in such small numbers—is demonstrably more equitable than expecting Camden and its poorer suburbs to remain concentrations of resource-poor people. Ten straight years of targeted movement of poor households into more affluent towns would lower Camden's economic segregation index to about 30.0, approximately the level in regions like San Francisco or Charlotte and a far more reasonable benchmark. Deconcentrating Camden's poor without negatively affecting wealthier communities also enhances the likelihood that the two other strategies will work there. For instance, jobs programs can have greater potential impact when demand is below the breaking point. And, as the second assumption shows, the city is deemed more attractive to new, energetic entrants when the ratio of poor residents to others is not so steep. Thus, the growth share strategy has the added benefit of simultaneously increasing the success of the other two strategies—raising local incomes through more effective resources, and attracting residents of higher income to Camden (or gentrification). (The converse is not true—raising incomes and attracting better-off residents would not also promote economic inclusion throughout the Camden region.)

### One Means: Inclusionary Zoning

But how would we accomplish these goals? There are many ways to achieve economic integration of high-growth suburban areas that follow the mixed-income emphasis HUD has adopted through various initiatives since the Clinton administration. New Jersey's own *Mount Laurel* doctrine is perhaps the best-known state-based means of demanding that regions distribute affordable housing equitably across towns. Let's assume for the moment that Rusk's idea of growth share dictates reform. In that case, the Camden three-county region could reach the goal of reducing economic segregation of the city's poor in ten years through the adoption of inclusionary zoning laws. These laws require that all participating jurisdictions enact affordable housing targets pegged to any new residential development. A certain percentage of units affordable to a chosen percentage of area median income (AMI) would be built or otherwise made available.[9] Housing advocates rightly recommend that additional units be set aside in especially high job-growth towns as a matter of efficiency (nearby workforce housing) and equity (to better share the employment gains they've captured by attracting development). This might add one housing unit per every five jobs. Thus, we have three potential variables—the basic set-aside, the AMI percentage, and the jobs-related set-aside. These percentages are the next arena of conflict in the equity context. Because of the fiscal logic of localism (and other factors we've discussed), towns want very low percentages of units for very high percentages of AMI—fewer units but pegged for more affluent new residents. Even when towns are compelled by law to accept their obligations, many find ways to resist or delay—thereby increasing the inequities on others. Equitable regionalism therefore entails serious enforcement at the state regulatory or state judicial level to ensure fairness for all municipalities sharing the burden.

So, to complete the exercise, imagine an aggressive target of 20 percent set-aside of new development. Before the housing bust, Camden and its three-county region saw 4,200 housing units built per year, which would have yielded 840 affordable units annually. If we add in the specific jobs-related units, there are 1,200 more for a total of 5,400. But the poor are not all the same. Many are elderly, and they are preferred by towns seeking to avoid the costs of child-related services. Other poor people are simply not so poor. They, too, are preferred. Camden's concentrated poor, we may assume, are very poor (i.e., below 30 percent of AMI) and frequently families with school-age children. Given this reality, a fair estimate is that only a quarter of the units available through inclusionary zoning would go to very poor working families with children. However, by these numbers, that's roughly 500 families—or 1,250 people—per year. Not a bad investment in social capital. At less aggressive target levels—say, 10 or 15 percent of new units a year—the goals will take longer to achieve, as in an economic downturn. This is the general logic of systematic, incremental, equitable change.

## Being Beloved

Pause for a moment to consider what's also beloved about this efficient strategy. Concentrated poverty is the best place to begin looking at metropolitan equity strategies because it represents the hardest, costliest case to a region, a municipality, and a neighborhood. But the greatest hardship, of course, resides within the person who is poor. That person is more often than not a child. A child of color. When we use a sterile term like inclusionary zoning, we are ultimately talking about including a child in a different world of options, influences, and resources. Ten years is a big chunk of childhood, and Camden's poorest areas have been poor for a lot longer than that. In the alternative, ten years of safe walks home from school, parents in stable employment, and the peace with which to emulate the opportunities of others are among the ingredients of a productive life. These don't always follow integration, but they often do. From the earliest families counseled and relocated to Chicago's suburbs under the *Gautreaux* program,[10] to Montgomery County, Maryland's scattered public housing formulas, even to Houston where so many Katrina survivors discovered new resources in middle-income communities—all over the country, in baby steps of faith, integrationist policies of economic inclusion have helped remake landscapes of opportunity for low-income kids.

Mutuality demands beneficiaries on both sides. The hard numbers on mixed-income mobility strategies like inclusionary zoning indicate no drop in local property values or school achievement. That doesn't mean they're entirely without costs, only that the costs are lower than typically (and hysterically) asserted. If shared equitably across a region, the

213

costs are largely recoverable in savings down the road. But beyond hard numbers are soft lives, made richer and better prepared by inclusiveness. Localism has not only helped manufacture a color-blind resegregation, as we saw in chapters 3 and 4. It has legitimated a dangerous social distance at odds with demography. Just as being a good student has always been more than the quantitative achievement of high scores, preparing for citizenship—let alone leadership—in a polyglot nation also requires the easy navigation of difference. At almost any level, understanding and gaining by difference requires meaningful integration.

## How Are a Region's Tax-Base Disparities Reduced?

The previous example showed how three principles of metropolitan equity—regional mixed-use housing, increasing the equitable distribution of opportunity, and deconcentrating inequities—may reduce disparities between the resources available to have and have-not households. The next scenario asks about ways to reduce the resource disparities between have and have-not municipalities within a region. There are many ways to measure resource disparities. Scholars often compare "fair shares of poverty," meaning a municipality's proportionate share of regional poverty. Another useful measure is a municipality's median family income as a percentage of the regional median, which provides a snapshot of a town's health within its metro area. Both of these measures will translate into relative tax capacity.

Let's look at the three-county Camden, New Jersey, area again and use some of David Rusk's figures before applying any policy remedy. The city of Camden is quite poor, we know. Relative to its region, it is disproportionately poor. If a proportionate share of regional family poverty scores 100 on an index, Camden's share is wildly one-sided. In 1970, for instance, it was 264; in 1980, 397. In 1990, Rusk calculates that it was 458. In 2000, it improved to 382—still almost four times its "fair share" of regional poverty; but in 2010, Camden's fair share of family poverty index resumed its upward climb to 585. Look further at its region's median family income. This measure involves no conversion to an index. It is simply expressed as a percentage of the regional median. Camden's postindustrial decline relative to its suburban neighbors is striking. In 1950, Camden's median family income was 94.0 percent of the tri-county bi-state Philadelphia region's median family income—almost equal. Then it dropped to 83.0 percent in 1960, 72.7 percent in 1970, then 48.5 percent in 1980, and so on until it was 35.0 percent in 2010. This is an awfully familiar story. Less well-known is the decline of area suburbs on the New Jersey side of the Delaware River. Lindenwold and Audubon Park have fallen to 66.0 from 84.0 and 73.0, respectively. Pennsauken went from 93.0 to 85.0, while Pine Hill, Brooklawn, and Magnolia have similarly declined. Even the more affluent suburbs like Stratford, Gibbsboro, and Cherry Hill have seen declines of almost ten points. Of course, income declines produce property tax deficits. Transformed by recession, the metropolitan landscape is seeing even more losers than winners by far.

Which is a good reason to share growth more equitably across the region. This is the essence of tax base revenue sharing policies. They are typically enacted by state legislation, such as Minnesota's Fiscal Disparities Act.[11] However, even New Jersey has such an arrangement under a fourteen-municipality agreement in the northern New Jersey Meadowlands.[12] What these arrangements do is to pool within a region a percentage—say, 10 percent—of each locality's combined tax capacity. The pooled proceeds may then be redistributed to the participating municipalities according to a need-based formula. As Myron Orfield explains, "With this distribution formula, the share a municipality receives is determined by the ratio of the metropolitan area average tax capacity per household and the municipality's tax base per household."[13] The precise numbers are initially a matter of political bargaining; they are ultimately adjusted and dispensed by a commission. Since its passage in 1971, the Minnesota law has been credited with keeping disparities among the 187 municipalities of the Twin Cities area within the range of four to one, rather than an estimated thirteen to one if the statutory mechanism didn't exist.[14]

Rusk demonstrates for the three-county, 101-municipality Camden area as follows. From 1997 to 2003, the area experienced an increase in its total equalized valuation from $52.1 billion to $72.6 billion. If each town had contributed 40 percent of its tax base growth into a pool beginning in the base year of 1997, the shared pool would have been $8.2 billion for redistribution over the period. Camden, for example, would have contributed a total of $31 million over six years. Suppose that the redistribution of the pooled tax base was made according to each municipality's percentage of regional household population as well as its tax capacity. (Tax capacity is tax base per household compared to the regional tax base per household.) During the period, Camden had 5.6 percent of the population, but its tax base per household was just a quarter of the regional average. Therefore, Camden would receive 20 percent, or $1.8 billion from the pooled tax base over six years.[15] Lindenwold would get a 12 percent average annual increase and Pennsauken would receive just 1 percent more. Meanwhile, the more affluent towns in the region would be giving up some growth. Moorestown, for instance, would make a net annual contribution to the regional tax base pool of $74 million and Mount Laurel Township would pay $53 million. Yet over six years these numbers reflect only a 3 percent and 2 percent reduction in tax base, respectively. That's considerable regional gain for little local cost.

## Socioeconomic Integration in Schools

The logic of socioeconomic segregation in schools follows the logic of housing segregation, since both hinge on the demarcation of place to establish eligibility for membership. This is why Kelley Williams-Bolar's ill-fated run for the jurisdictional walls in chapter 1 proved David Rusk's favorite line: "Housing policy is school policy." This is no accidental conundrum. It's a prime feature of localism, and accounts for higher levels of schools segregation in the Northeast and Midwest than in some other parts of the country. School district proliferation follows municipal fragmentation. What makes this especially harmful is the clear impact on educational opportunity. No variable is as important in creating a strong learning environment and reducing racial achievement gaps than the presence of a middle-class majority of kids in the classroom. As we saw in chapter 4, communities put up the greatest resistance to socioeconomic integration, however, even paying more in public revenues to equalize funding to poor students. Unfortunately, there is mounting evidence that funding equalization ends up favoring wealthier districts, or, when it does reach lower-income students, does not alone alter achievement gaps between wealthy and poor students, white/Asian, black/Latino, and so forth.[16] Metropolitan equity therefore demands strategies that promote economically balanced enrollments.

## County-Wide Districts and Inter-District Choice

If the tendency of localism is to constrict into small units and produce inequity, then reversing course typically entails expansion. Inclusionary zoning expands housing choices; expanding school districts to counties may open classrooms to more socioeconomic balance. In fact, regions characterized by larger school districts have lower indices of economic dissimilarity than do those characterized by multiple small ones. The reason is that larger districts provide greater options for all students based on factors other than place. A segregated school district has few internal options for achieving greater socioeconomic balance. This was the dilemma Detroit's segregated schools faced in the 1970s when the Supreme Court decided against cross-district desegregation remedies in *Milliken v. Bradley.* The city's white suburban residents fought bitterly against bearing the burden of desegregating a district from which they had benefited, then abandoned to the outlying suburban counties. On familiar localist grounds of self-determination, the Court agreed with them. Not surprisingly, Detroit's schools remained overwhelmingly black. Perhaps more surprisingly, those suburban districts often advertise for Detroit's black students today. Why? Because the numbers on declining student enrollment dictate that they do so. Without students, those fragmented suburban districts will lose funding and disappear. Few examples better demonstrate the point that our grandparents' policies will doom us today.

## Housing Choice
### Fair-Share Housing

The New Jersey Supreme Court employed most of the principles of metropolitan equity in its initial design of the *Mount Laurel* doctrine in 1975 and its subsequent codification by statute in the New Jersey Fair Housing Act of 1985. For all the flaws in execution and the myriad political attempts to reverse it, the doctrine spells out a theory of progressive mutuality for all to emulate (a few, but not many, states have). Fair-share housing obligates all municipalities—metro area by metro area—to provide their administratively determined share of the regional need for affordable housing. Connected to those obligations must be the affirmative responsibility to market those housing choices to eligible populations in those very places where they are presently concentrated. More successful programs have also included counseling services for families moving to unfamiliar areas. An improvement over many existing plans would be to designate some of the fair share housing allocation to local schools to better accommodate the costs of additional students.[17]

### "Affirmatively Furthering" Fair Housing

Less a plan than a principle, this language derives from the 1968 Federal Fair Housing Act.[18] It called on all housing programs that received any federal money to be designed in such a way as to "affirmatively further" the goal of fair housing—meaning economically and racially integrated housing. This is the first principle of mixed housing tied to a federal mandate (one ignored, ironically, by that same federal government for years, as we saw in chapter 3).[19] The Department of Housing and Urban

Development has been promulgating rules to specify just what the AFFH language (as it's known) should mean. Nevertheless, it is a legal norm, which may soon become binding. Rather than wait for enforcement, forward-thinking regions and municipalities may want to adopt it in their current housing policies.

Additional tools include community land trusts and community land banks in which land is deeded to the preservation of affordable land within areas ripe for gentrification.[20] Housing there may take many different forms, despite the common affordability restrictions. One in particular is the limited-equity cooperative.

## State Statutory Reforms
### Merger and Consolidation

Regional equity advocates like Manuel Pastor argue for a range of approaches, many of which are not legislative.[21] Nonetheless, the legal structure of localism is not easily amended without significant statutory reform, mostly at the state legislative level. One of the most direct ways of achieving the conditions of regional scale is by expanding communities through either merger or consolidation, a process that follows individual state laws that usually include consent by a majority of residents of each municipality.[22] Merged entities in theory find cost reductions through economies of scale. Equitable reforms are also made easier. By analogy, Rusk has long demonstrated that the typically more "elastic" cities of the West and Southwest have lower rates of economic and racial segregation than do the more "inelastic" cities of the East and Midwest.[23] This is not because one is more progressive than the other. Rather, it is because the former have more readily annexed unincorporated county land within the city's boundaries, which enables the population to spread out among the resources of a greater area. Inelastic cities are stuck with the region's wealth configuration and can do little to change things within each jurisdiction. Merger and consolidation are voluntary tools to effect benefits similar to annexation.[24]

## Urban Growth Management

The most well-known example of urban growth management as a means to effect more equitable distributions within a region is the urban growth boundary around Portland, Oregon.[25] This is essentially an anti-sprawl measure that prevents development beyond certain points, thereby increasing density. A tenet of Smart Growth advocacy, any policy that either prohibits or disincentivizes the second assumption—putting distance between the middle-class and low-income populations in order to preserve the status of both—assists in the conditions for regional equity and the benefits of integration.

## Metropolitan Government

This is typically what people assume when you mention metropolitan equity, but pure metro governments have rarely ever been tried (Minnesota, Oregon, and Louisville, Kentucky, are three notable exceptions).[26] However, metropolitan planning organizations that often discharge state planning law functions are a useful analogy to true metro governance (though their power is typically only advisory). They demonstrate that for certain limited purposes, a governmental authority can have regional authority beyond county government. Thus, hypothetically, a state could fashion metropolitan government to exercise plenary power over equity issues such as affordable housing or the siting of family services institutions.

## Home Rule Amendment

Home rule effectively delegates authority to local governments to regulate matters of local concern except where the state has expressly reserved power to itself.[27] Amending home rule authority in states that make this grant to municipalities is the most direct route to curbing the excesses of localism, but it is not the same thing as equitable regional-ism. However, amending home rule for the express purpose of transfer-ring local control of equity issues over to a regional or metropolitan authority for total control, conditional veto power, or oversight would be.[28] Such a frontal assault is not without its merits (and its unintended consequences), yet it seems far from here.[29]

Instead, the constriction of home rule authority has typically occurred through the backdoor of its own terms—that is, by states leg-islatively occupying a field once considered purely local, as New Jersey did with its requirement of regional fair-share housing obligations after the *Mount Laurel* litigation. This more piecemeal approach confronts formidable political obstacles, but offers the advantage of a clearer public purpose than a broader grant of authority and the possibility of experimentation. To give this approach more bite, however, state leg-islative curtailment of local powers over matters of equity should be mandatory and require some means of metropolitan oversight (as in the above discussion of metropolitan government).

Home rule may also be amended judicially where the original legisla-tive grant is construed more narrowly by courts interpreting its terms in a given case. This is, in fact, how home rule began, as a series of contests between growing municipalities reacting against Dillon's Rule.[30] Dillon's Rule was a mid-nineteenth-century doctrine of strict judicial construc-tion by which the authority of local governments was deemed always to be narrowly construed.[31] Given our very different context today, in contests over the *equitable effects* of challenged local decisions, we might expect judges to more narrowly interpret a municipality's home rule authority.

## Local Initiatives
### *Transit-Oriented Development Initiatives*

Many regional equity advocates focus on infrastructure development, because it connects municipalities, facilitates the movement of low-income residents to jobs and other opportunities (usually employing hundreds in the process), and comes with significant government conditions that can be negotiated.[32] Transportation best exemplifies the potential role of infrastructure development. Public transportation corridors connect regions and open up job-rich areas to people in job-poor areas, overcoming what some scholars have called the "spatial mismatch" between people and jobs. Since many low-income workers have limited access to cars (a fact known to areas that seek to exclude them), more robust public transportation options diminish the importance of obstacles to residential entry. In other words, transportation development mimics the logic of a large city, where people live in distant neighborhoods but can reach jobs all over on mass transit. Transit-oriented development is also associated with perfecting affordable housing choice; the two often need to go together.

## Inter-Local Services Agreements

In theory, any two jurisdictions can opt out of the constraints of localism by entering into shared services agreements with each other. The problem now is that localism creates a tight market for these agreements, with towns instead competing with others to provide a buyer town with services for less and less money. This potentially drives municipalities inward again. Therefore, the use of inter-local services agreements probably expands most when there is some mechanism for brokering them, or fitting them within a larger scheme of efficient deals.

## Living-Wage Ordinances

The movement for these laws began not coincidentally in the 1980s as service-sector wages fell well below inflation in many areas, and income inequality took off.[33] They have been criticized as driving up the cost of business in the city that adopts them and thereby putting it at a locational disadvantage. Whatever the merits of the criticism, it reflects the inter-local competition that comes naturally under localism. While these laws are critical at the local level—particularly in very expensive parts of the country like New York City—they would be much stronger were they more pervasive across an entire region. At its most basic level, metropolitan equity means promoting policies that encourage all workers to join the middle class.

## Services Siting Quotas

Reducing locational inequity often begins with ensuring that there is no concentration in just a few places of the things people don't want. As we have seen, it also means opening up housing opportunities to resource-rich parts of a region. However, people who need essential services—such as the disabled, drug-addicted adult children within a family of working-poor adults—may preclude a family's move because the high-opportunity area has no county social service offices nearby. They're all in the central city. Wealthier people with such needs take private transportation. Therefore, planning for a cap on social services siting in high-traffic areas as well as the provision of services in places where there are currently none is a local necessity of regional equity. Otherwise, people in need have no viable way to avoid concentration.

## Community Benefits Agreements

These are typically agreements between municipalities (and state financing agencies behind them) and developers that dictate some, but not all, of the hiring and labor rules associated with a large development project. Developers who win the right to develop such projects sign covenants to hire locally, pay equitable wages, sponsor training and apprenticeship programs, and use minority- and women-owned subcontractors. Some, like the Milwaukee Park East Redevelopment CBA, include provisions for the city's tax base.[34]

## A Note about Infrastructures and Territory

The culture of localism can be problematic for equitable regionalism even when the will is there. Most for-profit businesses are built for expansion into regions and beyond, but not local governments, many nonprofits, and particular agencies. They have more often grown out of a locally defined culture—a service area beyond which their expertise is deemed unneeded or otherwise unwelcome. This may lead either to the problem of duplicative services (and waste) or the dearth of services (and unmet need). For example, a nonprofit housing developer— "CDC"—is an established actor in Town A and has developed impressive expertise over twenty years. Town C, three towns away, has no such actor, a dearth of affordable housing development (other than low-market rents in blighted structures), and growing unmet need. But CDC is never consulted in Town C and views Town C as beyond its legitimate territory, even though it has valuable expertise and the perspective with which to increase capacity throughout both towns' region. This problem of localized infrastructure affects many potential areas of sharing and illustrates the imperative of planning for regional, not just local, capacity.

## The Critique

For many people of good faith on both the left and the right, these arguments for metropolitan equity could not be more ridiculous. On one hand, a leftist critic might say that, in addition to not going far enough, regional equity relies too heavily on racial integration, which is neither desirable nor realistic. Critics on the right might add that regional equity is politically unrealistic because it entails some degree of redistribution. It also vests too much faith in government—bigger government—to solve our problems. Both the left and the right might agree that regional equity is too quick to find fault with local authority, which is often the purest form of democratic decision making—something to be nurtured, respected, and empowered, not categorically criticized. Other forces are to blame for our deficits and equality gaps, and they are dangerously ignored by regional equity strategies.

My rejoinder is that the structure on which these critiques stand is broken and has to be transformed by acting on principles we long ago adopted. Integration is not the only way to do regional equity, but it is an unquestionably important part of it. The fact that people who need it want it in some form, and those who don't oppose it in all forms, is probably reason enough to pursue it. Yet it cannot be accomplished more radically because, indeed, that time has passed.[35]

The right's criticism of redistribution is short-sighted, decontextualized from the very cycles of life. Younger populations need the greater resources that foster opportunity so that they can one day support both the generation that helped them, their parents, and the one that will sustain them later, their children. It is the same order of redistribution one typically sees in the transmission of family wealth. Here, the "family" is a more broadly defined community of interests—the region and its myriad social capital. Yes, that idea challenges a long tradition of local decision making, but it doesn't end it. It merely recognizes that a different balance must be struck regarding what decisions are appropriate for fully local authority and what should be subject to equity—and therefore expanded to include other localities.

As to the complaint about the role of government, metropolitan equity is *precisely* what government can and should do at its best. Localism is a governmental arrangement that conditions the way private markets develop, and it does so in wildly lopsided fashion. Metropolitan equity is a necessary reformulation of our relationship to local government—the government that touches our lives most. I used the business analogy earlier in showing how profit-centered firms expand. However, there is no private entity charged with the duty of the common good. That is explicitly and exclusively the province of government.

I am not naive enough to suggest that regional equity, if implemented everywhere to the fullest, would solve all of our worst social and economic issues. For instance, we still need progress on banking and financial industry regulation, pension relief, and structural remedies for a service-based labor economy that employs too few workers in middle-class careers. Also, second-generation interventions must continue to expand in areas that have achieved some measure of quantitative diversity but struggle with qualitative diversity. Progressive mutuality is a multidimensional, profound, and difficult challenge. But sharing responsibilities for our spatially defined interests will make solving most of our social and economic issues substantially easier. That is, it will allow us to go from today's ridiculous to tomorrow's sublime, freeing us to reduce the costs of a paradise we've helped build for a few while remaking paths to opportunity for the many.

# ACKNOWLEDGMENTS

The list of people without whose help, guidance, or inspiration would have made such an ambitious project impossible is longer than I can accurately account, but it begins with my wife and soul partner, Shawn. My girls, Naima and Jasmine, were also patient, good-natured, and, at times, welcome distractions. My agent, Flip Brophy, was a tireless advocate for these ideas and a redeemer of my faith. My editor, Ilene Kalish, figured out what I was trying to do and helped me do it better. I'm grateful.

Many have heard me say over these years that this book was put together with shoelaces and bubblegum, but I had other, more indispensable resources—particularly an army of student researchers at Rutgers Law School (Newark), not one of whom worked for pay. They were David Acosta, Kathy Oviedo, Taraun Tice, Lauren Straub, and Suzanne Hoyes. A few deserve special recognition for having gone well beyond the call of duty, including Amani Abdellah, Tamarra Holmes, Enes Hajdarpasic, Awinna Martinez, Sal Sanchez, and Noelle van Baaren. Many of these concepts were developed in connection with the robust exchange of ideas and papers over years of teaching a Rutgers Law School class called "Race, Class, and Metropolitan Equity," and I am grateful to the many students whose insights contributed to this work. Pioneering student fellows with our Rutgers Center on Law in Metropolitan Equity (CLiME) contributed much at the end. Also at Rutgers I am indebted to the stop-everything support of librarians Dennis Kim-Prieto, Evelyn Ramones, and Minglu Wang. My colleagues Paul Tractenberg, Ronald Chen, Esther Canty-Barnes, Randi Mandelbaum, and Jennifer Valverde all contributed important insights and leads at key moments. I have learned much from the Rutgers Property Tax Discussion Group. Colleagues in the field, like Solangel Maldonado, revealed to me what lay under rocks I'd missed, or challenged my assumptions, like Olympia Duhart. I am also thankful for the support of my dean, John Farmer, and the New Jersey first-ring suburb tours by Marianne Moore, Linda Garbaccio, Robert Holmes, and Charles Auffant.

I learned a lot about this country from my visits to the field where I am indebted to the work and insights of David Alexander in Miami, as well as Gihan Perara, Antoinette Pierre (and her Miami Gardens staff), Jim Murray (FAU Center for Urban and Economic Studies), Phillip Bacon (Collins Center), Elizabeth Williams and Timothy Barber (Miami Black Archives); in Houston, Anne-Marie Balthazar, Parnell Herbert, Ellen Marrus, Pat Jasper, Yvette Mitchell, and Steve Klineberg (Rice University), Jeff Taebel (Houston Division of Community Environmental Planning), Xavier Burke, Carlos Lopez, Carl Lindahl, and many others who gave me time; in Detroit, Steven Jackson, Regina Jackson, Riley Ford, Dr. Melba Joyce Boyd (Wayne State University), Claudia Peek Corbin, James Bush, the Reverend Juanita Peek-Vary, Danny Abdul Kauthar, and a host of family and wonderful Detroiters who assembled in focus groups on my behalf; in New Orleans, the very generous Jordan Flaherty and Morgan Williams; in Los Angeles, my dear friend Mary Lee; in Baltimore, Garrett Power (University of Maryland Law School) for his comprehensive tour and generous materials, and Muhammed, the cabdriver, who, unlike me and last names, remembers everything; in Trevose, Janis Risch, Chrissy Thomas, Alice Swan, Charles Ellzy, and Frederick D. James Jr.; in Philadelphia, Patricia Stewart; and in northern New Jersey, the Reverend Anthony Johnson and former Montclair mayor Jerry Fried. I would not have known many of the finer points without the subject-matter expertise of my regional equity forerunners Manuel Pastor, David Rusk, Angela Glover Blackwell, and Myron Orfield. I also appreciate the insights of Kathe Neuman (Rutgers), Elvin Wyly, and Dr. Elizabeth Dickey of Bank Street College.

Nothing ever works for long without the love of my sisters, Eve Troutt Powell and Margot Troutt Keys. Everything I ever do reflects the hard work and enduring love of my late parents, Bobbye Vary Troutt and George David Troutt, who taught me how to think. You have my eternal gratitude and more.

# NOTES

NOTES TO THE INTRODUCTION

1. *See* Sharon Otterman, *Diversity Debate Convulses Elite High School*, New York Times, Aug. 4, 2010.
2. G. William Domhoff, *Wealth, Income, and Power*, Oct. 2012, *available at* http://www2.ucsc.edu/whorulesamerica/power/wealth.html.
3. John R. Logan and Brian Stults, *The Persistence of Segregation in the Metropolis: New Findings from the 2010 Census*, Census Brief prepared for Project US2010, Mar. 2011, *available at* http://www.s4.brown.edu/us2010.
4. Douglas S. Massey, *Segregation and Stratification: A Biosocial Perspective*, 1 Du Bois Review: Social Science Research on Race 1 (2004).
5. Charles M. Tiebout, *A Pure Theory of Local Expenditures*, 64 Journal of Political Economy 464 (1956).

NOTES TO CHAPTER 1

1. *See, Annual Report: Budget Review*, Board of Governors of the Federal Reserve System, 2012, *available at* http://www.federalreserve.gov/pubs/alpha.htm.
2. *See generally* Ed Meyer, *Judge Says Prosecutors Rejected Lesser Charges in Copley Schools Residency Case*, Jan. 21, 2011, *available at* http://www.ohio.com/; Andrea Canning, *Ohio Mom Kelley Williams-Bolar Jailed for Sending Kids to Better School District*, ABC News, Jan. 26, 2011, *available at* http://abcnews.go.com/US/ohio-mom-jailed-sending-kids-school-district/story?id=12763654#.UHTspphLWSo.
3. What's also interesting is how few people actually make such runs for the walls. The prosecution and school officials from nearby districts all acknowledged that sneaking kids into a better school district is quite rare.
4. The following statistics come from Jennifer Wheary, Thomas M. Shapiro, and Tamara Draut, *By a Thread: The New Experience of America's Middle Class*, Institute on Assets and Social Policy at Brandeis University, 2007, *available at* http://iasp.brandeis.edu/pdfs/Author/draut-tamara/By%20A%20Thread.pdf.
5. *See generally* Richard Briffault, *Our Localism: Part I—The Structure of Local Government Law*, 90 Colum. L. Rev. 1 (1990).
6. Briffault argues that localism engenders a privatization of interests that erodes concern for a wider public sphere. *See, Our Localism: Part I, supra*, at 6.
7. *See* United States Census Bureau, *Most Children Younger Than Age 1 Are Minorities, Census Bureau Reports*, May 17, 2012, *available at* http://www.census.gov/newsroom/releases/archives/population/cb12-90.html. *See also* Jeffrey Passel, Gretchen Livingston, and D'Vera Cohn, *Explaining*

*Why Minority Births Now Outnumber White Births*, Pew Research Center, May 17, 2012, *available at* http://www.pewsocialtrends.org/2012/05/17/explaining-why-minority-births-now-outnumber-white-births/.

8. The specific census findings that follow may be found at http://diversitydata.sph.harvard.edu/.

9. Let's pause and think about what this does *not* mean. Families are not everyone. People are getting married and not having kids. More people are choosing not to get married at all. And more and more women of all races are heading their own households with young children. The traditional notion of families is clearly in flux along with the historical significance of families with children. Spatial context is also important. The metropolitan area is the important geographic measure because it's the interconnected seat of both population and economic growth. Yet people do live outside of these areas. And within them, central cities—which may yet regain their cultural and economic importance—attract millions of single adults.

10. *See* Myron Orfield, American Metropolitics: The New Suburban Reality (Brookings 2002).

11. They are Atlanta, Boston, Chicago, Cincinnati, Cleveland, Dallas–Fort Worth, Denver, Detroit, Houston, Kansas City, Los Angeles, Miami, Milwaukee, Minneapolis–St. Paul, New York–Newark, Philadelphia, Phoenix, Pittsburgh, Portland, San Diego, San Francisco–Oakland, Seattle, St. Louis, Tampa, and Washington DC–Baltimore.

12. Angela Woodall, *Cost of Oakland Bloodshed Overwhelms Police, Social Services*, Oakland Tribune, Oct. 14, 2009.

13. Winnie Hu, *Obesity Ills That Won't Budge Fuel Soda Battle by Bloomberg*, New York Times, June 12, 2012. "[T]his isn't your crisis alone—it is a crisis for our city and our entire country," Bloomberg told an audience in the Bronx, where 70 percent of adults are overweight.

14. Rich McKay, *What Urban Sprawl Costs You*, Orlando Sentinel, Mar. 27, 2006.

15. Meyer, *supra*.

16. *Disparities in Neighborhood Poverty of Poor Black and White Children*, May 2007, *available at* http://diversitydata.sph.harvard.edu/Publications/brief7.pdf.

### NOTES TO CHAPTER 2

1. *See, e.g.*, an examination of the development and effects of "streetcar suburbs" on Boston in Sam Bass Warner Jr., Streetcar Suburbs: The Process of Growth in Boston (1970–1900) (2nd ed., Harvard 1978).

2. Lewis Mumford, The City in History: Its Origins, Its Transformations, and Its Prospects 485–86 (Harcourt, Brace and World 1968).

3. Kenneth T. Jackson, Crabgrass Frontier: The Suburbanization of the United States 52 (Oxford 1985).

4. *Vill. of Belle Terre v. Boraas*, 416 U.S. 1, 9 (1974).

5. *Vill. of Euclid, Ohio v. Ambler Realty Co.*, 272 U.S. 365, 369 (1926).
6. Richardson Dilworth, The Urban Origins of Suburban Autonomy (Harvard 2005).
7. Jackson, *supra*, at 205.
8. *Id.*, at 215.
9. *See* Richard F. Weingroff, *Federal-Aid Highway Act of 1956: Creating the Interstate System*, 60 Public Roads (1996), *available at* http://www.tfhrc.gov/pubrds/summer96/p96su10.htm.
10. See Federal Housing Administration, *Underwriting Manual: Underwriting and Valuation Procedure under Title II of the National Housing Act*, sec. 9 (1938); Kenneth T. Jackson, *Race, Ethnicity, and Real Estate Appraisal: The Home Owners' Loan Corporation and the Federal Housing Administration*, 6 J. Urb. Hist. 419 (1980).
11. *See* W. Benjamin Pigott, *The "Problem" of the Black Middle Class: Morris Milgram's Concord Park and Residential Integration in Philadelphia's Postwar Suburbs*, Pennsylvania Magazine of History and Biography, Apr. 2008.
12. *See, e.g.*, United States Census Bureau, *Historical Census of Housing Tables*, *available at* http://www.census.gov/hhes/www/housing/census/historic/values.html.
13. Thomas M. Shapiro, The Hidden Cost of Being African American: How Wealth Perpetuates Inequality 32 (Oxford 2004).
14. Robert Carroll et al., *Costs and Benefits of Housing Tax Subsidies*, Pew Fiscal Analysis Initiative and Subsidyscope 2–3 (2011). According to the study, the government's Joint Committee on Taxation reached a slightly higher total subsidy amount of $120.1 billion in 2010. *See also* Internal Revenue Service, *Publication 936: Home Mortgage Interest Deduction*, 2011, *available at* http://www.irs.gov/pub/irs-pdf/p936.pdf.
15. *Id.*
16. Shapiro, *supra*, at 135.
17. *Id.*, at 116–18.
18. *See* Lauren J. Krivo and Robert L. Kaufman, *Housing and Wealth Inequality: Racial–Ethnic Differences in Home Equity in the United States*, 41 Demography (2004).
19. *Id.*
20. *See generally* United States Census Bureau, *Housing Vacancies and Home Ownership*, *available at* http://www.census.gov/hhes/www/housing/hvs/qtr212/files/q212press.pdf; and Joint Center for Housing Studies of Harvard University, *Homeownership*, *available at* http://www.jchs.harvard.edu/sites/jchs.harvard.edu/files/son2012_homeownership.pdf.
21. *See* Melvin Oliver and Thomas Shapiro, Black Wealth/White Wealth: A New Perspective on Racial Inequality (Routledge 1997).
22. Wheary, Shapiro, and Draut, *supra*.
23. *See* Joseph Serna and Mike Anton, *Nearly Half of Costa Mesa City Employees Get Layoff Notices*, Los Angeles Times, Mar. 18, 2011.

24. *See, Costa Mesa Mourns City Worker Who Killed Himself after Getting Layoff Notice*, Los Angeles Times, Mar. 21, 2011.

## NOTES TO CHAPTER 3

1. Norimitsu Onishi, *Lucas and Rich Neighbors Agree to Disagree: Part II*, New York Times, May 21, 2012.
2. For instance, a Habitat for Humanity study of hundreds of units of affordable housing for low-income renters in San Francisco found no reduction in property values caused by the projects. From Homebase/The Center for Common Concerns, San Francisco, *Why Affordable Housing Does Not Lower Property Values*, 1996, *available at* http://www.habitat.org/how/propertyvalues.aspx. Researchers at NYU conducted one of the most detailed, longitudinal studies of project-based housing in New York City and found not only a negligible negative impact on surrounding property values, but in some cases an actual *increase* in value (perhaps because the existing neighborhood benefited from the improvements that accompanied the new housing). Michael H. Schill and Denise Previti, *The State of New York City's Housing and Neighborhoods* (2003, 2004, 2005). In the very New Jersey township that provoked decades of litigation around exclusionary zoning, researchers led by Douglas Massey studied property values in Mount Laurel after the Ethel Lawrence Homes (named for the first plaintiff in the lawsuit) were built. According to Massey, "Even in neighborhoods immediately adjacent to the project, we found no effect of ELH on crime, property values or taxes. Indeed, in a survey we conducted among neighbors, one-third did not know affordable housing even existed in the neighborhood, and among those who did know, only 40 percent could successfully name the project. Despite dire predictions and outsized fears expressed before the fact, when ELH finally opened, it was not with a bang, but a whimper." Douglas S. Massey, *Lessons from Mount Laurel: The Benefits of Affordable Housing for all Concerned*, 21 Poverty & Race Research and Action Council 3, 7 (2012).
3. *See generally* Stacy E. Seicshnaydre, *How Government Housing Perpetuates Racial Segregation: Lessons from Post-Katrina New Orleans*, 60 Cath. U. L. Rev. 661 (2011).
4. *See* Greater New Orleans CMTY Data Center, *Neighborhood Statistical Data Profiles*, 2010, *available at* http://www.gnocdc.org/NeighborhoodData/Orleans.html; *see also* United States Census Bureau, 2003, *available at* http://www.census.gov/.
5. *Id.*
6. *Greater New Orleans Fair Hous. Action Ctr. v. St. Bernard Parish*, 641 F.Supp. 2d 563 (E.D. La. 2009).
7. Jennifer Ludden, *Allegations of Racism and Classism Rattle New Orleans Community*, National Public Radio, Aug. 26 2009, http://www.npr.org/templates/story/story.php?storyId=112247357.
8. *S. Burlington County NAACP v. Mount Laurel Twp.*, 336 A.2d 713 (1975); *S. Burlington County NAACP v. Mount Laurel Twp.*, 456 A.2d 390 (1983).

9. *See* Naomi Balin Wish and Stephen Eisdorfer, *The Impact of Mount Laurel Initiatives: An Analysis of the Characteristics of Applicants and Occupants* 27 Seton Hall L. Rev. 168 (1997).

10. *See* Patch Staff, *Livingston Planning Board to Consider Housing Complex*, Apr. 3, 2012, *available at* http://millburn.patch.com/articles/livingston-planning-board-to-consider-housing-complex.

11. David Dante Troutt, *Ghettoes Made Easy: The Metamarket/Antimarket Dichotomy and the Legal Challenges of Inner-City Economic Development* 35 Harv. C.R.–C.L. L. Rev. 427 (2000).

12. *See, e.g.*, Jason DeParle, Robert Gebeloff, and Sabrina Tavernise, *Older, Suburban, and Struggling, "Near Poor" Startle the Census*, New York Times, Nov. 19, 2011.

13. See 2010 census data for select U.S. tracts in interactive map form at *Mapping the 2010 U.S. Census*, New York Times, *available at* http://projects.nytimes.com/census/2010/map.

14. *See generally* Melanie Shell-Weiss, Coming to Miami: A Social History (Florida 2009).

15. Michael N. Danielson and Jameson W. Dolg, New York: The Politics of Urban Regional Development 302 (California 1982).

16. *See, e.g.*, Kevin Mumford, Newark: A History of Race, Rights, and Riots in America 72 (NYU 2007).

17. Thomas Sugrue, The Origins of the Urban Crisis: Race and Inequality in Postwar Detroit 63 (Princeton 2005).

18. Mindy Thompson Fullilove, Root Shock: How Tearing Up City Neighborhoods Hurts America and What We Can Do about It (One World 2005).

19. *Id.*, at 14.

20. *See generally* Martha Mahoney, *Law and Racial Geography: Public Housing and the Economy in New Orleans*, 42 Stan. L. Rev. 1251 (1990).

21. U.S. Housing and Community Development Act, Pub. L. No. 93-383, 88 Stat. 633 (1974) (requiring local government approval before public housing may be developed within a jurisdiction and requiring separate local authorization for additional projects); 42 U.S.C. §§ 1437c(e), 439(a–d) (1988 & Supp. IV 1992) ("[i]t is the policy of the United States . . . to vest in local public housing agencies the maximum amount of responsibility in the administration of their housing programs"); 24 C.F.R. § 882.209(a)(4)(1993) (§ 8); Pub. L. No. 93-383, 88 Stat. 633 (1974) (providing a federal basis for local control); *see also* Conn. Gen. Stat. § 8–39 (1993); N.Y. Pub. Hous. Law § 31 (McKinney 1989); Ind. Code Ann. § 36-7-18-41 (Burns 1989); Ill. Ann. Stat. ch. 310, para. 10/3, 17(b), 30 (Smith-Hurd 1993); Mo. Ann. Stat. §§ 90.080, 99.320 (Vernon 1989) (for examples of state law that upholds policy of requiring local approval to build public housing authorities [PHAs]); *see, e.g.*, *Housing Authority of the Town of East Hartford v. Papandrea*, 610 A.2d 637 (Conn. 1992) (where a local PHA avoided control of a local state agency in their town).

22. *See, e.g., Housing Authority of the Town of East Hartford v. Papandrea*, 610 A.2d 637 (Conn. 1992) (where a local PHA avoided control of local state agency in their town); *City of Hartford v. Town of Glatonbury*, 561 F.2d 1032 (1977) (limiting the federal effort to impose federal obligations on local governments).
23. 416 U.S. 1 (1974).
24. 422 U.S. 490 (1975).
25. 429 U.S. 252 (1977).
26. 411 U.S. 1 (1973).
27. 418 U.S. 717 (1974).
28. Arbitrarily limiting consideration to the 1970s, there were others from the Burger Court. *See, James v. Valtieri*, 422 U.S. 490 (1971); *Salyer Land Co. v. Tulare Lake Basin Water Storage Dist.*, 410 U.S. 719 (1973); *City of Eastlake v. Forest City Enters*, 426 U.S. 668 (1976); *Rizzo v. Goode*, 423 U.S. 362 (1976). *But see, Hills v. Gautreaux*, 425 U.S. 284 (1976); *Moore v. East Cleveland*, 431 U.S. 494 (1977).
29. "If the ordinance segregated one area only for one race, it would immediately be suspect under the reasoning of *Buchanan v. Warley*, 245 U.S. 60, where the Court invalidated a city ordinance barring a black from acquiring real property in a white residential area by reason of an 1866 Act of Congress, 14 Stat. 27, now 42 U.S.C. § 1982, and an 1870 Act, § 17, 16 Stat. 144, now 42 U.S.C. § 1981, both enforcing the Fourteenth Amendment. 245 U.S., at 78–82." 416 U.S. at 6 (citation omitted).
The issue had begun to receive some attention from legal commentators, too. See Lawrence Sager, *Tight Little Islands: Exclusionary Zoning, Equal Protection, and the Indigent*, 21 Stan. L. Rev. 767 (1969); *Note: Exclusionary Zoning and Equal Protection*, 84 Harv. L. Rev. 1645 (1971); *Note: The Responsibility of Local Zoning Authorities to Nonresident Indigents*, 23 Stan. L. Rev. 774 (1971).
Of course, race easily could have become an issue, since a related-persons restriction—like the blood-only ordinance struck down more recently in St. Bernard Parish, Louisiana—has clear racial implications.
30. *Id.*
31. *See, e.g., Berman v. Parker*, 348 U.S. 26 (1954), an urban slum removal case from Washington DC, from which the Court quoted as follows: "The concept of the public welfare is broad and inclusive. . . . The values it represents are spiritual as well as physical, aesthetic as well as monetary. It is within the power of the legislature to determine that the community should be beautiful as well as healthy, spacious as well as clean, well-balanced as well as carefully patrolled." *Id.*, at 32–33.
32. Richard Briffault points out that timing also prevents cities from engaging in such regulation in that their spatial and demographic diversity developed well before the rise of localist legal principles in defining a municipality's police powers. Zoning protects parochial interests against *future* incursions. *Our Localism II: Localism and Legal Theory*, 90 Colum. L. Rev. 346, at 373–74 (1990).
33. *Id.*, at 9 (emphasis added).
34. 348 U.S. 26 (1954).

35. Interestingly, this outcome was explicitly rejected by the Court's greatest champion of civil rights, Justice Thurgood Marshall, and utterly ignored by Justice Brennan, both of whom dissented in *Belle Terre*. "This is not a case where the Court is being asked to nullify a township's sincere efforts to maintain its residential character by preventing the operation of rooming houses, fraternity houses, or other commercial or high-density residential uses. Unquestionably, a town is free to restrict such uses. Moreover, as a general proposition, I see no constitutional infirmity in a town's limiting the density of use in residential areas by zoning regulations which do not discriminate on the basis of constitutionally suspect criteria." 416 U.S. at 17 (Marshall, J., dissenting).

36. 422 U.S. at 496. This is akin to the successful argument that plaintiffs made in the *Mount Laurel* case.

37. *Id.*, at 509. Quoting precedent, the majority began by saying, "'Of course, pleadings must be something more than an ingenious academic exercise in the conceivable.' We think the complaint of the taxpayer–petitioners is little more than such an exercise. Apart from the conjectural nature of the asserted injury, the line of causation between Penfield's actions and such injury is not apparent from the complaint. Whatever may occur in Penfield, the injury complained of—increases in taxation—results only from decisions made by the appropriate Rochester authorities, who are not parties to this case." *Id.*, at 509 (citation omitted). *But see, e.g., NAACP v. City of Kyle, Tex.* (where the NAACP, the Home Builders Association of Greater Austin Inc., and National Association of Home Builders Inc. brought a claim after the city of Kyle adopted changes to its zoning ordinances. The plaintiffs argued that the changes, which required a minimum garage size, an increase in the minimum home size, and an increase in the minimum lot size, would cause the average price of a single-family residence to increase by about $38,000. This increase would thus have a disparate impact on African Americans and Hispanics and would "have a segregative effect on the community." The Court held that the disparate impact on minority communities was a viable injury. The Court also held that such injury could be traced to the zoning ordinances because generally, "more stringent zoning and subdivision ordinances . . . cause[ ] the price of entry level homes to increase and that . . . price increase has . . . a disproportionate negative effect on the ability of minorities to purchase starter homes in the City's jurisdiction").

38. *Vil. of Arlington Heights v. Metropolitan Housing Development Corp.* 429 U.S. 252, 257 (1977).

39. *Id.*, at 258.

40. 82 Stat. 81, 42 U.S.C. § 3601 *et seq.*

41. *Washington v. Davis*, 426 U.S. 229 (1976).

42. 429 U.S. at 270–71.

43. 272 U.S. 365 (1926). For instance, *Euclid's* language with respect to the "parasitic" effect of apartment houses resonates today:

With particular reference to apartment houses, it is pointed out that the development of detached house sections is greatly retarded by the coming of apartment houses, which has sometimes resulted in destroying the entire section for private house purposes; that in such sections very often the apartment house is a mere parasite, constructed in order to take advantage of the open spaces and attractive surroundings created by the residential character of the district. Moreover, the coming of one apartment house is followed by others, interfering by their height and bulk with the free circulation of air and monopolizing the rays of the sun which otherwise would fall upon the smaller homes, and bringing, as their necessary accompaniments, the disturbing noises incident to increased traffic and business, and the occupation, by means of moving and parked automobiles, of larger portions of the streets, thus detracting from their safety and depriving children of the privilege of quiet and open spaces for play, enjoyed by those in more favored localities,—until, finally, the residential character of the neighborhood and its desirability as a place of detached residences are utterly destroyed. Under these circumstances, apartment houses, which in a different environment would be not only entirely unobjectionable but highly desirable, come very near to being nuisances. (Id., at 394–95)

44. *See* Angela Woodall, *Cost of Oakland Bloodshed Overwhelms Police, Social Services*, Oakland Tribune, Oct. 14, 2009 (detailing the death of Shaneice Davis).

45. *See generally* Christian Henrichson and Ruth Delaney, *The Price of Prisons: What Incarceration Costs Taxpayers*, Vera Institute of Justice, Jul. 20, 2012.

46. In finding violations of the constitutional right against cruel and unusual punishment, Justice Anthony Kennedy cited mental and medical health concerns in a prison system where suicide rates are 80 percent higher than the nationwide average for inmates. *Brown v. Plata*, 131 S.Ct. 1910 (2011); *Coleman v. Schwarzenegger*, 2010 U.S. Dist. LEXIS 2711 (N.D. Cal., Jan. 12, 2010). The requirement of releasing prisoners has set off a new policy conundrum for the state. *See* Mac Taylor, *State Should Consider Less Costly Alternatives to CDCR Blueprint*, Cal. Legislative Analyst Office, May 16, 2012, *available at* http://www.lao.ca.gov/analysis/2012/crim_justice/cdcr-blueprint-051512.pdf.

## NOTES TO CHAPTER 4

1. Steven Thrasher, *Inside a Divided Upper East Side Public School*, Village Voice, Feb. 23, 2010, *available* at http://www.villagevoice.com/2010-02-23/news/inside-a-divided-nyc-public-school/3/.

2. *See, Manhattan Community District 8*, *available at* http://www.nyc.gov/html/dcp/pdf/lucds/mn8profile.pdf. For a look at the New York census tracts *see*, *NYC Census Factfinder*, *available at* http://gis.nyc.gov/census/.

3. Myron Orfield and Thomas Luce, *America's Racially Diverse Suburbs: Opportunities and Challenges*, Institute on Metropolitan Opportunity, University of Minnesota Law School, Jul. 20, 2012.

4. *Id.*, at 8.
5. *Id.*, at 21–22.
6. *Id.*
7. *Id.*, at 26.
8. Logan and Stults, *supra.*
9. *Id.*, at 6–8.
10. *Id.*, at 12.
11. *Id.*, at 18.
12. Thomas Massey and Nancy Denton, American Apartheid (Harvard 1993).
13. Rima Wilkes and John Iceland, *Hypersegregation in the Twenty-First Century*, Demography, Feb. 2004, *available at* http://www.wilkes.rima.ca/PDF/1515211.pdf.
14. *Id.*, at 29.
15. Nancy McArdle, Theresa Osypuk, and Delores Acevedo-Garcia, *Segregation and Exposure to High Poverty Schools in Large Metropolitan Areas: 2008–09*, Sept. 2010, *available at* http://diversitydata.sph.harvard.edu/Publications/school_segregation_report.pdf.
16. *See, e.g., Grutter v. Bollinger*, 539 U.S. 306, 328 (2003).
17. McArdle, Osypuk, and Acevedo-Garcia, *supra.*
18. We could take it a step further. Perhaps smart, financially comfortable kids are expected to lead society in the future, as their parents currently may. Those unfit to sit beside them will probably work for them, goes the unspoken assumption. OK, but does anyone seriously believe that's a sustainable plan for a well-educated employer? Is that the training we would expect of our leaders as they compete with Chinese and Indian companies, for instance? I doubt it.
19. *See, e.g.*, Matthew Lassiter, The Silent Majority: Suburban Politics in the Sunbelt South (Princeton 2006).
20. 411 U.S. 1.
21. 418 U.S. 717.
22. 411 U.S. at 4.
23. *Id.*, at 14n35.
24. *Id.*, at 17–18.
25. *Id.*, at 44. "[I]t would be difficult to imagine a case having a greater potential impact on our federal system than the one now before us, in which we are urged to abrogate systems of financing public education presently in existence in virtually every State." *Id.* However, the New Jersey Supreme Court reached a contrary conclusion on state constitutional grounds at about the same time. In *Robinson v. Cahill*, 62 N.J. 473 (1973), that court held that New Jersey's overreliance on local property taxation in its method of school finance deprived children in property-poor districts of their state right to a thorough and efficient education.
26. 411 U.S. at 50–51.
27. *Id.*, at 49–50.

28. *Id.*, at 84 (Marshall, J., dissenting). The Court, he argued, ignored its own education precedent when, in the desegregation context, it had ruled that unequal resources for black law students amounted to a denial of equal protection notwithstanding a baseline of law school curricula. *Id.* (citing *Sweatt v. Painter*, 339 U.S. 629, 633–34 [1950]). Justice Marshall's voluminous dissent suggests disagreement among the justices so bitter as to imply genuine animus over the meaning of the case. For example, Marshall asserts that the majority violated basic rules of appellate procedure by allowing the appellants to argue against facts that had gone unchallenged at trial for the first time at oral argument before the Court. 411 U.S. at 95n56. Further, he argued that the majority's indifference to fiscal disparities was blind to the lineup of wealthy school districts who filed amicus curiae briefs on behalf of Texas. *Id.*, at 85, and text accompanying note 42.

29. 411 U.S. at 54.

30. 422 U.S. 490 (1975).

31. 418 U.S. at 738–39. Specifically, the trial judge wrote that "while [they] would provide a racial mix more in keeping with the Black–White proportions of the student population [they] would accentuate the racial identifiability of the [Detroit] district as a Black school system and would not accomplish desegregation."

32. 418 U.S. at 741–42.

33. The oft-quoted language is the following: "No single tradition in public education is more deeply rooted than local control over the operation of schools; local autonomy has long been thought essential both to the maintenance of community concern and support for public schools and to quality of educational process." *Id.*

34. *See generally* Sugrue, *supra*, 209–29. Detroit, like New Orleans, has a history as one of the most segregated cities in the United States.

35. The use of economic proxies for racial struggles is relevant in another important respect here: it obscured the extent to which affluent whites benefited from localist rules far more than did middle- and lower-middle-class whites. The latter could be vociferous antibusing segregationists in part because they were the whites whose lives were altered by desegregation orders. However, in Charlotte, North Carolina, where "busing equalization" took hold across the metropolitan area, a coalition of whites and blacks worked successfully to spread the effects of school desegregation across classes. According to Matthew Lassiter, "The Charlotte case reveals that the long-term viability of urban school systems undergoing court-ordered desegregation depended upon spatial and socioeconomic remedies that encompassed the entire metropolitan region and pursued racial stability through policies sensitive to the demands of class fairness." *"Socioeconomic Integration" in the Suburbs*, 140, in Kevin Kruse and Thomas Sugrue, eds., The New Suburban History (Chicago 2006).

36. The Court's willingness to use colorblindness to trump even local control continues in its most recent school desegregation decisions. *See, Parents Involved in Community Schools v. Seattle School District No. 1*, 551 U.S. 701 (2007). In *Parents Involved*, the Court struck down two voluntary school assignment plans in Seattle,

Washington, and Jefferson County, Kentucky, on the grounds that their binary classification schemes sought racial balance in violation of the Equal Protection Clause and the non-racial desegregation dictates of the *Brown* case. Although the school districts' explicit use of race in making assignment decisions compelled heightened scrutiny, the plurality gave little of the deference suggested by earlier cases to the educational policy decisions made by elected local school officials acting on behalf of the affected local communities.

37. This was especially true for Southern whites. *See* Jason Sokol, There Goes My Everything: White Southerners in the Age of Civil Rights (Knopf 2000). See also Derrick Bell, Silent Covenants: Brown v. Board of Education and the Unfulfilled Hopes for Racial Reform (Oxford 2004).

38. Lassiter describes these sentiments within the terms Richard M. Nixon used to great effect with voters he called the "Silent Majority." "The ascendance of color-blind ideology in the metropolitan South, as in the rest of the nation, depended upon the establishment of structural mechanisms of exclusion that did not require individual racism by suburban beneficiaries in order to sustain white class privilege and maintain barriers of disadvantage facing urban minority communities." Silent Majority, *supra*, at 4.

39. Briffault makes a similar observation. *See, Our Localism: Part II, supra*, at 373n122.

40. *QuickFacts from the US Census Bureau, available at* http://www.infoplease.com/us/census/data/michigan/detroit/.

41. *Combined Data Book, 2005–2006*, prepared by the Office of Health, Information, Planning, Evaluation, and Research, *available at* http://www.detroitmi.gov/Portals/0/docs/healthandwellness/PDF/2005-2006%20DHWP%20Databook_Master%20(2007).pdf.

42. *Population Change in Metro Detroit*, Detroit News, Jul. 19, 2007.

43. Orfield and Luce, *supra*, at 5.

44. Sugrue, *supra*, at 251.

45. *See* United States Census Bureau, *State and County QuickFacts, available at* http://quickfacts.census.gov/qfd/states/26/2622000.html; *see also, Population Change in Metro Detroit, supra*.

46. Shapiro, *supra*, at 155–82.

47. To say nothing of tracking, special education, charter schools, and the proliferation of attention deficit hyperactivity disorder diagnoses and their pharmacological treatments.

48. Shapiro, *supra*, at 143.

49. For example, in New Jersey, the three lowest-ranking high schools all have over 90 percent Hispanic and black populations, and more than half of the students are eligible for discounted or free lunch. Woodrow Wilson High (Camden, NJ): 61.0 percent Hispanic, 36.9 percent black, 56.1 percent eligible for discounted or free school lunch. *See* http://www.schooldigger.com/go/NJ/schools/0264001348/school.aspx; Barringer (Newark, NJ): 62.5 percent Hispanic, 36.2 percent black,

69.2 percent eligible for discounted or free school lunch. *See* http://www. schooldigger.com/go/NJ/schools/1134002190/school.aspx; Asbury Park High (Asbury Park, NJ): 18.2 percent Hispanic, 79.0 percent black, 72.7 percent eligible for discounted or free school lunch. *See, More Must Be Done for Failing Schools*, June 5, 2012, State of New Jersey Department of Education, *available at* http:// www.schooldigger.com/go/NJ/schools/0093003732/school.aspx.

50. *See* Ronald F. Ferguson, Toward Excellence with Equity: An Emerging Vision for Closing the Achievement Gap (Harvard Education Press 2008); and *see generally* James S. Coleman et al., Equality of Educational Opportunity Study (Coleman Report) (1966).

51. James E. Ryan, Five Miles Apart: One City, Two Schools, and the Story of Educational Opportunity in Modern America (Oxford 2011).

52. *Id.*, at 94–95.

53. *Id.*, at 273–76.

54. *Id.*, at 277.

55. *Id.*, at 278.

56. Chris Cert, *More Must Be Done for Failing Schools*, State of New Jersey Department of Education, June 5, 2012, *available at* http://www.nj.gov/education/ news/2012/0605oped.htm.

57. Ryan, *supra*, at 185.

58. I realize there is another view here that asserts that culture and attitude play an unacknowledged role. First-generation Asian students, for instance, may achieve well beyond their family income precisely because their parents devote scarce resources to test preparation and tutoring as a means of mobility. This reality is nothing short of amazing (and is not unusual among immigrant groups from a variety of countries). Yet it doesn't alter the fact that *most* of those coveted spots are going to students whose socioeconomic advantage is reflected in their parents' educational backgrounds, resourcefulness, information networks, linguistic comfort, help at home, and, yes, financial resources to pay for expensive test-prep classes and tutorials.

59. Dr. Martin Luther King Jr., *The Ethical Demands for Integration*, Dec. 27, 1962, in James M. Washington, ed., A Testament of Hope: The Essential Writings and Speeches of Martin Luther King, Jr. (HarperOne 2003).

60. *See* Ryan, *supra*, at 215–38.

61. john a. powell, *The Tensions between Integration and School Reform*, 28 Hastings Const. L.Q. 655, 658 (2001).

62. Louis Uchitelle, *Even a Wealthy Suburb Faces Pressure to Curb School Taxes*, New York Times, Mar. 8, 2011.

NOTES TO CHAPTER 5

1. *See* Manny Fernandez, *Teenager Testifies about Attacking Latinos for Sport*, New York Times, Mar. 29, 2010.

2. Wesley Yang, *Paper Tigers*, New York, May 28, 2011.
3. Mary D. Edsall and Thomas Byrne Edsall, Chain Reaction: The Impact of Race, Rights, and Taxes on American Politics 183 (Norton 1992).
4. *Id.*, at 164.
5. *Id.*, at 182.
6. *See also* George Packer, *Poor, White, and Republican*, New Yorker, Feb. 14, 2012.
7. *See, e.g.*, Michael Ettlinger and Michael Linden, *The Failure of Supply-Side Economics: Three Decades of Empirical Economic Data Shows That Supply-Side Economics Doesn't Work*, Center for American Justice, Aug. 1, 2012, *available at* http://www.americanprogress.org/issues/economy/news/2012/08/01/11998/the-failure-of-supply-side-economics/.
8. Edsall and Edsall, *supra*, at 193.
9. *Id.*, at 218.
10. Linda Villarosa, *A Radical "Parkway" Plan to Slow Down Cars on Park Ave.*, New York Times, Apr. 19, 2012, *available at* http://fort-greene.thelocal.nytimes.com/2012/04/19/a-radical-parkway-plan-to-slow-down-cars-on-park-avenue/.
11. *See generally* facts assembled by the Delco Alliance, *available at* http://www.ejnet.org/chester/. *See also* Mike Ewall, *Environmental Injustice in Delaware County, PA*, *available at* http://www.ejnet.org/chester/delco-ej.pdf; *see also* Sanjay Gupta, *Toxic America*, cnn, *available at* http://www.cnn.com/SPECIALS/2010/toxic.america; *see also* Public Interest Law Center of Philadelphia, *Environmental Racism in Chester*, *available at* http://pilcop.org/chester-2/.
12. Center of Excellence in Environmental Toxicology, *Community Outreach and Engagement: Target Communities*, available at http://www.med.upenn.edu/ceet/community_outreach/target_comm.shtml.
13. *Chester Residents Concerned for Quality Living v. Com., Department of Environmental Resources*, 668 A.2d 110 (1995).
14. Exec. Order No. 12898, 59 FR 7629 (Feb. 11, 1994).
15. Carleton Waterhouse, *Failed Plans and Planned Failures*, 169, in J. Levitt and M. Whitaker, eds., Hurricane Katrina: America's Unnatural Disaster (Nebraska 2009).
16. *See* Gabriel Nelson, *Oil Refinery Group Sues EPA over Request for Emissions Data*, New York Times, June 1, 2011.
17. *See* Kathe Newman, *Post-Industrial Widgets: Capital Flows and the Production of the Urban*, 33 International Journal of Urban and Regional Research (2009).
18. Kathe Newman and Elvin K. Wyly, *Geographies of Mortgage Market Segregation: The Case of Essex County, New Jersey*, 19 Hous. Studies 53 (2004).
19. *See* Kathleen C. Engel and Patricia A. McCoy, *From Credit Denial to Predatory Lending: The Challenge of Sustaining Minority Homeownership*, Segregation: The Rising Costs for America, Sept. 2, 2007, *available at* http://ssrn.com/abstract=1011489.
20. *See generally* Constance M. Ruzich and A. J. Grant, *Predatory Lending and the Devouring of the American Dream*, 32 Journal of American Culture 137 (2009).

21. *See* Larry Schwartztol, *Predatory Lending: Wall Street Profited, Minority Families Paid the Price*, ACLU Racial Justice Program, Sept. 16, 2011, available at http://www.aclu.org/blog/racial-justice/predatory-lending-wall-street-profited-minority-families-paid-price.

22. U.S. Department of Housing and Urban Development, *Unequal Burden: Income and Racial Disparities in Subprime Lending in America*, 2000, *available at* http://www.huduser.org/Publications/pdf/unequal_full.pdf.

23. *Id.*

24. *Id.*

25. Association of Community Organizations for Reform Now, *Separate and Unequal: Predatory Lending in America*, 2004, *available at* http://www.evaluationtoolsforraci-alequity.org/evaluation/resource/doc/separate_and_unequal_2004.pdf.

26. Furman Center for Real Estate and Urban Policy NYU School of Law and Wagner School of Public Service, *The High Cost of Segregation: Exploring the Relationship Between Racial Segregation and Subprime Lending*, 2009, *available at* http://furmancenter.org/files/publications/The_High_Cost_of_Segregation_Furman_Center_Policy_Brief_November_2009.pdf.

27. *See* Marc Mauer, Race to Incarcerate (New Press 1999).

28. *See* Michelle Alexander, The New Jim Crow: Mass Incarceration in the Age of Colorblindness 96–97 (New Press 2010).

29. *Id.*, at 59.

30. *Id.*, at 150–52.

31. *Id.*, at 47–49.

32. *Id.*, at 53.

33. *Id.*, at 124.

34. *Id.*, at 97.

35. *Id.*, at 98.

36. *Id.*, at 74.

37. Eric Blumenson and Eva Nilsen, *Policing for Profit: The Drug War's Hidden Economic Agenda*, 65 U. Chicago L. Rev. 35, 45 (1998).

38. Alexander, *supra*, at 86–87.

39. *Id.*, at 70.

40. *Id.*, at 133.

41. *See* New York Civil Liberties Union, *Analysis Finds Racial Disparities, Ineffectiveness in NYPD Stop-and-Frisk Program; Links Tactic to Soaring Marijuana Arrest Rate*, May 22, 2013, *available at* http://www.nyclu.org/news/analysis-finds-racial-disparities-ineffectiveness-nypd-stop-and-frisk-program-links-tactic-soar.

42. *See* Tracey Maclin, *Race and the Fourth Amendment*, 51 Vand. L. Rev. 333 (1998).

### NOTES TO CHAPTER 6

1. *See* Alan Berube and Elizabeth Kneebone, Confronting Suburban Poverty in America (Brookings Institution Press 2013).

2. *See* U.S. Department of Labor Statistics, *A Profile of the Working Poor*, 2010, *available at* http://www.bls.gov/cps/cpswp2010.pdf.

3. Stephanie Hoopes Halpin and United Way of Northern New Jersey, *ALICE: Asset Limited, Income Constrained, Employed Study of Financial Hardship in New Jersey*, August 2012.

4. For a description of how states manage the work requirements mandated under the federal Temporary Assistance to Needy Families program, *see* Liz Schott, *Policy Basics: An Introduction to TANF*, Center on Budget and Policy Priorities, Dec. 4, 2012.

5. *See* Katherine S. Newman and Rourke O'Brien, Taxing the Poor: Doing Damage to the Truly Disadvantaged (California 2011).

6. *See, e.g.*, Deneen L. Brown, *The High Cost of Poverty: Why the Poor Pay More*, Washington Post, May 18, 2009; David Dante Troutt, *The Thin Red Line: How the Poor Still Pay More*, Consumers Union Publications, 1993.

7. *See* Angela Donkin, Peter Goldblatt, and Kevin Lynch, *Inequalities in Life Expectancy by Social Class, 1972–1999*, Health Statistics Quarterly, Autumn 2002. Relatedly, low-income patients may receive disparate treatment in seemingly innocuous ways, despite devastating results. For instance, low-income mothers giving birth at several New York City hospitals that serve Medicaid patients disproportionately were tested for marijuana use, a policy rarely applied to insured mothers. Mothers who tested positive were investigated by city child-welfare agencies, and some lost parental rights. *See* Oren Yaniv, *Weed Out: Hosps Test Poor Moms for Pot*, New York Daily News, Dec. 26, 2012.

8. *See, e.g.*, Oscar Lewis, La Vida (Vintage 1968).

9. *See, e.g.*, Charles Murray, Losing Ground: American Social Policy, 1950–1980, 1986; and Coming Apart: The State of White America, 1960–2010, 2012.

10. *See, e.g.*, William Julius Wilson, The Truly Disadvantaged: The Inner City, the Underclass, and Public Policy (Chicago 1990).

11. *See* Patricia Cohen, *Scholars Return to "Culture of Poverty" Ideas*, New York Times, Oct. 17, 2010.

12. Oscar Lewis, *The Culture of Poverty*, 1966, *available at* http://lenguaix.pbworks.com/f/Culture+of+Poverty.pdf.

13. *See, e.g.*, Sheila Fitzgerald Krein and Andrea H. Beller, *Educational Attainment of Children from Single-Parent Families: Differences by Exposure, Gender, and Race*, 25 Demography 2 (May 1988).

14. *See* National Center for Health Statistics Data Brief, *Changing Patterns of Nonmarital Childbearing in the United States*, May 2009.

15. Kathryn Edin and Maria Kefalas, Promises I Can Keep: Why Poor Women Put Motherhood before Marriage 204 (California 2005).

16. *Id.*, at 6.

17. *Id.*, at 33.

18. *Id.*, at 205 (citing a range of studies).

19. *Id.*, at 137. This is the second time Edin has done this—altered a deep intuition by living with and reporting the words of poor women in the United States. The first time was in 1997 when she published a study along with Laura Lein called Making Ends Meet (Russell Sage 1997), an intimate look at the financial shortfalls that women on welfare routinely faced and the ingenuity and hard work with which most made up the difference. The study might have made a huge impact on the way Americans understood welfare, but it happened to come on the heels of a vast overhaul of the federal system that changed all the rules. The point is that Kathryn Edin is a dedicated mythbuster when it comes to the lives of poor women. She is keenly aware of the assumptions most Americans have about people whose lives are lived at a deliberate distance, and she has succeeded in showing the key factual misconceptions to which many of us cling.

20. Again, the names of social workers and their organization have been changed to protect patient confidentiality.

21. *See* the series by Robert Coles, Children of Crisis (1967–80).

22. *See, e.g.*, Bruce McEwen and Elizabeth Lasley, The End of Stress as We Know It (National Academies Press 2002).

23. *See generally* Judith Herman, Trauma and Recovery: The Aftermath of Violence—From Domestic Abuse to Political Terror (Basic Books 1997).

24. Andrea J. Sedlak et al., *Fourth National Incidence Study of Child Abuse and Neglect (NIS-4)*, U.S. Department of Health and Human Services, Jan. 2010, p. 11, *available at* http://www.acf.hhs.gov/sites/default/files/opre/nis4_report_congress_full_pdf_jan2010.pdf.

25. *Id.*, at 12.

26. *Id.*, at 9.

27. "As with previous results, the recent observations cannot plausibly be explained by the claim that lower socioeconomic families are simply more visible to the community professionals who provide most of the data. The NIS sentinels observe substantial numbers of children and families at the middle- and upper-income levels. Sentinels in schools alone recognized the majority of the maltreated children." *Id.*, at 21.

28. Kathryn Collins et al., *Understanding the Impact of Trauma and Urban Poverty on Family Systems: Risks, Resilience, and Interventions*, Family Informed Trauma Treatment Center, 2010, *available at* http://www.nctsn.org/products/nctsn-affiliated-resources/understanding-impact-trauma-and-urban-poverty-family-systems.

29. *Id.*, at 11.

30. *Id.*

31. *Id.*, at 21–22.

32. *Id.*, at 4.

33. Jody Miller, Getting Played: African American Girls, Urban Inequality, and Gendered Violence 65 (NYU 2008).

34. *Id.*, at 57.
35. *Id.*, at 113.
36. Massey, *Segregation and Stratification, supra*, at 13.
37. McEwen and Lasley, *supra*, at 56.
38. *Id.*, at 67–68; Massey, *supra*, at 14.
39. Massey, *supra*; McEwen and Lasley, *supra*, at 58–59.
40. Collins et al., *supra*, at 12: "In relation to the symptoms affecting attention, concentration, and memory, these children often experience disruptions in academic learning and skill development. Their hypervigilance, heightened sense of alert, and posttraumatic play may set them apart from peers, restrict the normalcy of their social interactions, and place them at risk for delays in social competence."
41. Massey, *supra*, at 14.
42. Nor have we focused on the usual issues that dominate conversations about high-poverty areas—drugs, gangs, crime, and dependence on entitlement programs like cash payments, food stamps, and disability support.
43. This follows a similar point I wrote about years ago in the context of low-income communities I call "antimarkets." "Antimarket" is a more apt word than "ghetto" because it better describes its relationship to the type of community from which it is systematically separated by policy, the "metamarket." *See* Troutt, *Ghettoes Made Easy, supra.*
44. Ingrid Gould Ellen and Karen Mertens Horn, *Do Federally Assisted Households Have Access to High-Performing Schools?* Poverty and Race Research Action Council, Nov. 2012.
45. Organizations called the First Suburbs Project and Building One Pennsylvania organized local communities in order to pressure HUD to make funds available for mobility programs, including counseling. HUD agreed to allocate $500,000 to the demonstration project that could affect as many as two hundred households. *See* Loretta Rodgers, *HUD Gives $500k for Housing Voucher Reform*, Daily Times, Dec. 5, 2012, *available at* http://www.delcotimes.com/articles/2012/12/05/news/doc50c01f8982f65067266921.txt. *See also, Thompson v. HUD*, 404 F.3d 821 (4th Cir. 2005), a fair housing case filed in 1995 against HUD by black public housing tenants in Baltimore frustrated by federal housing policies that reinforced segregated residential patterns. The settlement in the case included an important regional housing mobility program that placed low-income African American tenants in lower-poverty areas.
46. *See* Lora Engdahl, *New Homes, New Neighborhoods, New Schools: A Progress Report on the Baltimore Housing Mobility Program*, Baltimore Regional Housing Campaign and Poverty and Race Research Council, Oct. 2009, *available at* http://www.prrac.org/pdf/BaltimoreMobilityReport.pdf.
47. HUD's Moving to Opportunity program (MTO), a demonstration project of the Clinton administration begun in 1994, released a study of its tenants after between

ten and fifteen years of mobility housing. *See* Lisa Sanbonmatsu et al., *Moving to Opportunity for Fair Housing Demonstration Program: Final Impacts Evaluation*, U.S. Department of Housing and Urban Development, Nov. 2011, *available at* http://www.huduser.org/publications/pdf/MTOFHD_fullreport_v2.pdf. The results are mixed and puzzling, at times cryptic. The clear benefits include much reduced stress, violence, and obesity, reinforcing the conclusion that opportunity may begin with improved public health. However, the report also makes clear that mobility as a strategy is incomplete without closer attention paid to both racial and economic integration. Even the most successful MTO residents ("compliers") moved to communities that were nearly as overwhelming black as the ones they left and not much more affluent.

### NOTES TO CHAPTER 7

1. Indeed, so coercive is the aspiration that it precludes learning about racial identity on the obviously erroneous grounds that such education is no longer necessary. In this feedback loop, we ensure generational ignorance about race topics by avoiding—fearfully—all study of race as if it were redundant to a generation of people who supposedly "no longer think like that." This makes the treatment of race rare among complex social fields. It also makes us more likely doomed to repeat past generational understandings of racial conflict.
2. This is in fact a tenet of critical race theory as demonstrated in Neil Gotunda, *A Critique of "Our Constitution is Color-Blind,"* 44 Stan. L. Rev. 1 (1991); Ian Haney-Lopez, White by Law: The Legal Construction of Race (NYU 1997); Richard Delgado and Jean Stefancic, Critical Race Theory: An Introduction (NYU 2001); Derrick A. Bell, Silent Covenants: Brown v. Board of Education and the Unfulfilled Hopes for Racial Reform (Oxford 2005).
3. Except perhaps in California and the Pacific Northwest where Asian Americans occupy such great numbers that the racial and ethnic dynamic defies generalization.
4. Tanya Kateri Hernandez, Racial Subordination in Latin America: The Role of the State, Customary Law, and the New Civil Rights Response 179 (Cambridge 2012).
5. *Id.*, at 180.
6. *See* Josh Sides, *Straight into Compton: American Dreams, Urban Nightmares, and the Metamorphosis of a Black Suburb*, 56 Am. Q. 583 (2004).
7. See Albert M. Camarillo, *Cities of Color: The New Racial Frontier in California's Minority–Majority Cities*, 76 Pac. Hist. Rev. 1 (2007).
8. Patrick J. McDonnell, *As Change Again Overtakes Compton, So Do Tensions*, Los Angeles Times, Aug. 21, 1994. (The "tough little city in South Los Angeles County was the most populous community west of the Mississippi where blacks held political sway, a national symbol of political empowerment despite its persistent poverty. Here refugees from the Jim Crow South acquired their piece of the American Dream, using the ballot box to overcome discrimination.")

9. The following quotes were collected during interviews with primarily Latino residents of Compton by one of my student research assistants, Sal Sanchez, a Latino resident of Compton who spoke with his subjects in Spanish during the late fall of 2010 and winter of 2011. I am grateful for his insights.

10. The ambivalence corroborated comments made in a National Public Radio report that documented local Latino opinions about Compton's political murals. See Krissy Clark, *Compton's Latinos Want Council Elections Revamped*, National Public Radio, Jan. 18, 2011, *available at* http://www.npr.org/2011/01/18/133012346/ Latinos-Want-Comptons-City-Council-Elections-Overhauled.

11. For instance, according to the *Compton Unified School District in California: District Profile, Local School Directory*, there were 20,919 Latino students enrolled in the schools in 2010–11 compared to only 6,694 black students. Yet the majority of teachers are black, and black staff members overall outnumber Latino staff two to one.

12. Ann M. Simmons and Abby Sewell, *Suit Seeks to Open Compton to Latino Voters*, Los Angeles Times, Dec. 20, 2010.

13. Nicolas Vaca, The Presumed Alliance: The Unspoken Conflict between Latinos and Blacks and What It Means for America 139 (HarperCollins 2004).

14. Camarillo, *supra*, at 37.

15. Vaca, *supra*, at 145.

16. *See, e.g., Westminster School District of Orange County v. Mendez*, 161 F.2d 774 (9th Cir. 1947).

17. Ordinarily, we would embark here on a discussion of national-origin discrimination, which is the official civil rights category for discrimination based on ethnicity. I will refrain from doing that, however, because I'm not sure what an exhaustive analysis would add. Obviously, as I discussed in chapter 5, national-origin discrimination is real; it produces significant harms at both an individual and structural level. In some places it can be especially harsh. Yet, fortunately, it is not as widely documented, litigated, or studied as either racial or economic exploitation. Ironically, it may at times distract us from more common yet subtle forms of marginalization based on vulnerability, lack of economic sophistication, or spatial concentration. The alternative questions we might ask include, are these disadvantages visited on this person because of her national origin, and would this person be the object of marginalization if these other structural disadvantages were not in play?

18. Camille Zubrinsky Charles, Won't You Be My Neighbor? Race, Class, and Residence in Los Angeles (Russell Sage 2006).

19. *Id.*, at 100.

20. *Id.*, at 103.

21. *Id.*, at 127.

22. These findings on stereotypes, however, do not mean that minorities do not detect discrimination against themselves or others. Nonwhites believe there is much more racial discrimination in the United States, first against blacks, then against

Latinos, and last faced by Asians. Whites in Charles's study more often do not share this belief.

23. *Id.*, at 128 (rivaled only by native Asians). These results confirm findings by Thomas Shapiro and others. *See* Shapiro, *supra.*

24. Charles, *supra*, at 182–84.

25. *Id.*, at 43–44.

26. *Id.*, at 44.

27. *Id.*, at 93.

28. *Id.*

29. *Id.*, at 94.

30. *Id.*

31. That oft-cited public choice economist Charles Tiebout was right back in the 1950s about how preferences help drive residency. However, he failed to explain why. *See* Charles M. Tiebout, *A Pure Theory of Local Expenditures* 64 J. of Political Economy 416 (1956).

32. Charles, *supra*, at 159.

33. *Id.*

34. *See, e.g.,* George Yancey, Who Is White? Latinos, Asians, and the New Black/Non-black Divide (Lynne Rienner 2003), who argues that a variety of social processes have worked to form a new binary of blacks in one category and nonblacks in another. Further, as Gerald Torres and Lani Guinier write in The Miner's Canary: Enlisting Race, Resisting Power, Transforming Democracy (Harvard 2002) at 248, the pressure is strong for Asians to be considered honorary whites and for Latinos still to choose their race.

35. Massey and Denton, *supra.*

36. *See, e.g.,* Charles, *supra*, at 42.

37. Paul A. Jargowsky, *Immigrant and Neighborhoods of Concentrated Poverty: Assimilation or Stagnation?* National Poverty Center, Nov. 2006, *available at* http://www.npc.umich.edu/publications/u/working_paper06-44.pdf.

38. *See, e.g.,* Urban Flight from Los Angeles: Straight Outta Compton, The Economist, Feb. 14, 2008, *available at* http://www.economist.com/node/10697106.

39. *See* Noel Ignatiev, How The Irish Became White (Routledge 2008); David R. Roediger, Working toward Whiteness: How America's Immigrants Became White: The Strange Journey from Ellis Island to the Suburbs (Basic Books 2006); Karen Brodkin, How Jews Became White Folks and What That Says about Race in America (Rutgers 1998).

40. Gerald Torres and Lani Guinier have a similar idea they call "political race." See *supra*, at 243.

NOTES TO CHAPTER 8

1. *See, e.g.,* Manuel Pastor, Chris Benner, and Martha Matsuoka, This Could Be the Start of Something Big: How Social Movements for Regional Equity Are

Reshaping Metropolitan America (Cornell 2009); *Shared Prosperity, Stronger Regions: An Agenda for Rebuilding America's Older Core Cities*, PolicyLink, 2006, *available at* http://www.policylink.org/; M. Paloma Pavel, *Breakthrough Communities: Sustainability and Justice in the Next American Metropolis*, 2009; Peter Dreier, John Mollenkopf, and Todd Swanstrom, Place Matters: Metropolitics for the Twenty-First Century (Kansas 2000).

2. *See, Housing and Economic Development: Developers Guide*, Sept. 24, 2012, *available at* http://www.mass.gov/hed/community/40b-plan/developers-guide.html, for an example a of mixed-income development initiative. *See also* Margery Austin Turner et al., *Benefits of Living in High Opportunity Neighborhoods: Insights from the Moving to Opportunity Demonstration*, Sept. 2012, *available at* http://www.urban.org/UploadedPDF/412648-Benefits-of-Living-in-High-Opportunity-Neighborhoods.pdf, for a report on the benefits of such mixed-income housing.

3. Judith Bell and Mary M. Lee, *Why Place and Race Matter: Impacting Health through a Focus on Race and Place*, PolicyLink, 2011, *available at* http://www.policylink.org/.

4. Orfield, *supra*.

5. Pastor, Benner, and Matsuoka, *supra*.

6. *See* David Rusk, Inside Game, Outside Game: Winning Strategies for Saving Urban America (Brookings 2001); David Rusk, Cities without Suburbs: A Census 2000 Update (Woodrow Wilson 2003).

7. A similar Camden-area simulation by Rusk is discussed in *Housing Policy Is School Policy*, 227, in David K. Hamilton and Patricia Atkins, eds., Urban and Regional Policies for Metropolitan Livability (M. E. Sharpe 2008).

8. This index is calculated by the traditional methodology—that is, the segregation of all persons that fall below the official poverty line from everyone else.

9. Often the affordable housing set-aside is made a statutory condition of receiving state financial assistance. In New Jersey, for example, the Housing Reform Act of 2008 requires that all state aided housing developments have at least 20 percent of the units be affordable at less than 80 percent of AMI, but also requires that at least one quarter of those (or 5 percent of the total development) must be affordable at less than 30 percent of AMI.

10. This refers initially to an important federal fair housing case, *Gautreaux v. Chicago Housing Authority*, 296 F.Supp. 907 (N.D. Ill. 1969); 475 F.3d 845 (7th Cir. 2007), which led to an innovative mobility program. For a history of the litigation, *see* Alexander Polikoff, Waiting for Gautreaux: A Story of Segregation, Housing, and the Black Ghetto (Northwestern 2007); and for highlights of the program *see* Leonard Rubinowitz, *Imagining Gautreaux*, foreword to 1 NW. J. of L. & Soc. Pol'y (2006).

11. Act of Jul. 23, 1971, ch. 24, §§ 1–13, 1971 Minn. Laws 2286 (codified as amended at Minn. Stat. § 473F [2004]); *see* Myron Orfield and Nicholas Wallace, *The Minnesota Fiscal Disparities Act of 1971: The Twin Cities' Struggle and Blueprint for Regional*

*Cooperation*, 33 Wm. Mitchell L. Rev. 591, for a discussion of the Act; *see, Bill no. 170: An Act to Reform the Municipal Territorial Organization of the Metropolitan Regions of Montréal, Québec and the Outaouais*, Assemblée nationale du Québec, *available at* http://www.assnat.qc.ca/en/travaux-parlementaires/projets-loi/projet-loi-170-36-1.html, for a look at a Canadian bill for city reorganization and merger.

12. The Intermunicipal Tax Sharing Program was established to create a fair and equitable method of distributing the benefits and costs of economic development and land use decisions made by the New Jersey Meadowlands Commission (NJMC) among the fourteen Meadowlands District municipalities. The legal basis for the program can be found in the enabling legislation at NJSA 13:17–60 at 76. The NJMC receives no money from the fund and serves as the routing agent for monies distributed to district municipalities.

13. Orfield, *supra*, at 195.

14. Orfield and Wallace, *supra*, at 603.

15. Note that this is not direct receipt of revenues. Rather, it is increased tax base, or what Camden might have "received" in increased ratables had the equivalent amount of office parks and new condos arrived. The same is true for the reductions experienced by the wealthier towns in the region. In revenue terms, assuming a median regional rate of $2.71 per $1,000 of assessed valuation, Camden would receive an additional $786,000 in annual property tax revenues under this simulation.

16. *See, e.g.*, Gary Burtless, ed., Does Money Matter? The Effect of School Resources on Student Achievement and Adult Success (Brookings 1996).

17. New Jersey eventually did just that in its 2008 School Funding Reform Act.

18. Fair Housing Act of 1968, 42 U.S.C. §§ 3608(e)(5) (1988); 24 C.F.R. sections 91.225(a), 570.601(a)(2) (2011).

19. Westchester County, New York, also ignored the seriousness of the requirement while filing false claims of compliance in order to get federal reimbursement for segregated housing it built. The result was a costly settlement for the county in a case of first impression, *United States ex rel. Anti-discrimination Center v. Westchester County* 668 F.Supp.2d 548 (S.D.N.Y. 2009).

20. "The purposes of a Community Land Trust are to provide access to land and housing to people who are otherwise denied access; to increase long-term community control of neighborhood resources; to empower residents through involvement and participation in the organization; and to preserve affordability of housing permanently." National Community Land Trust Network, *available at* http://www.cltnetwork.org/. *See,* Community Investments, *Community Land Trusts: Preserving Long-Term Affordable Housing*, Spring 2008, *available at* http://www.frbsf.org/publications/community/investments/0805/land_trusts.pdf, for a brief history of the benefits and challenges of community land trusts. *See* Twin Cities Community Land Bank, *available at* http://www.tcclandbank.org/, for an example of a community land bank.

21. Pastor, Benner, and Matsuoka, *supra*. *See also* Chris Benner and Manuel Pastor, Just Growth: Inclusion and Prosperity in America's Metropolitan Regions (Routledge 2012).

22. Osborne M. Reynolds Jr., Local Government Law, sec. 75 (West 2009). For an example of a planned community merger/consolidation, *see* North Carolina Planned Community Act, N.C. Gen. Stat. § 47F-1-102 (2012).

23. *See* Rusk, Cities without Suburbs, *supra*.

24. For an illuminating account of a failed effort at inter-municipal consolidation, *see* Craig R. Bucki, *Regionalism Revisited: The Effort to Streamline Governance in Buffalo and Erie County, New York*, 71 Alb. L. Rev. 117 (2008).

25. *See* H. Jeffrey Leonard, Managing Oregon's Growth: The Politics of Development Planning 134–37 (Conservation Foundation 1983); *see also, Urban Growth Boundary*, Metro, http://www.oregonmetro.gov/index.cfm/go/by.web/id=277, for an overview of the Oregon urban growth boundary.

26. For a look at some of Minnesota's legislation for its pure metro government, *see* Legislative Commission on Metropolitan Government, Minn. Stat. § 3.8841 (2012); *see also* Council's Submissions to Legislative Commission, Minn. Stat. § 473.246 (2012). For a look at some of Oregon's legislation for its pure metro government, *see* Or. Rev. Stat. § 197.298 (2011); Or. Rev. Stat. § 197.296 (2011); Or. Rev. Stat. § 456.060 (2011); on Louisville, *see* http://www.louisvilleky.gov/.

27. Briffault, *Our Localism: Part I, supra*, at 10–18.

28. David D. Troutt, *Katrina's Window: Localism, Resegregation, and Equitable Regionalism*, 55 Buff. L. Rev. 1109, 1173 (2008).

29. *See* David J. Barron, *Reclaiming Home Rule*, 116 Harv. L. Rev. 2255 (2003).

30. *City of Clinton v. Cedar Rapids*, 24 Iowa 455 (1868).

31. *See* John F. Dillon, Commentaries on the Law of Municipal Corporations 449 (1911).

32. For an example of approaches, *see, Equitable Development Toolkit: Building Regional Equity, Transit Oriented Development*, PolicyLink, 2008, *available at* http://www.polcitylink.org/.

33. *See* Clayton P. Gillette, *Local Redistribution, Living-Wage Ordinances, and Judicial Intervention*, 101 NW. U.L. Rev. 1057 (2007); *Local Living-Wage Laws and Coverage*, National Employment Law Project, *available at* http://www.nelp.org/page/-/Justice/2011/LocalLWLawsCoverageFINAL.pdf?nocdn=1, for a list of municipalities with living-wage laws as current through July 2011. *See also* Terrence T. McDonald, *Jersey City Council Adopts "Living Wage" Ordinance to Boost Minimum Pay for Some Low-Level Workers*, Jul. 19, 2012, *available at* http://www.nj.com/jjournal-news/index.ssf/2012/07/jersey_city_council_adopts_liv.html.

34. *See, e.g.*, Amy Lavine, *Milwaukee Park East Redevelopment CBA*, Jan. 30, 2008, *available at* http://communitybenefits.blogspot.com/2008/01/milwaukee-park-east-redevelopment-cba.html.

35. powell, *supra*, 658.

# SELECTED BIBLIOGRAPHY

Alexander, Michelle, The New Jim Crow: Mass Incarceration in the Age of Colorblindness (New Press 2010).

Anderson, Michelle Wilde, *Cities Inside Out: Race, Poverty, and Exclusion at the Urban Fringe*, 55 UCLA L. Rev. 1095 (2008).

Attkisson, Lesley R., *Putting a Stop to Sprawl: State Intervention as a Tool for Growth Management*, 69 Vand. L. Rev. 979 (2009).

Barron, David J., *Reclaiming Home Rule*, 116 Harv. L. Rev. 2255 (2003).

Benner, Chris, and Manuel Pastor Jr., Just Growth: Inclusion and Prosperity in America's Metropolitan Regions (Routledge 2012).

Berube, Alan, David Erickson, Caroline Reid, Lisa Nelson and Anne O'Shaughnessy, eds., The Enduring Challenge of Concentrated Poverty in America: Case Studies from Communities across the U.S., available at http://www.brookings.edu/~/media/research/files/reports/2008/10/24%20concentrated%20poverty/1024_concentrated_poverty.pdf (2008).

Blackwell, Angela Glover, *It Takes a Region*, 31 Fordham Urb. L.J. 1303 (2004).

Bollens, Scott A., *Concentrated Poverty and Metropolitan Equity Strategies*, 8 Stan. L. & Pol'y Rev. 11 (1997).

Briggs, Xavier de Souza, ed., The Geography of Opportunity: Race and Housing Choice in Metropolitan America (Brookings 2005).

Briffault, Richard, *The Local Government Boundary Problem in Metropolitan Areas*, 48 Stan. L. Rev. 1115 (1996).

———, *Our Localism: Part I, The Structure of Local Government Law*, 90 Colum. L. Rev. 1 (1990).

———, *Our Localism: Part II, Localism and Legal Theory*, 90 Colum. L. Rev. 346 (1990).

Brown, Michael K., Martin Carnoy, Elliott Currie, and Troy Duster, eds., White Washing Race: The Myth of a Color-Blind Society (California 2003).

Buzzbee, William W., *Urban Sprawl, Federalism, and the Problem of Institutional Complexity*, 68 Fordham L. Rev. 57 (1999).

———, *Urban Sprawl and Legal Reform*, in Sprawl City: Race, Politics, and Planning in Atlanta 161–86 (Robert D. Bullard, Glenn S. Johnson, and Angel Torres, eds., 2000).

Calmore, John O., *A Call to Context: The Professional Challenges of Cause Lawyering at the Intersection of Race, Space, and Poverty*, 67 Fordham L. Rev. 1927 (1999).

Cashin, Sheryll, *Federalism, Welfare Reform, and the Minority Poor: Accounting for the Tyranny of State Majorities*, 99 Colum. L. Rev. 552 (1999).

———, *Localism, Self-Interest, and the Tyranny of the Favored Quarter: Addressing the Barriers to New Regionalism*, 88 Geo. L.J. 1985 (2000).

———, *Middle-Class Black Suburbs and the State of Integration: A Post-integrationist Vision for Metropolitan America*, 86 Cornell L. Rev. 729 (2001).

Charles, Camille Zubrinsky, Won't You Be My Neighbor? Race, Class, and Residence in Los Angeles (Russell Sage 2006).

DeBray-Pelot, Elizabeth, and Erica Frankenberg, *Federal Legislation to Promote Metropolitan Approaches to Educational and Housing Opportunity*, 17 Geo. J. on Poverty L. & Pol'y 265 (2010).

Dilworth, Richardson, The Urban Origins of Suburban Autonomy (Harvard 2005).

Dreir, Peter, John Mollenkopf, and Todd Swanstrom, Place Matters: Metropolitics for the Twenty-First Century (Kansas 2004).

Edin, Kathryn, and Maria Kefalas, Promises I Can Keep: Why Poor Women Put Motherhood before Marriage (California 2005).

Eitle, David, *Dimensions of Racial Segregation, Hypersegregation, and Black Homicide Rates*, 37 J. Crim. Just. 28 (2009).

Ellis, Mark, Richard Wright, and Virginia Parks, *Work Together, Live Apart? Geographies of Racial and Ethnic Segregation at Home and at Work*, 94 Annals of the Ass'n Am. Geographers 620 (2004).

Fallah, Belal N., Mark D. Partridge, and Rose Olfert, *Urban Sprawl and Productivity: Evidence from U.S. Metropolitan Areas*, 90 Papers Regional Sci. 451 (2011).

Fennell, Lee Anne, *Properties of Concentration*, 73 U. Chi. L. Rev. 1227 (2006).

Flagg, Kinara, *Mending the Safety Net through Source of Income Protections: The Nexus between Antidiscrimination and Social Welfare Laws*, 20 Colum. J. Gender & L. 201 (2011).

Flaherty, Jordan, Floodlines: Community and Resistance from Katrina to the Jena Six (Haymarket 2010).

Frank, Robert, Falling Behind: How Rising Inequality Harms the Middle Class (California 2007).

Frug, Gerald E., City Making: Building Communities without Building Walls (Princeton 2001).

Frug, Jerry, *The Geography of Community*, 48 Stan. L. Rev. 1047 (1996).

Fullilove, Mindy Thompson, Root Shock: How Tearing Up City Neighborhoods Hurts America and What We Can Do about It (One World 2005).

Goetz, Edward G., *The Politics of Poverty Deconcentration and Housing Demolition*, 22 J. Urb. Aff. 157 (2000).

Greenstein, Rosalind, and Wim Wiewel, eds., Urban-Suburban Interdependencies (Lincoln Instit. 2000).

Gullen, Jamie, *Colorblind Education Reform: How Race-Neutral Policies Perpetuate Segregation and Why Voluntary Integration Should Be Put Back on the Reform Agenda*, 15 U. Pa. J. L. & Soc. Change 251 (2012).

Haney Lopez, Ian F., *"A Nation of Minorities": Race, Ethnicity, and Reactionary Color-blindness*, 59 Stan. L. Rev. 985 (2007).

Hernandez, Elizabeth Pierson, *Twice Uprooted: How Government Policies Exacerbate Injury to Low-Income Americans Following Natural Disasters*, 14 The Scholar: St. Mary's Law Review on Minority Issues 219 (2011).

Hudnut, William H., III, Halfway to Everywhere: A Portrait of America's First-Tier Suburbs (ULI 2003).

Hutch, Daniel J., *The Rationale For Including Disadvantaged Communities in the Smart Growth Metropolitan Development Framework*, 20 Yale L. & Pol'y Rev. 353 (2002).

Iceland, John, and Kyle Anne Nelson, *Hispanic Segregation in Metropolitan America: Exploring the Multiple Forms of Spatial Assimilation*, 73 Am. Soc. Rev. 741 (2008).

Inman, Robert P., ed., Making Cities Work: Prospects and Policies for Urban America (Princeton 2009).

Jackson, Kenneth T., Crabgrass Frontier: The Suburbanization of the United States (Oxford 1985).

Jargowsky, Paul, Poverty and Place: Ghettos, Barrios, and the American City (Russell Sage 1998).

Johnson, Olatunde, *The Last Plank: Rethinking Public and Private Power to Advance Fair Housing*, 13 U. Pa. J. Const. L. 1191 (2011).

Katznelson, Ira, When Affirmative Action Was White: An Untold History of Racial Inequality in Twentieth-Century America (Norton 2012).

Kodras, Janet E., *The Changing Map of American Poverty in an Era of Economic Restructuring and Political Realignment*, 73 Econ. Geography 67 (1997).

Kruse, Kevin M., and Thomas J. Sugrue, The New Suburban History (Chicago 2006).

Ladd, Helen F., and John Yinger, America's Ailing Cities: Fiscal Health and the Design of Urban Policy (Johns Hopkins 1989).

Lareau, Annette, Unequal Childhoods: Class, Race, and Family Life (California 2003).

Lassiter, Matthew D., The Silent Majority: Suburban Politics in the Sunbelt South (Princeton 2006).

Levitt, Jeremy I., and Matthew Whitaker, eds., Hurricane Katrina: America's Unnatural Disaster (Nebraska 2009).

Lucy, William H., and David L. Phillips, Confronting Suburban Decline: Strategic Planning for Metropolitan Renewal (Island 2000).

Mallach, Alan, *The Mount Laurel Doctrine and the Uncertainties of Social Policy in a Time of Retrenchment*, 63 Rutgers L. Rev. 849 (2011).

Massey, Douglas S., Categorically Unequal: The American Stratification System (Russell Sage 2007).

Massey, Douglas S., and Nancy A. Denton, American Apartheid (Harvard 1994).

———, *Hypersegregation in U.S. Metropolitan Areas: Black and Hispanic Segregation along Five Dimensions*, 26 Demography 373 (1989).

Massey, Douglas S., and Mitchell L. Eggers, *The Ecology of Inequality: Minorities and the Concentration of Poverty, 1970–1980*, 95 Am. J. Soc. 1153 (1990).

Massey, Douglas S., Andrew B. Gross, and Kumiko Shibuya, *Migration, Segregation, and the Geographic Concentration of Poverty*, 59 Am. Soc. Rev. 425 (1994).

McDonald, Janet D., Mary F. Hughes, and Gary W. Ritter, *School Finance Litigation and Adequacy Studies*, 27 U. Ark. Little Rock L. Rev. 69 (2004).

Meyer, Stephen Grant, As Long as They Don't Move Next Door: Segregation and Racial Conflict in American Neighborhoods (Rowman & Littlefield 2000).

Miller, David Y., The Regional Governing of Metropolitan America (Westview 2002).

Miller, Jody, Getting Played: African American Girls, Urban Inequality, and Gendered Violence (NYU 2008).

Minow, Martha, *Reforming School Reform*, 68 Fordham L. Rev. 257 (1999).

Mumford, Kevin, Newark: A History of Race, Rights, and Riots in America (NYU 2007).

Oliver, Melvin L., and Thomas M. Shapiro, Black Wealth/White Wealth: A New Perspective on Racial Inequality (Routledge 1997).

Orfield, Myron, American Metropolitics: The New Suburban Reality (Brookings 2002).

———, *Racial Integration and Community Revitalization: Applying the Fair Housing Act to the Low-Income Housing Tax Credit*, 58 Vand. L. Rev. 1747 (2005).

Pastor, Manuel, Jr., Chris Benner, and Martha Matsuoka, This Could Be the Start of Something Big: How Social Movements for Regional Equity Are Reshaping Metropolitan America (Cornell 2009).

Pastor, Manuel, Jr., Peter Dreir, J. Eugene Grigsby III, and Marta Lopez-Garza, Regions That Work: How Cities and Suburbs Can Grow Together (Minnesota 2000).

Poindexter, Georgette C., *Towards a Legal Framework for Redistribution of Poverty-Related Expenses*, 47 Wash. U. J. Urb. & Contemp. L. 3 (1995).

Pollard, Oliver A., III, *Smart Growth: The Promise, Politics, and Potential Pitfalls of Emerging Growth Management Strategies*, 19 Va. Envtl. L.J. 247 (2000).

powell, john a., *The Tensions between Integration and School Reform*, 28 Hastings Const. L.Q. 655 (2001).

Reiff, David, Going to Miami: Exiles, Tourists, and Refugees in the New America (UPF 1987).

Resnik, David B., *Urban Sprawl, Smart Growth, and Deliberative Democracy*, 100 Am. J. Pub. Health 1852 (2010).

Rhomberg, Chris, No There There: Race, Class, and Political Community in Oakland (California 2004).

Robinson, Russell K., *Perceptual Segregation*, 108 Colum. L. Rev. 1093 (2008).

Roediger, David R., Working toward Whiteness: How America's Immigrants Became White (Basic 2005).

Roisman, Florence Wagman, *Intentional Racial Discrimination and Segregation by the Federal Government as a Principal Cause of Concentrated Poverty: A Response to Schill and Wachter*, 143 U. Pa. L. Rev. 1351 (1995).

Rusk, David, Cities without Suburbs: A Census 2000 Update (Woodrow Wilson 2003).

———, Inside Game, Outside Game: Winning Strategies for Saving Urban America (Brookings 1999).

Ryan, James E., Five Miles Away, a World Apart: One City, Two Schools, and the Story of Educational Opportunity in America (Oxford 2011).

———, Schools, Race, and Money, 109 Yale L.J. 249 (1999).

———, The Supreme Court and Voluntary Integration, 121 Harv. L. Rev. 131 (2007).

Schill, Michael H., and Susan M. Wachter, The Spatial Bias of Federal Housing Law and Policy: The Concentrated Poverty in Urban America, 143 U. Pa. L. Rev. 1285 (1995).

Seitles, Marc, The Perpetuation of Residential Racial Segregation in America: Historical Discrimination, Modern Forms of Exclusion, and Inclusionary Remedies, 14 J. Land Use & Envtl. L. 89 (1998).

Self, Robert O., American Babylon: Race and the Struggle for Postwar Oakland (Princeton 2003).

Shah, Seema Ramesh, Having Low-Income Housing Tax Credit Qualified Allocation Plans Take into Account the Quality of Schools at Proposed Family Housing Sites: A Partial Answer to the Residential Segregation Dilemma? 39 Ind. L. Rev. 691 (2006).

Shapiro, Thomas, The Hidden Cost of Being African American: How Wealth Perpetuates Inequality (Oxford 2004).

Shell-Weiss, Melanie, Coming to Miami: A Social History (Florida 2009).

Sherraden, Michael, Assets and the Poor: A New American Welfare Policy (M. E. Sharpe. 1991).

Sibley, David, Geographies of Exclusion: Society and Difference in the West (Routledge 1995).

Sokol, Jason, There Goes My Everything: White Southerners in the Age of Civil Rights (Knopf 2000).

Sugrue, Thomas J., The Origins of the Urban Crisis: Race and Inequality in Postwar Detroit (Princeton 1996).

Troutt, David Dante, Ghettoes Made Easy: The Metamarket/Antimarket Dichotomy and the Legal Challenges of Inner-City Economic Development, 35 Harv. C.R.–C.L. Rev. 427 (2000).

———, Katrina's Window: Localism, Resegregation, and Equitable Regionalism, 55 Buff. L. Rev. 1109 (2008).

Tuttle, Brad R., How Newark Became Newark: The Rise, Fall, and Rebirth of an American City (Rivergate 2009).

Vaca, Nicolas C., The Presumed Alliance: The Unspoken Conflict between Latinos and Blacks and What It Means for America (HarperCollins 2004).

Venkatesh, Sudhir Alladi, Off the Books: The Underground Economy of the Urban Poor (Harvard 2006).

Wagmiller, Robert L., Jr., Race and Spatial Segregation of Jobless Men in Urban American, 44 Demography 539 (2007).

Wen, Ming, et al., Poverty, Affluence, and Income Inequality: Neighborhood Economic Structure and Its Implications for Health, 57 Soc. Sci. & Med. 843 (2003).

Wilkes, Rima, and John Iceland, *Hypersegregation in the Twenty-First Century*, Demography, Feb. 2004.

Wilkinson, Richard, and Kate Pickett, The Spirit Level: Why Greater Equality Makes Societies Stronger (Bloomsbury 2009).

Wilson, William Julius, More Than Just Race: Being Black and Poor in the Inner City (Norton 2009).

——, The Truly Disadvantaged: The Inner City, the Underclass, and Public Policy (Chicago 1990).

Yancey, George, Who Is White? Latinos, Asians, and the New Black/Nonblack Divide (Lynne Rienner 2003).

# INDEX

AFFH language, 218–219

affordable housing: class antagonism, 64; fear of "lowlifes," 64; hate speech against, 63–64; inclusionary zoning, 212; Marin County, California, 63–64; middle-class and, 172; *Mount Laurel* doctrine, 68, 70, 211, 218; New Orleans, 65; percentage of area median income (AMI), 212; poor whites' ability to find, 64, 206; property values, 64; public housing, 74, 75, 78, 79–80, 232n2; racism, 64; regional contribution agreements (RCAs), 69–70; set-asides for, 249n9; trading away obligations to build, 69–70; Westchester County, New York, 121; zoning laws, 83

African Americans. *See* blacks

Aid to Families with Dependent Children, 152

Akron, Ohio, 18–19

Alameda County, California, 31, 88

Alexander, Michelle, 140, 143, 145–147

allostatic load, 161–162, 167–170

allostatic response, 167

*American Apartheid* (Massey and Denton), 100

American Dream: access to, 9; coroner of, 135; home ownership, 134–135; jurisdictional governance underlying, 23 (*see also* localism); middle-class status, 10; selective generosity, 56; self-sufficiency, 61; social capital, 33; suburbs, 42; threshold assumption of, 10; upward mobility, 45

"Angry White Male," 128

Anti-Drug Abuse Act (1988), 142

antimarkets, 72–74, 86, 88, 137

antiracism, 196

apartment houses, 235n43

Arlington Heights, Illinois. See *Village of*

*Arlington Heights v. Metropolitan Housing Development Corp.*

Army Corps of Engineers, 134

Asbury Park, New Jersey, 9

Asbury Park High School (Asbury Park, New Jersey), 239n49

Asians: blacks, 180, 190, 192; Chinese in New York City, 197; class consciousness among, 192; desire to live among whites, 191–193; first-generation students, 240n58; Latinos, 190; neighborhood proximity to whites, 193–194; social mobility, 193; stereotypes of, 191; uncertain status of, 178; Vietnamese in Houston, 89; Vietnamese in Louisiana, 197

Asset Limited, Income Constrained, Employed (ALICE), 151–152, 154

Association of Community Organization for Reform Now (ACORN), 138

assumptions about American ideals, 6–7, 37–38, 194, 205–208

Atlanta, 137

*Atlanta Journal-Constitution* (newspaper), 137

at-risk suburbs, 29–31

Audubon Park, New Jersey, 215

backlash politics, 127

Baltimore, 101, 245n45

Baltimore Housing Mobility Program, 174–175

"Bamboo Ceiling," 124–125

Barringer High School (Newark, New Jersey), 239n49

"beaner hopping," 124

Bedford-Stuyvesant (Brooklyn), 2

"bedroom-developing" suburbs, 30

Belle Terre, New York, 82. See also *Village of Belle Terre v. Boraas*

# ABOUT THE AUTHOR

David Dante Troutt is a writer and Professor of Law and Justice John J. Francis Scholar at Rutgers Law School–Newark, where he directs the Center on Law in Metropolitan Equity. In addition to his regular journal scholarship and popular commentary, he is the author of *The Monkey Suit: Short Fiction on African Americans and Justice* (New Press 1998); a novel, *The Importance of Being Dangerous* (HarperCollins 2007); and the editor of *After the Storm: Black Intellectuals Explore the Meaning of Hurricane Katrina* (New Press 2006). Troutt's work examines policy and cultural issues involving race, economic opportunity, and mobility amid changing ideas about place. He lives in Montclair, New Jersey, with his family.